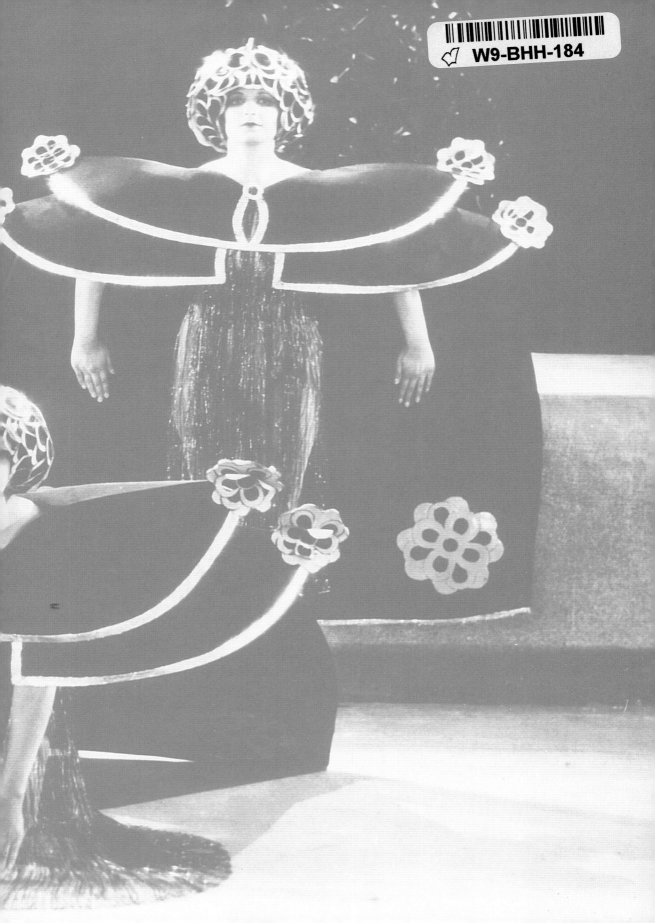

Madam Valentino

The Many Lives of Natacha Rambova

By Michael Morris

With all best wishes from the author, Michael Morris

Abbeville Press   Publishers

New York   London   Paris

*To Sarah with love
and many memories
Fred.*

To my grandmother,
Elizabeth Wismer Kuykendall

EDITOR: Alan Axelrod
DESIGNER: Renée Khatami
PRODUCTION EDITOR: Cristine Mesch
PRODUCTION SUPERVISOR: Hope Koturo

〜 〜

Library of Congress Cataloging-in-Publication Data
Morris, Michael (Michael Thomas)
   Madam Valentino: the many lives of Natacha Rambova / by Michael Morris.
      p.   cm.
   Filmography: p.
   Includes bibliographical references and index.
   ISBN 1-55859-136-2
   1. Valentino,   Rudolph,   1895–1926—Marriage.
2. Rambova, Natacha.   3. Motion picture actors and actresses—United   States—Biography.   4. Set designers—United States—Biography.   I. Title.
PN2287.V3M6   1991
791.43′028′092—DC20
[B]   91-16131

JACKET FRONT: *The "Royal Portrait," a photographic study of Rudy and Natacha by James Abbe. "Their joint popularity was so great," wrote Abbe, "one might imagine the double image appearing on our silver dollars."*
JACKET BACK: *A portrait of Natacha Rambova painted by Svetoslav Roerich, 1931*
ENDPAPERS: *The attendants of the Judæan princess in* Salome; *costumes designed by Rambova*
FRONTISPIECE: *Rambova in a publicity photo for her role in the play* Creoles, *1927*
TITLE PAGE: *Valentino and Rambova dancing the tango; photograph by James Abbe, 1923*
THIS PAGE: *Rambova, in a costume she designed for "The Aztec Dance," 1917*

CONTENTS

My interest in Natacha Rambova began in graduate school at the University of California, Berkeley, while I was working on a master's thesis in art history. My subject was Aubrey Beardsley's illustrations for the English edition of Oscar Wilde's play *Salome,* published in 1894. As I was researching the material, one of my colleagues pointed out to me that a silent film had been made of Wilde's play, and the costumes and sets had been designed by Rudolph Valentino's wife in a style à la Beardsley. Coincidentally, the film was being reprised a short time later at the Roxie Theatre in San Francisco. So I made an effort to see it.

I went. I saw. And I was conquered.

The acting was dated and appeared camp. The print was old, filled with scratches and bad splices. But the visual concept of the film, its costumes and its sets, were still a marvel to behold. I left the movie wanting to find out more about the curious woman who had designed it. In so doing, my interest in Natacha Rambova gradually turned into an obsession. I read everything about her and saw every film in which her character was depicted. Finally, I traveled to New York in order to read her will, and began to interview the people who had known her. The picture that began to develop was a far cry from the image portrayed of her in the media. A television movie, *The Private Life of Rudolph Valentino* (1975), starring Franco Nero as Valentino and Yvette Mimieux as Rambova, based its characters more on fabrication than on fact. Ken Russell's

A rare photo of Rambova with her hair unbound, 1926

self-indulgent *Valentino* (United Artists, 1977), starring Rudolph Nureyev as Valentino and Michelle Phillips as Rambova, proved to be nothing more than a burlesque of these two fascinating historical figures. A number of books written about Valentino and his wife, fifty years after his death and a decade after hers, only contributed to the farce.

I continued to study Rambova as a hobby while living in England, gathering data for my doctoral dissertation on Victorian painting. This hobby proved to be a richly rewarding experience; the woman who was an enigma to me ten years ago has emerged as one of the most fascinating females of our century.

She would not have wanted her biography written. She would have considered it unimportant in her quest to see the greater scheme of things. But the time is overdue to set the record straight. The uncovered facts put the fiction written about her to shame. In the case of Natacha Rambova, art has not even attempted to imitate the remarkable adventures of life.

A number of film scholars and historians came to my aid as my research on Rambova progressed. These included Kevin Brownlow, David Chierichetti, William K. Everson, and Alexander Walker. I wish to extend special thanks to Anthony Slide at the Motion Picture Academy Library, Brian Taves at the American Film Institute, and John Wayne at the Library of Congress, for the special attention they have given me over the years.

It was my good fortune to interview a number of people who knew Natacha Rambova and/or Rudolph Valentino personally. For their insights I am indebted to the following: Agnes de Mille, Winifred Edwards (Vera Fredova), Mark Hasselriis, Flower Hujer, L. Fred Husson, Paul Ivano, Buffie Johnson, Stella Kramrisch, Anne McGuire, William McGuire, Patsy Ruth Miller, Alden Nash, Dorothy Norman, Dian Provo, Madeline Mahoney Reid, Lois Wilson, and Loretta Young.

Numerous institutions and agencies assisted me in this project. I would like especially to thank the following: the Film Library and Special Collections of the University of Southern California, and the law firm of Gianelli and Morris, in Los Angeles; Paul Chamberlain International, and the Margaret Herrick Library of the Academy of Motion Picture Arts and Sciences, in Beverly Hills; the Bancroft Library of the University of California, the Pacific Film Archives, and the Graduate Theological Union Library, in Berkeley; the Historical Department of the Church of Jesus Christ of Latter Day Saints, the Utah Museum of Fine Arts at the

University of Utah, and the Utah State Historical Society, in Salt Lake City; the Library of Congress in Washington, D.C.; the Museum of the City of New York, the Museum of Modern Art, the Nicholas Roerich Museum, the Billy Rose Theatre Collection of the New York Public Library, and the Washburn Gallery, in New York City; the Philadelphia Museum of Art; Lancaster Ultra-Graphics, Inc. in Lancaster, Pennsylvania; the Princeton University Press; the Reading Room of the British Museum, and the National Film Archives and Stills Library, in London.

I would also like to thank a number of people whose support and assistance in this work has been greatly appreciated: Kathryn Abbe, Doug Adams, John Adams, Antonio Altamirano, Diane Apostolos-Cappadona, Nancy Baxter, Dewitt Bodeen, Susan Dinwoodey Burton, Peter Cameron, Michael Carey, Paul and Patricia Chamberlain, Diane Choquette, Elizabeth Hudnut Clarkson, Samson DeBrier, John and Jane Dillenberger, C. Robert Dumbacher, Daniel Entin, Erté, Mary Fabilli, Don Fehr, Norbert Fihn, John Flannery, Leslie Flint, Donald Goergen, Donald Grant, Harold Grieve, Jane Hampton, Jerome Henson, the Hon. James Ideman, Charles Kidd, John Kobal, Craig H. Long, Elizabeth Mariani, Reginald Martin, Antonio Moreno-Elosequi, Charles and Elizabeth Morris, Timothy Morris, Joaquin Nin-Culmell, Sean O'Gara, Katherine Peterson, Mark Peterson, Svetoslav Roerich, the Countess of Romanones, Edward Samaniego, E. F. Sanguinetti, Jack Scagnetti, Peter Selz, Joseph Simms, Jack Spears, Esther Vescey, Emmerich Vogt, and William Yates.

I wish to especially thank my agent, Charlotte Gordon, for finding the best possible publisher for this story. At Abbeville, I am grateful to Alan Axelrod for his patient and cheerful editing of this work, and to Renée Khatami for its elegant design.

But my greatest gratitude goes to Natacha Rambova's cousin, Ann Wollen, who, for the past ten years, has generously provided me with letters, family photographs, artwork, and memories of her celebrated relative. If I have captured but a portion of Rambova's captivating personality as she related it to me, then my work will not have been in vain.

Michael Morris
Berkeley, California, 1991

On August 23, 1926, Rudolph Valentino, Hollywood's biggest movie star, known to millions as "the Latin Lover" and "the Sheik," died at the age of thirty-one of a perforated ulcer. On the afternoon of August 15, the actor, who had always taken great pride in his physical perfection, was rushed to New York's Polyclinic Hospital after having collapsed in his hotel room. Three physicians were carefully chosen to cut into his body and arrest the poison spreading as a result of peritonitis. As he fought for his life on a white enameled iron bed located in a guarded suite on the eighth floor of the hospital, he did not know that below him an emotional frenzy was mounting. The hospital lobby had been transformed into a vast information center to dispense bulletins to the crowds who had gathered there demanding some news of the screen idol. Extra operators were placed on the hospital switchboard, which was receiving thousands of calls hourly. The mailroom was flooded with bundles of telegrams sent from all over the world, praying for Valentino's recovery. On station WEAF Major Bowes asked the radio public to think encouraging thoughts for the stricken actor. National and international newspapers carried headline reports on the film star's progress.

A few days after the operation, Valentino's health seemed to improve. This hopeful news allowed analysts to reflect on the powerful anxiety that the actor's hospitalization had brought upon millions. The *New York Times* promptly published an editorial on the amazing power of the cinema to create heroes of such mythic proportions:

Edward Weston photographed Rambova in this costume she designed for the Dance of the Seven Veils in Salome, c. 1921.

Strength and beauty, and that indefinable something variously called charm or personality, have ever commanded the admiration of the multitude. The fame of mighty men . . . in ancient stories is of the same fabric as the luster that in these days surrounds our movie sheiks. The brilliance may not be so enduring, but while it lasts it flashes as blinding a light as ever dazzled the enthralled listeners of Homer. A young man whose ardent acting on the screen has caught the imagination of millions all over the world falls suddenly ill. He is rushed to a hospital, whence issue bulletins of the precise state of his pulse, respiration and temperature. Inquiries by the thousand necessitate special arrangements to answer them. Whole gardens of flowers are transported to his bedside. When the rumor of his death is circulated the world's heart skips a beat. Authentic information of his improvement brings relief, and the crisis is awaited with baited breath. He is one of our modern heroes.

But the crisis did not abate. On Saturday, August 21, the actor's health suddenly took a turn for the worse. His pulse rate increased, and a raging fever plunged him into delirium. Pleurisy developed, and his breathing became labored. Priests were ushered in to administer Extreme Unction. A second wave of anxiety swept over the public, until Monday, when the dreaded news was released. Valentino had entered into immortality.

In his most popular films, Valentino had either been gallantly wounded or died the death of a hero. Now the film god's real life agony brought with it a maelstrom of misfortune for others. Of his three attending physicians, Dr. Durham experienced a heart attack, Dr. Manning suffered from exhaustion, and Dr. Meeker hastened to write an apologia claiming that the medical attention given the actor had been sound and proper. Barclay Warburton, Jr., a broker who had entertained Valentino in his apartment shortly before the collapse, disappeared into a sanitarium. In the frenzy of despair that gripped the globe, several suicides were reportedly committed in reaction to the actor's death. The most notable took place in London where a twenty-seven-year-old actress named Peggy Scott took an overdose of sleeping pills in a room where she had hung Valentino's autographed images.

"The immense interest shown in the outcome of Valentino's illness," declared the *New York Times*, "is a striking sign of what moving pictures have done to create a new mental attitude in vast multitudes of people. They come to regard a favorite screen actor as one whom they have known intimately."

The power of that media-generated image was tested most dramatically when Valentino's corpse was transferred under a cloth of gold to Campbell's Funeral Church on Broadway at Sixty-sixth Street in preparation for public viewing. Crowds gathered there before dawn, twelve hours before the doors were scheduled to open. By noon the numbers had swelled to over ten thousand, in spite of the heat and humidity of a torrid summer day. Police reinforcements were called in, for fear that the crowd might storm the funeral parlor. Fifty patrolmen and more than a dozen mounted police tried desperately to contain the growing chaos that had halted traffic for blocks around Campbell's. By two o'clock, the size of the crowd had tripled. Additional police squadrons were rushed to the scene. A thickening gloom gathered in the skies as the horde pushed and shoved, chanting for Campbell's doors to open early.

Gotham was tensing for a suitably cinematic Götterdammerung. Shortly after two, the heavens opened on the screaming mob. Steam rose from the hot pavement, creating a Dantesque inferno. The crowd surged forward, breaking through the police lines and Campbell's plate-glass windows. Three patrolmen, a photographer, and seven women were injured by flying glass. When the doors of the funeral parlor suddenly swung open, a wave of humanity rushed in and began to gut Campbell's stately interior. Outside, the crescendo of hysteria mounted to a chain reaction, as more store windows were broken and parked cars were overturned. The mounted police charged the crowd, cracking skulls with their clubs and trampling bodies under their horses' hooves.

Inside Campbell's Gold Room, which had been transformed into a flower-filled tabernacle, the body of Valentino, dressed in formal evening wear, lay on a catafalque surrounded by the solemn symbols of religion: a statue of the Madonna, an elaborately bound edition of the Vulgate Bible, lit altar candles, a rosary, and an embroidered antependium. Attendants, reporters, and the film star's manager, George Ullman, tried to halt the crazed fans, who suddenly poured into the room, knocking over potted palms and breaking furniture.

Miraculously the movie idol's bier was not disturbed, and in a matter of minutes the police had cleared the funeral parlor. The harder task was outside. Only after several charges were the patrolmen finally successful in expelling the mob to a distance of several hundred feet away from Campbell's battered facade. Over one hundred people had been injured. Ambulances carried away those who were bleeding and

A mourner kneels
before the body of
Rudolph Valentino in
Campbell's Funeral
Church, 1926.

those unable to walk. Debris littered the street: umbrellas, hats, torn clothing, and twenty-eight separate shoes. The police claimed that the riot, both in size and behavior, was without precedent in the history of the city.

After the police commissioner himself took charge of the situation and order had been restored, the schedule of public viewing began. Nine thousand people per hour passed through Campbell's doors, ten hours each day, for three days. During that time the drama did not abate, as everyone—from fascists to antifascists, from an ex-wife he did not love to a lover he did not marry—saluted, posed, paraded, collapsed, and, in general, lapped up the stardust that surrounded the fallen luminary. John Dos Passos, who would become famous as the author of the novel *U.S.A.*, wrote critically of the funerary escapade:

hundreds of women groggy with headlines got in to view the poor
body, claiming to be exdancingpartners, old playmates, relatives from
the old country, filmstars; every few minutes a girl fainted in front of
the bier and was revived by the newspapermen who put down her
name and address and claim to notice in the public prints. Frank E.
Campbell's undertakers and pallbearers, dignified wearers of black
broadcloth and takersup of crape, were on the verge of a nervous
breakdown.

The Vatican took a harsher view of the hysteria surrounding Valentino's death, calling it "collective madness, incarnating the tragic comedy of a new fetishism."

Fetishism it was, but of the most potent and numinous kind. The relatively new art form of film had created a love god whose cult was celebrated the world over in opulent shrines designed like Chinese temples, Arabian palaces, and Egyptian tombs. Movie theaters aspired to the same magic one might find in a Gothic cathedral; the hushed silence broken only by the strains of organ music, the darkened interior, the pewlike regularity of seats arranged before a curtained Holy of Holies. Few knew Valentino the man, but the apotheosis of his image, incarnated in these cinematic temples, made him universally recognized.

If the cult of Valentino were to claim its chief vestal, she would be none other than his second wife, Natacha Rambova, the woman who stood behind the myth and to a large degree created it. When they met in Hollywood in the winter of 1920 he was an impoverished Italian-born actor with but one hit on his résumé. She was a dancer turned designer, attempting to bring a more sophisticated look to the art of film. He was reeling from a short-lived and reportedly unconsummated marriage. She had fled from an unfaithful and manipulative lover. Together, their creative energies left an indelible mark on Hollywood history, and they became one of the most attractive and talked-about couples in the western world. Their story was Pygmalion and Galatea in reverse, the only time in Hollywood history that a woman fashioned a male star to an image of her imagination and shared that image with millions.

From the very beginning of their relationship Rambova molded Valentino into an effigy made to her liking. Under her spell, the well-groomed, muscular sophisticate emerged with his polished European manners and romantic bearing. George Ullman saw how much power the exotic and beautiful woman had over Valentino: "It is only fair to say that her culture, which she painstakingly but subtly communicated to her husband, was one which others recognized and which in my opinion put him forever in her debt. He was truly, and in the highest sense, elevated by his association with Natacha."

In her own right she designed America's first "art film." But her greatest and most lasting creation was the image of Valentino as a love god, Hollywood's first great male idol. This was accomplished subtly at first, by designing costumes for him that complemented his physical endowments. Later, as she took greater control of his career, she sought to find and develop specific film projects that would showcase not only his corporeal attributes and athletic prowess, but also manifest his noble spirit to an audience hungry for romance, legend, and lore. As his popularity grew, Rambova guided, negotiated, and defended Valentino's image while jealous studio moguls tried to gain possession of it. That he deferred to her judgment was manifest by a platinum bracelet of interlocked chain, a "slave bracelet" she had designed for him—and that he wore faithfully, always, even to the grave.

The slave bracelet was a symbol not only of Rambova's dominating artistic spirit, but of Valentino's unquestioning love. This image of the "Latin lover" was not a shrewdly calculated concept invented by Hollywood studios, nor was it even an artistic idea that sprang from Rambova's fertile mind. Rather, it was the reflection of a very passionate physical and emotional relationship that existed between them in the mere six years of their association together.

When that relationship finally ended and Rambova left Valentino in a much-publicized departure at a Los Angeles train station, the wheels were set in motion for the love god's eventual collapse. As he pursued her to France where she filed for divorce, photographers were able to record the lines of tension and fatigue that had etched their way into his famous face. Sorrow and distress over her departure had noticeably ravaged his outer appearance, but what was not known to him or others at the time was the damage that was taking place inside of him. Gastric acids had eaten through his stomach. Eight months after the divorce had been finalized, during which Valentino had pursued a reckless and even suicidal life-style, doctors finally discovered what the emotional loss had cost him. With graphic realism Dos Passos recorded their discovery:

When the doctors cut into his elegantlymolded body they found that peritonitis had begun; the abdominal cavity contained a large amount of fluid and food particles; the viscera were coated with a greenish-grey film; a round hole a centimeter in diameter was seen in the anterior wall of the stomach; the tissue of the stomach for one and onehalf centimeters immediately surrounding the perforation was necrotic. The appendix was inflamed and twisted against the small intestine.

In the end, Valentino could not live without Rambova. Her loss destroyed him from within.

Who was that woman who was the center of Valentino's life, whose

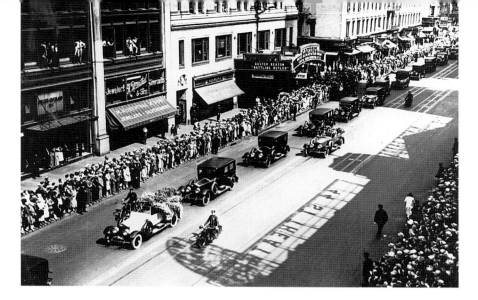

absence was noted at the grand funerals held for him in New York and Hollywood? Was his marriage to her the "sordid comedy" that H. L. Mencken called it, or was it the tragic love story of the century? Did she have other loves beside Valentino? Was she an opportunist and a domineering lesbian, as her enemies in Hollywood chose to believe? What of her other accomplishments as a stage actress, dress designer, crime reporter, health therapist, author, spiritualist, and scholar of symbolism and ancient Egyptian religion?

For over sixty years, Natacha Rambova has remained an enigma, a turbaned and exotically robed mystery to the score of biographers who have poured over every episode in the life of her illustrious husband. For the most part, authors and filmmakers have chosen to portray her central role in Valentino's career as that of a meddlesome harpy rather than a female Svengali. The image of an interfering wife in a male-dominated industry is ready-made for opprobrium. Rambova became a symbol not of Valentino's inspiration, but of his ruination.

Her story is far more complex than any simple-minded image would portray it. Hers was a life of remarkable talent, filled with unparalleled passion, adventure, and misadventure. It unfolded itself on three continents, from Hollywood and New York to the capitals of Europe; from an island in the Mediterranean to the pyramids of Egypt. And it began not in the strange and beautiful world of Imperial Russia, but in the American desert and the shore of the Great Salt Lake.

atacha Rambova. The name carries with it visions of onion-domed citadels and faraway places. But the fact is that its bearer was born Winifred Kimball Shaughnessy in Salt Lake City, Utah. Her family nicknamed her "Wink."

Not that her origins were humble. Far from it. Winifred Kimball Shaughnessy never set foot on Russian soil, but she was something of an American exotic. Her father was a Civil War hero, the retired federal marshal of two states, and a millionaire who made his fortune in the mining business. Her mother, a Kimball, was a descendant of a great Mormon patriarch and a member of one of the great pioneer families of the western frontier.

Writers of old-fashioned biography were fond of exploring their subject's geneology in search of clues to character. In the case of Rambova, the search proves to be more than idle literary convention. For in that collective pool of genes one finds the traits that marked her character: independence, industry, fair-mindedness, a fiery temper coupled with a fighting spirit, a brash self-confidence, a penchant for female bonding, and an inclination toward the symbolic and the mystical.

Her father, Michael Shaughnessy, was born in New York City on October 11, 1844. As a first generation American of Irish ancestry, he proved himself a staunch patriot during the Civil War by enlisting at age seventeen in the Second Cavalry. He quickly made a name for himself as

Winifred Kimball Shaughnessy as a toddler

19

a tough warrior who could endure much pain and hardship. Placing himself at the front of his command, he was wounded in the battles of Brandy Station and Cold Harbor. He recovered quickly and reentered the fray, until he was severely wounded at Gettysburg on July 3, 1863. He lay all night, bleeding on the field between the two contending armies before Confederate forces carried him off to Virginia as a prisoner. With eighty-seven other officers captured on that day, he was consigned to Libby Prison, a converted Richmond warehouse, where he remained for seven months without so much as a change of clothing. Finally, in an exchange of prisoners, he was returned North, to Annapolis, Maryland, where he was discharged, broken and emaciated.

But it was then that Shaughnessy's resilient vitality manifested itself most dramatically. He recovered and not only rejoined the army, but brought with him a volunteer company of infantry. Appointed captain, he fought in several battles around Mobile, was again wounded and transferred to St. Louis Officer's Hospital in New Orleans, where he underwent four months of painful recuperation. Appointed quartermaster until the war's end, Shaughnessy was breveted a lieutenant colonel "for conspicuous gallantry and meritorious conduct in action." Thereafter he was called by friend and foe alike "the Colonel."

After the war Shaughnessy decided to settle in Alabama and pursue the life of a planter, but changed his plans when President Andrew Johnson appointed him assessor of internal revenue. A hero in the conquest of the Confederacy, the Colonel now directed his attention to another kind of campaign, capturing the heart of a belle from Alabama named Eudora Mustin. Her family had been slave owners who lost their land and most of their money in the defeat of the South. After three years of courtship, the Colonel resigned his government post and married Eudora in Mississippi, where the governor appointed him brigadier general of the militia.

The Colonel's fortunes ascended more rapidly from that point on. His friendship with black senator Blanche K. Bruce catapulted him to the position of United States Marshal for the Southern District of the State of Mississippi. Shaughnessy took office at the critical moment when Ku Klux Klan trials were beginning, and he helped convict many of the organization's leaders, which led to the disbanding of the Klan's forces in the state.

In the eyes of many Mississippi whites, the Shaughnessys were "carpetbaggers," for they lived in high style and were friendly with the newly powerful black politicians. Eudora was particularly disturbed by the death threats leveled against her husband and begged him never to leave the house at night alone. He ignored her pleas. Refusing to be intimidated, his bravery may have been laced with equal portions of pig-headedness and Irish bravado, but he nevertheless carried a gun with him wherever he went.

In 1876 the Colonel became a Mississippi delegate to the Republican National Convention held in Cincinnati. He was elected vice president of that convention and forged many political alliances. Upon his return to Mississippi he was nominated by the Republicans as candidate for the Third Congressional District, which encompassed the territory between Jackson and the Gulf Coast. He campaigned vigorously on the Rutherford B. Hayes ticket throughout the district and was elected, but the opposition engineered a bogus vote count, which cheated him of the office. Shaughnessy filed a protest with the House of Representatives, but while the case was being heard, the Colonel became involved in two incidents that changed the course of his entire career.

In the spring of 1877, Judge Chisolm of Kemper County, a close friend of Colonel Shaughnessy's, was ambushed in his home by an enraged mob after he had been unjustly accused of conspiracy in the murder of a local Democratic leader and fund-raiser. During a shoot-out that lasted for several days, the judge and two of his children were wounded. Word reached Colonel Shaughnessy that his friends were in trouble, and he beseeched the governor to allow him to lead a militia party into Kemper County to rescue the Chisolm family. The governor forbade him to act, and, as a result, the judge and his children died of their wounds. Shortly afterward, the Vicksburg *Herald* published an editorial charging the Colonel with duplicity in his fruitless efforts to rescue the Chisolms. The Colonel published a letter in the rival Vicksburg *Commercial* condemning the charges against him as "false and infamous," whereupon the *Herald*'s editor, Charles Wright, challenged Shaughnessy to a duel.

On the day appointed, Colonel Shaughnessy and his friends waited several hours for the editor to arrive. Finally, they received word that Wright had lingered in Vicksburg in order that he might be arrested for his unlawful challenge and deposited safely in jail. Undaunted, the Colonel immediately sent two of his friends to Vicksburg to post bail for Wright. Thirty-six hours after the original time set for the duel, the editor appeared, but again sought to postpone the fight, claiming that the impending darkness and the evening fog rolling off the Mississippi would unfairly impede the duelists' vision. When the Colonel ordered that bonfires be built for illumination, Wright apologized and publicly retracted his charges.

In a second incident shortly thereafter, it was the Colonel who gave challenge. This time, it was no mere journalist who had roused Michael Shaughnessy's anger, but the bombastic Democratic senator of Mississippi, Lucius Quintus Cincinnatus Lamar. Noted for his flamboyant speeches in defense of "the unconquered and unconquerable Saxon race," Lamar was inevitably the sworn enemy of Blanche K. Bruce— and, therefore, of Colonel Shaughnessy. Challenge did not bring the Colonel the satisfaction he had expected. The penalty for dueling in Mississippi was disenfranchisement. Lamar saw to it that the law was enforced in this case, thereby bringing to summary conclusion the Colonel's political aspirations in the state.

Now the jobless father of four, Shaughnessy seemed to have grim prospects in the South, but the political friendships the Colonel had made at the Republican National Convention of 1876 came to his rescue. On February 20, 1878, President Rutherford B. Hayes appointed him the eleventh U.S. marshal of Utah Territory. Within a month, the Colonel had moved his family to Salt Lake City and took up his assignment at Fort Douglas.

While the politics of slavery had been the burning problem in the reconstructed South, the marshal of Utah had to deal with polygamy, advocated in the early Mormon creed and the chief target at which the federal government took aim in its efforts to curb the sect's domination of the region. In 1863 Congress passed the Morrill Law, which forbade plural marriage. The U.S. marshal was responsible for enforcing that law. Soon after he took office, Shaughnessy was sent to Nebraska to retrieve George Reynolds, a prisoner found guilty of polygamy and sentenced to two years in prison. Authorities in Washington wanted Reynolds to be kept in the Territorial Prison in Utah, where he could serve as an example. The Colonel pleaded with his superiors to allow the prisoner to remain in Nebraska, but to no avail. While escorting Reynolds back to Utah, Shaughnessy was so impressed with the man's innocence—not of the fact, but based on the sincerity of his faith—that he championed a drive for an immediate pardon. This was denied, but the Colonel's reputation among the Mormons benefited mightily.

Indeed, the Colonel earnestly befriended the leading Mormon families of Salt Lake City, where mansions on Brigham Street were the most elegant between Denver and San Francisco. Heber P. Kimball's family was particularly fond of the Colonel, and it was in their mansion, situated on a hill above Eagle Gate, that he met the person who would become the mother of Natacha Rambova.

An old family story relates how the Colonel first set eyes on Rambova's mother as she sat on a porcelain chamber pot. It was an unusual although practical chair to drag into the crowded parlor whenever company arrived, and was excusable only because the sitter was a six-year-old child at the time.

Her name was Winifred, but the family called her Winnie. Little did thirty-three-year-old Shaughnessy know then that this blonde infant —only three years older than his own daughter, Mary—with her infectious smile and flirtatious attitude, would two decades hence be his wife. At the moment, Shaughnessy was more interested in the little girl's family, one of the most prominent in Utah. Her father was a businessman of fortune, a wealthy cattle rancher, the owner of a stage coach line, and a former officer in the Territorial Militia, which defended the Mormon flock against the Indians. His Canadian-born wife, Phoebe Judd, bore him seven children—four sons and three daughters. Of these, Winnie was the youngest daughter. The family maintained its formidable home in Salt Lake City and a large ranch outside of town in Tooele County.

The size of Heber P. Kimball's family shrinks into insignificance beside that of his father, Heber C. Kimball—Rambova's most illustrious ancestor, one of the founding apostles of Mormonism, and Brigham Young's right-hand man. Heber C. sired what may have been the largest family in the Mormon Church, if not the western world: sixty-five children by forty-five wives. Before his conversion to Mormonism in 1832 Kimball had been a simple potter happily married to his wife, Vilate, and busy raising two children in Mendon, New York. After his conversion, he sacrificed all security to take up active ministry in the church. He proselytized for a year in England (the land of his ancestors, one of whom, Alice Freeman, is a forebear of Lady Diana Spencer, the Princess of Wales, making Rambova her eighth cousin, twice removed, and the future King William of England Rambova's eighth cousin three times removed). After his return to America, he shared a covered wagon with Brigham Young as they led the persecuted sect from Ohio to Missouri to Illinois to Utah. Kimball laid the cornerstone of the Salt Lake Temple, and in the early days of that desert theocracy he held the office of first

The Mormon patriarch, Heber C. Kimball

Vilate, his first wife

counselor, chief justice, and lieutenant governor of Deseret, later known as the Territory of Utah. No less than Mark Twain referred to Heber as a saint of "high degree" and a "mighty man of commerce." Credited as a pioneer who turned barren land into a prosperous commonwealth, Kimball died in 1868 and was accorded a funeral worthy of Valentino himself.

By the late 1870s a horde of non-Mormons, or "gentiles," were beginning to mine copper and silver in the Utah Territory. The Colonel observed how a number of these newcomers got rich practically overnight, and he decided to try his own hand at mining. He bought land in the Big Cottonwood Canyon and in the American Fork Canyon, and he struck it rich. His investments rapidly displaced his enthusiasm for his job as marshal. As dutiful zeal waned, so did his reputation. He argued over conflicting land claims. In one dispute, Shaughnessy hurled R. C. Chambers of the Ontario Silver Mining Company to the ground, cocked his pistol, and pointed it at the man's head ordering him to get off of "his" land. Chambers filed charges against the Colonel, which were eventually dropped, but the cordial and fair-minded U.S. marshal was viewed by many thereafter as a man of fiery temperament and bold ambition, lusting after land and money.

It was only a matter of time before the Colonel's mining interests demanded his full attention and prompted him to resign his federal post, leave Utah, and move his family to his home state of New York. He left the territory with a million-dollar fortune.

The Colonel purchased an estate called Bellevue in Suffern, New York, and spent thousands making it into a showplace, filled with Old

The Colonel's estate, "Bellevue," in Suffern, New York

An engraving of Colonel Michael Shaughnessy, shown with his signature below

Master paintings. He also established a pied-à-terre at the Hoffmann House in New York City, where he joined the Thirteen Club, a prestigious clique of wealthy politicians and merchants. Affluence and comeliness were two qualities that marked the Colonel in the prime of his life, just as they would one day characterize Rambova at the height of her celebrity. In May of 1888 the *Rockland County Journal* commented that "One of the most magnificent specimens of physical manhood in New York is Colonel Shaughnessy. Seen about Wall Street and in the public places up town, he is two or three inches above six feet in height, elegantly formed, with a pleasant, well-rounded face, blond mustache and goatee." Having enjoyed so much success in life, he could look forward to a genteel retirement. But soon the fissures in his moral character began to widen. A weakness for gambling led him to wager an enormous amount of money on the Blaine-Cleveland presidential campaign of 1884; Shaughnessy bet on Blaine. He also invested $103,000 with a New York broker, who absconded with his money. The *Salt Lake Herald* observed on July 10, 1885: "He should have protected it like he got it, with his sixshooter."

The greatest catastrophe was the death of his wife, Eudora, at thirty-nine. She had been the loving mother of his seven children, and her death plunged Shaughnessy into deep depression. He increasingly sought comfort in alcohol, which provoked a furious temper. He recklessly continued to gamble and saw his fortune dwindle to nothing.

The painful disintegration of his physical, emotional, and financial well-being was mitigated somewhat by the terms of his late wife's will. Her estate was worth $50,000, with valuable land holdings in Idaho and Utah, all of which was left in trust to her children with the Colonel authorized to develop the property as he saw fit. This became Shaughnessy's life raft in a sea of adversity. Crippled but not killed by bad luck, he returned to Utah to fulfill his wife's bequest. He took his daughter Mary with him and set out to regain his fortune.

Salt Lake City in the 1890s was vastly different from the town he had known a decade before. Taller, more elaborate buildings of brick and stone had been raised in the commercial district once dominated by single-story wooden structures. New businesses flourished on Main Street, where one could find clothing stores, pharmacies, restaurants, saloons, bakeries, photography studios, elegant hotels, and even a Masonic Hall. Over all of these towered the newly completed Great Salt Lake Temple, a gray granite behemoth quarried from the mouth of Little

Cottonwood Canyon. The temple walls rose to a height of 107 feet, and the towers soared an additional 103 feet. The Mormons had built it to withstand every natural disaster. Forty years of careful construction had followed that day in 1853, when Heber C. Kimball laid the cornerstone. It stood guard over the city, waiting to usher in the millennium.

On his arrival, the Colonel visited the home of his old friends, the Kimballs. Things had changed dramatically there as well. Heber Parley Kimball, son of the revered patriarch, had died of dropsy in the winter of 1885, leaving his wife, Phoebe, as head of the household. The curly-haired infant, Winifred, who had so charmed him by dragging a chamber pot into the parlor, had grown into a sophisticated and beautiful woman of twenty. In time she came to view the Colonel not so much as a widower almost thirty years her senior who was trying to piece his life together, but a mature embodiment of adventure and daring enterprise.

Winifred Kimball may have abandoned her childish ways, but she was still rebellious, clever, full of fun, and willing to take risks. After a brief and unhappy marriage to an eastern army lieutenant named Butts, Winnie had returned to the house of her mother. All the men in her family had either died or left home to start families of their own. The insulated matriarchal family consisted of her mother, Phoebe, her elder sister Teresa (with whom she would have a lifelong friendship), and two nieces.

Michael Shaughnessy entered this world as a figure of dreamy valor, and he and Winifred began to see each other frequently. He found again the drive and energy he had felt in his youth, and he began to rebuild his lost fortune. The Tiewaukee Mine in Bingham, which he had developed as part of his wife's trust, proved lucrative. After more than a year and a half of moderate success, he began to talk about remarriage. When he finally proposed to Winifred, no one was particularly surprised or shocked. But they *were* skeptical. The differences in age and religion seemed to spell trouble. Yet Phoebe ultimately gave them her blessing, and as a wedding gift—they married in 1895—she presented her daughter with some of her finest pieces of jewelry.

From the beginning Winifred Shaughnessy tried her very best to make this union a successful one. She refrained from wearing her favorite imported perfumes, because her friends had told her that the wives of Catholic gentlemen would never tolerate such vanities. She gave up the idea of having a home of her own, because the Colonel preferred to take up residence at the Knutsford Hotel. It was a temporary arrangement, he said, until his finances would allow them to return to New York. "Temporary" stretched into years.

The Colonel spent much of his time and money carousing with his Irish mining buddies. Winifred was not so much unhappy at first as she was bored. The Colonel was a celebrity in Utah, and she enjoyed basking in his fame, however local. But it was soon evident that Michael Shaughnessy's life was not set on the new beginnings he had dreamed of and she had hoped for. Instead, in a dissipated state of endless reflection on the past, the Colonel behaved like a man whose glory days had long gone. Newspapers repeatedly asked him for a series of stories based on his career as marshal, but he never actually got down to writing them. He preferred to sit in a bar and mesmerize the locals with tales of the wild and romantic days of the old West, a place and time the Colonel had never really left.

Disappointed once again in marriage, Winifred found herself often sitting alone at the Knutsford Hotel, looking forward to the twentieth century and all its promise as the Colonel sat regaling admirers in a saloon forever looking backward at the nineteenth.

Clearly, the most noteworthy event of the Shaughnessy union occurred on January 19, 1897, with the birth of a daughter. The child was christened six months later at the Church of the Madeleine and given her mother's name, Winifred. In order not to confuse mother with daughter, Aunt Teresa nicknamed the little girl Wink.

Winifred proudly hovered over her infant daughter, sparing no expense to array her in imported lace, satins, and velvets. At the same time, the Colonel periodically raided his wife's closet to extract some of her finest gowns, which he sold against his mounting gambling debts.

As befitting the daughter of a Celtic warrior and a Mormon princess, Wink's childhood was sequestered, pampered, and ultrafashionable. Winifred encouraged her daughter to play with her Kimball cousins, but the child was often alone and learned early on to delve into a world of fantasy and make-believe. She kept under her bed pieces of material for making costumes, paper for drawing, and clay to fashion figures.

Wink could do nothing to bridge the widening rift between Winifred and Michael Shaughnessy. Had she been born a boy, the situation might have developed differently; for Shaughnessy had taken a keen interest in his sons and closely directed their development. His daughters, however, were entrusted to their mothers. Indeed, the Colonel neglected both Wink and Winifred. At last, as the Colonel's drunken temper flared more frequently and his gambling debts mounted, Winifred resolved to leave him quietly and return to her parents' home. She dared not tell her husband she was leaving, for fear that his possessive rage might turn violent. Walking out on the proud old soldier was risky business, but it was not altogether devoid of humor.

One night mother and daughter packed their bags and dressed for their final departure. At the very moment they were taking their luggage downstairs toward the lobby, they heard the Colonel singing a barroom ballad and making his way upstairs. Hurriedly Winifred and Wink retreated back into the bedroom, flung their suitcases under the bed, and dashed under the covers. When Shaughnessy entered the room, he was so drunk that he did not observe the obvious sign that something was amiss: in the bed, feigning sleep, were his wife *and* daughter, covers up to their chins—and fancy feathered bonnets on their heads.

Their second attempt at escape was successful. Winifred refused to return to the hotel with Michael Shaughnessy, even when his whiskey-induced anger turned to sober, tear-filled pleading. The marriage was dead. The five years Winifred had spent with the Colonel had been little more than a contest of endurance that rekindled her own desire for independence. Wink was her one consolation.

Winifred and her daughter,
"Wink," 1897

After procuring a divorce in 1900, Winifred moved to San Francisco with her daughter. As to the Colonel, his dissolute saloon life and gambling continued to take its toll on his body and business affairs. On January 10, 1910, he died—nearly broke—of "cerebral anemia" after an illness of many months.

Although he often neglected her, the Colonel left Wink a strong legacy in the form of a volcanic temper, steely resolve, and the ability to endure physical hardship. Just as the Colonel loved to duel—and suffered for it—so Rambova would battle Hollywood moguls and be vilified in the press. Colonel Shaughnessy had been jealously hated for his ambition; his daughter would be despised similarly.

As her great-grandfather, Heber C. Kimball, had helped bring civilization to the Rockies, so Natacha Rambova would attempt to bring high-brow culture to the pioneer and proletarian film industry. Those close-knit female ties that her mother had experienced in the Kimball household would be forged in Rambova's own life. And while this would at times cause her some frustration, it would also bring her the only long-lasting security and happiness that she would ever know.

*S*he was a stunning child. Winifred marveled at how clear Wink's complexion was, and how the coloring of her brown eyes, her auburn hair, and even the reddish, fleshy tones of her mouth and lips blended together in dramatic counterpoise to that translucent skin. The child's beauty was shown to full advantage in the variety of costumes Winifred provided or Wink herself made, costumes in which the girl performed her precocious, interpretive dances before her mother's friends at tea.

After the divorce from Colonel Shaughnessy, the independent-minded Winifred determined that she should support her daughter and herself by taking up a profession. She was particularly interested in the new field of interior decoration, an area of expertise in which women were finding that they could become arbiters of taste—*and* get paid for it. Before she left the Colonel, she had taken note of an article in *Outlook* magazine by Candice Wheeler, "Interior Decoration as a Profession for Women." Winifred realized that she was already qualified to speak on the subject since she had a well-developed knowledge of art and textiles and was familiar with the coordination of domestic interiors as manifested in the finest mansions of Salt Lake City. With a shrewd business sense appended to her own self-confident good taste, she launched herself as a professional decorator, first in Salt Lake City, then on to the more lucrative market of San Francisco's high society.

Wink as a pensive young artist

In order to pursue a profession that demanded much travel, Winifred had to make arrangements for Wink's care. Following instinctively upon the lines of her polygamous Mormon ancestors, she depended on the notion of the extended family, the bonding of wives and their offspring in the absence of a resident father. Winifred left Wink in the care of her sister, Mrs. Teresa Werner. Both women found themselves in similar circumstances as divorcees; and both had daughters. They pooled their sisterly resources in order to raise their fatherless children. A third sister in the Kimball family, Margaret, had died of appendicitis at twenty-five. Her daughter, Katherine, was also incorporated into a family that now numbered five females. It was agreed that Winifred would earn the money needed for everyone's support, and Teresa would take care of the home and watch after the girls. An only child, Wink suddenly had sisters, and in many ways, Teresa Werner became the girl's surrogate mother. A relationship of love was nurtured between aunt and niece that would last a lifetime.

Having established herself as a decorator and moved to San Francisco, Winifred Shaughnessy met and soon married Edgar de Wolfe, the brother of Elsie de Wolfe—the woman who is generally recognized as America's first interior decorator. What Edgar lacked in intelligence, he made up for in charm, and the marriage gained for Winifred not only pleasant male companionship, but entrée into the top echelon of a new multimillion-dollar enterprise spearheaded under the de Wolfe name. Together, Winifred and Elsie began to sweep Victorian clutter aside to make way for the sparer and more classical lines of eighteenth-century decor.

Born in 1865 in New York and educated in Scotland, where she had family roots, Elsie de Wolfe first gained public notice as a would-be society girl who turned to the stage with the hope of following in the footsteps of Sarah Bernhardt. While she failed in that endeavor, she did succeed in gaining some notice before the turn of the century as a fashion plate in Europe and America. She then turned her attention to the revolutionary changes taking place in interior decoration. With the death of Queen Victoria in 1901, a monarch to whom she had once been presented as an aspiring debutante, the overblown fashion and heavy culture of the era given the queen's name came to an end. In 1904 Elsie accurately forecast the new century's emerging taste for simplicity and coordination in environmental decoration, and she set up her own decorating shop in New York. The first big commission, which established her name and her career, was undertaken in 1905 at the Colony Club, the first women's club in New York. There she created a sensation by taking visual elements borrowed from the country—garden trellises, tiled floors, wicker furniture, chintz fabric—and translating them into city chic. Her taste for Georgian architecture, French antiques, Louis XV furniture, and artists like Fragonard made her a natural choice as a decorator of Henry Frick's Fifth Avenue mansion. Thereafter, the social elite came begging for her services. While her business could well have kept her occupied full time in America, she preferred to make her home in Europe, becoming a mainstay of the fashionable social set that circulated in London, Paris, and the French Riviera.

When Elsie allowed Edgar to take charge of the business of her New York office, his new bride was delighted to be part of that undertaking. Elsie and Winifred saw eye to eye. They enjoyed circulating in the same social stratosphere, they shared the same aesthetic tastes, and they both pursued a creative spirit, which led them away from the traditional feminine ties to hearth and home. Like generals coordinating an attack, the two women divided the United States in half. Commissions undertaken on the East Coast would fall to Elsie de Wolfe, those on the West Coast went to Winifred de Wolfe, who became a millionaire as she decorated private mansions and grand hotels.

There was one discordant note in the seemingly effortless triumph of Winifred's professional career: Wink disdained Edgar de Wolfe. It was as if the child discovered the core of disingenuousness behind Edgar's creamy charm, a sybaritic and a self-absorbed laziness that floated atop the industry, brains, and financial success of his sister and his wife. Wink began to exhibit two opposing traits that would often become manifest whenever she encountered stress. She either became cool, quiet, and withdrawn, or else the genetic chemistry in her Shaughnessy blood exploded, and she charged for the attack. Once, Wink up and punched Edgar in the nose, bloodying it, when he playfully attempted to wrestle with her in the middle of a family picnic.

In an effort to let the girls enjoy themselves away from home and grammar school, Muzzie and Aunt Tessie (Wink's nicknames for Winifred and Aunt Teresa) sent them to summer camp at Raw Denim, a resort compound in the mountains near Santa Cruz. Wink and her cousins loved to vacation there, where they could discover the pleasures of horseback riding, swimming, mountain climbing, and, as they grew older, the company of boys. Although they were not yet even teenagers,

Wink and her cousin Katherine were tall for their age, and many of the older boys at camp had a crush on them. The girls liked the attention and greeted the boys' innocent overtures with giggles and jokes. One of their jokes went too far.

On a sultry evening, as Wink and Katherine were preparing for bed in their second-story dormitory room, they found themselves being serenaded by a group of boys standing beneath their balcony. Like two Juliets responding to their Romeos, the girls stood on the balcony in their nightgowns, trying to suppress their smiles at the sight of the ragtag suitors who were so intent on impressing them with song. Whispering in each other's ear, the two girls excused themselves for a moment, then returned to the balcony with a bucketfull of water, which they poured over the boys' heads. As they dove into their beds, shaking with laughter, little did they think that the camp directors would fail to share their sense of humor. They sent the girls home for the unladylike conduct of standing barefoot on their balcony clad only in their nightgowns.

Shortly thereafter, Winifred de Wolfe decided to place Wink in a boarding school for girls, where she could be properly educated in the arts, the humanities, and the social graces. Elsie de Wolfe suggested to her sister-in-law that the girl enroll in a qualified school in London. As she had recently purchased a fashionable home in Versailles, the Villa Trianon, Elsie further suggested that Wink come and visit her during the summer months, take ballet lessons in Paris, learn French, and be exposed to some of the glitterati of European society who passed through her salon. On Elsie's recommendation, Winifred selected Leatherhead Court, an exclusive boarding school for girls, in Leatherhead, a town not far from London in the county of Surrey. Wink accepted her mother's plans with all the eagerness of a prison sentence. She begged Winifred to let her stay with Aunt Tessie and the other girls. But Muzzie would not be moved. She was firmly convinced that what she was doing was in her daughter's best interest. So, after a brief tour of Europe, Winifred and Edgar deposited the girl at Leatherhead Court and sailed back to America. Wink was only eight years old.

Described in the *Leatherhead Directory* at that time as "a high class school for young ladies," Leatherhead Court was situated on Randalls Road, on the outskirts of the town, in an area surrounded by park lands and meadows. The forty-year-old half-timbered and brick building was an eclectic pile, part Tudor and part Georgian, with a multitude of leaded windows, gables, and chimneys. To Wink it must have seemed a strange

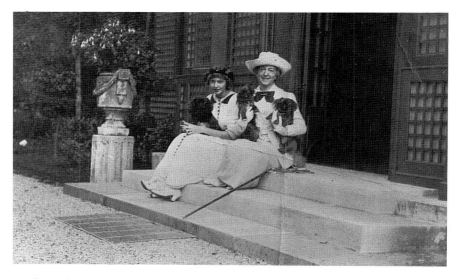

castle, where girls from all over the world were deposited by their wealthy parents, to be both coddled and sternly corrected by the headmistress, Miss Tullis.

There, in a foreign land steeped in fable, Wink compensated for acute loneliness by voracious reading. As she later remarked, "My interest in mythology and legend began as a child, as I never read any other kind of book." Greek mythology, Roman mythology, Nordic legends, nothing escaped her insatiable need to lose herself in myth. This also had an effect on her artistic abilities, which tended to the fantastic, and it likewise encouraged her already well-established penchant for dance.

In the nearly nine years that Wink spent at Leatherhead Court, she was most enthusiastic about field trips to museums and the ballet. The British Museum was a veritable sanctuary of visual stimulation. It provided her with solid evidence of those mythic people she read about, from the wrapped mummies and decorated sarcophagi of the mysterious Egyptians to the marble deities found in the Parthenon fragments of the ancient Greeks. And when the Russian Ballet visited London, Wink clamored to see that one idol who was a myth in her own day: Anna Pavlova.

The Russian prima ballerina made her English debut at the Palace Theatre in London in 1910, accompanied by her partner, Mikhail Mordkin. Starting with that engagement and Pavlova's two London appearances the following year, Wink faithfully stationed herself at the stage door after each performance in order that the legendary dancer might sign the ballet scrapbook she had made with the pictures pasted in it of

her favorite Russian stars: Pavlova, Tamara Karsavina, Vaslav Nijinsky, and Mikhail Mordkin. In Wink's pantheon of Russian dancers there was one other, Theodore Kosloff. He had had a brief debut appearance in London at the Coliseum Theatre, but the memory of that performance on a gray July day in 1909 would prove fateful for the young girl.

The program in which he starred with Tamara Karsavina was titled *L'Oiseau de Feu,* a pas de deux with music chosen from Tchaikovsky. Ballet historian Arthur Applin, who viewed the performance, later wrote of Kosloff's stunning presence that afternoon:

It is more than probable a portion of the audience thought he slid down from the flies on an invisible tight wire, and that his wonderful leaps and bounds and flights through the air were caused by some hidden mechanism concealed either in the dancer or on the stage. . . .

Here also was the spirit of youth. There is nothing effeminate about Kosloff; to those whose standard of manhood is gauged by the weighing machine at the apothecary's or the railway station he hardly seems flesh and blood; manly, yet scarcely human man. . . .

While we remained holding fast to the arms of our fauteuils, part of us, the spiritual, which, thank God, can at times break all natural laws, went up on the stage and danced in the Forest of Imagination with Karsavina and Kosloff.

At the Coliseum Theatre that day, there was coincidentally another woman in the audience for whom this performance would have its long-lasting effect. Her name was Winifred Edwards, and neither she nor Wink nor Theodore Kosloff had any idea then how their lives would be intimately connected to each other in the future.

During the summer months, when most of the girls at Leatherhead Court left the school to rejoin their families, Wink remained in Europe. Except for those rare occasions when Muzzie came to take her on visits to Germany and Italy, the girl was sent to France, to live with her Aunt Elsie at the Villa Trianon in Versailles. Elsie's nineteenth-century residence was situated on the outskirts of the property that had once belonged to the former royal palace. Deserted and in disrepair when she purchased it in 1905, the villa was transformed into a small palace infused with the spirit of the ancien régime.

A vigorous social climber, Elsie used the Villa Trianon and its surrounding gardens to attract interesting and fashionable people. During the many summers she spent there, Wink would have encountered the likes of Sarah Bernhardt, Henry Adams, Count Robert de Montesquiou, Bernard Berenson, Loïe Fuller, Paul Poiret, and a smattering of political dignitaries, from the papal nuncio to Constantine, crown prince of Greece. Elsie made sure that her niece's education was properly continued during her French sojourns. She enrolled Wink in ballet classes conducted by Rosita Mauri at the Paris Opera and had her take courses in French, Italian, art, and architecture.

While she loved her classes, Wink did not care for Elsie de Wolfe any more than she liked Elsie's brother, Edgar. The fact that her mother

Russian dancers Tamara Karsavina and Mikhail Mordkin

Theodore Kosloff as a student in the Moscow Imperial Ballet School

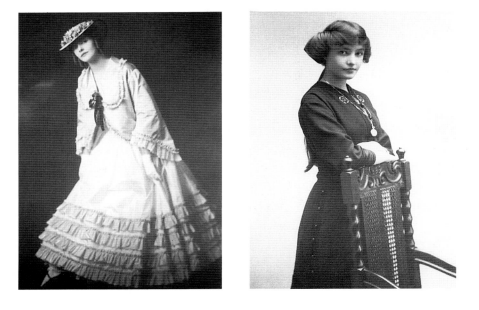

had imposed these two people on her life at that most vulnerable time
of transition from childhood to lonely adolescence contributed to conflicts Wink would have with Muzzie in later years. Wink was shy, intellectual, and contemplative—serious about life around her. The
shallowness and pretension that marked so much of Elsie's existence at
the Villa Trianon did not agree with her. Elsie's memorable response
when she first viewed the Parthenon—"It's beige! *My* color!"—was
typical of all that Wink found irritating in her aunt.

As plain as she was pretentious, Elsie relied on her knowledge of
theatrical make-up to enhance her looks before resorting to more drastic
measures like face lifts. She was also a health fanatic, given to strenuous
exercise, and loved to stand on her head for long periods of time to the
amazement of her guests. Finally, when age turned the decorator's hair
pure white, she was the first to introduce to society the rage for blue
rinse. Elsie's celebration of artifice, her love of wit, gossip, and gaiety
were qualities she shared with her sister-in-law, but not with young
Wink. Later, when she would read about some social event Elsie had
participated in, Wink would wryly comment, "Aunt Elsie is still doing
the same thing. She never changes."

One thing that never changed—though she later made a marriage
of convenience and picked up a title, Lady Mendl, in the process—was
Elsie's preference for the intimate company of women over that of men.
During the years when Wink was a regular visitor at Villa Trianon, Elsie

was involved in a sapphic relationship with the elephantine Elizabeth "Bessie" Marbury, a theatrical agent, hostess, and driving force in Democratic Party politics. For years the two had been called "The Bachelors," until a third woman, Ann Morgan, the youngest daughter of financier J. P. Morgan, joined them at the Villa Trianon. The three were known thereafter as the "Versailles Triumvirate."

They attempted to keep a tight reign on Wink, who, as she grew older and more aware, must have felt they were grooming her for membership in their lesbian clique. While they indulged her every artistic interest, they strictly policed contact with the opposite sex. As a consequence, her regular adolescent frustrations developed into a smoldering resentment against the Villa Trianon and the ladies who inhabited it. But in the mounting battle of wills, Elsie had met her match. After many skirmishes, in which Wink accused her aunt of being superficial and manipulative, a final clash thundered through the well-appointed halls of the villa, and Wink was sent packing back to America.

As it turned out, she was leaving just in time. A greater conflict had been ignited by a shot fired at Sarajevo. In a matter of weeks, Europe was caught in the ferocious grip of a world war.

*W*ink was able to escape the outbreak of war in Europe, but it was not long before she found herself locked in combat with her mother on the home front.

The issue was dance: Muzzie had always assumed that her daughter would enter San Francisco's high society after receiving the polished education of a European. She viewed Wink's absorption in dance as nothing more than an avocation, an activity that contributed to physical grace and good health. For Wink, however, dance was not a means to an end, but a way of life. The thought of becoming a social butterfly repelled her; she wanted to dedicate her heart and soul to the art of Pavlova and Karsavina.

Winifred de Wolfe failed to appreciate how history was repeating itself. Just twenty years earlier, she herself had left Utah and the claustrophobia of a matriarchy. Now, seventeen-year-old Wink was feeling that same compelling need for independence. The elder Winifred had deviated from Mormon custom, leaving her family to marry a man outside her faith; the younger Winifred rejected the eighteenth-century creed of de Wolfian taste and social elitism in favor of a more modern, even Bohemian, life-style. But, like her mother before her, Wink chose a man as her means of escape. He was Theodore Kosloff, the brilliant graduate of the Moscow Imperial Ballet School, whom she had first seen dance with Karsavina at the London Coliseum in 1909. Now, in 1914,

With a new name and fresh artistic resolve, Natacha Rambova poses with her maestro, Theodore Kosloff.

he had arrived from Europe to establish a dance studio in New York City.

As was often the case when mother and daughter were at odds, Aunt Teresa suggested a compromise. Wink would go to New York, where she would live with Teresa for one year and enroll in Kosloff's school. Then, after she had had her fill of Terpsichore, she would return to San Francisco with a new appreciation of genteel society.

Kosloff's dance studio on 42nd Street was far removed from the ballet academies of Moscow and Saint Petersburg. Nevertheless, he hoped that by locating near Broadway he would be able to prosper, training the dancers used in the big musical productions so popular in the American theater. He established his school in a shabby brownstone that had once been an illegal gambling parlor. Down the hall, past the front entrance of the place, was a steel door opening into a large, bleak, windowless room.

Kosloff had come to America with the sole object of making money. It was not his first venture in the United States. After dancing in Diaghilev's Ballets Russes for a year, he formed his own company, which toured the capitals of Europe until Gertrude Hoffmann persuaded him in 1911 to perform in America. One of his partners in that American tour was Maria "Alexandra" Baldina, with whom he had been linked romantically ever since their performance together at the London Coliseum. Soon, they were living together. When Baldina became pregnant by Kosloff, Gertrude Hoffmann insisted that the couple marry immediately. They did so, and the two were legally husband and wife when the troupe reached San Francisco.

Kosloff and Baldina returned to Europe, where she gave birth to a baby girl they named Irina. In 1912, while the family was on a tour of Italy, little Irina contracted what seemed to be a persistent cold. It was later diagnosed as meningitis. The child survived, but would spend the rest of her life an invalid. Barred by immigration policy from reentering the United States with such a dependent, Maria Baldina lovingly cared for their child in a home Kosloff had purchased for her in Bournemouth, England. In the meantime, the dancing master set sail for America, where he hoped—as so many immigrants did—to find his fortune.

When the daughter of the wealthy Winifred de Wolfe applied to Kosloff's studio, he accepted her immediately. It was his practice never to turn away a student of means. Another young woman, by the name of Marilyn Miller, applied and was also accepted; Kosloff knew her father, who held a managerial position with the Shubert Theater conglomerate,

which had sponsored the Russian's immigration. Money, influence, and connections were what the maestro sought, and he found them in the handful of students he gathered at his 42nd Street studio. Later, when Marilyn Miller and another pupil, Mary Eaton, developed into celebrated Ziegfeld stars, Kosloff took credit for their success.

Despite his ulterior motives, by Kosloff's exacting standards, Wink was the wrong type for classical dance: she was too tall—five feet, eight inches, an inch taller than Kosloff himself. Yet she had an ingenious facility for pantomime invention, and her originality in interpretive dance extended to designing her own costumes. But most of all, Kosloff thought her the most beautiful student he had ever encountered, with her perfect complexion and finely chiseled features, her auburn hair parted and coiled in braids on either side of a long, elegant swan neck.

The fascination was mutual.

Kosloff told Wink that she had the potential of becoming a pre-mière danseuse, under his tutelage, of course. But two things were necessary if she hoped to pursue a career in dance. First, she must never again wear shoes with heels; they destroyed a dancer's posture. Second, she must change her name.

Years later the story circulated that Wink was given the name of a dead Russian ballerina, one of Kosloff's previous partners, whose career had been tragically cut short before she had reached her full potential. Perhaps this is true, but there is no doubt that any marquee advertising exotic Russian dance would have looked incongruous listing Winifred

Shaughnessy as one of its stars. But the colorful myth that the memory of Kosloff's late beloved could be made to live on in his new protégée served yet another purpose. In adopting the name Natacha Rambova, Winifred Kimball Shaughnessy assumed a new maturity that left her childhood behind. She graduated from being Kosloff's pupil to Kosloff's lover.

Winifred Edwards, an Englishwoman who likewise adopted a Russian name (Vera Fredova) in order to dance in Anna Pavlova's troupe, attached herself to Kosloff's studio later that year as an assistant instructor. She too, had been attracted to Theodore Kosloff when she first saw him perform in London. "I saw him at the Coliseum, not knowing from Adam who he was. I was enormously struck by him," she later recalled. She compared him favorably with other stars of the Russian ballet: "Mordkin was a massively built man, but Kosloff was extremely lithe and beautifully faceted." "He was all male, that's for sure!" said Agnes de Mille, who would later study with him. "But what a ménage of females he had around him—and mistresses!" she added.

Fredova befriended Natacha, who was two years her junior, and the young women became like sisters. Natacha sought Fredova's advice on how to handle the man who was at once her mentor, her father figure, her dance partner, her artistic idol, and her lover.

Vera Fredova poses in costumes Rambova designed for the Imperial Russian Ballet.

"Natacha was only seventeen and a virgin when Kosloff first made love to her," Fredova later recalled. "But I knew this romance would not last, because she was so young and had never been in love before."

Patiently, and not without some cunning, Fredova dispensed her wisdom to the young woman, whose emotions teeter-tottered between exhilaration and depression. Kosloff's volcanic temper and boundless ego were difficult to endure, but as a lover he had totally mesmerized Rambova and won from her a fidelity that would be dramatically demonstrated as soon as their affair became known to her family.

If Aunt Teresa had ever been suspicious of her niece's sexual involvement with Theodore Kosloff, she did not act upon it, notwithstanding the dramatic change of name and the long hours spent with the Russian dancer. With Fredova acting as confidante, it is possible that Natacha was able to hide her romance entirely from the custodial eyes of Teresa Werner.

Natacha's eventual betrayal came in the form of the Broadway theatrical manager Morris Gest. A Russian-born immigrant, Gest disguised his troll-like appearance behind long coats, slouch hats, and flowing ties. He made his first money in America by painting sparrows yellow and selling them as canaries and launched his career on Broadway acting as an "authorized" ticket scalper for Hammerstein productions. In 1909 he married the daughter of the renowned dramatist and producer David Belasco, capitalizing on his new respectability to sponsor theatrical ventures, which proved enormously successful. In 1911 his firm introduced the Russian ballet to New York City, where he was the lessee and director of several theaters. When Gest became aware of Kosloff's affair with the underage Rambova, he relayed this information to his distinguished father-in-law. The San Francisco–bred Belasco was a good friend of Natacha's mother, whom he immediately notified.

Kosloff had commenced negotiations to play the Keith-Orpheum vaudeville circuit with an assembled troupe of twelve dancers, which he named Theodore Kosloff's Imperial Russian Ballet. He had taken over the contracts of several members of Diaghilev's organization and had local painters copy Leon Bakst's designs for scenery (the artist later tried to sue Kosloff for this, but the case was thrown out of court). Rambova was to have a featured part in the production as a soloist, and she had been counting on her mother's help to pay for the cost of her costumes. But Mrs. de Wolfe's response to the news that Kosloff was "molesting" her daughter resounded like a thunderclap on Broadway, alerting police

Portraits of the Kimball sisters: Natacha's mother (left), and her aunt Teresa Werner (right)

and the press to what had heretofore been a private affair. She ordered Natacha to return home immediately, and with all the influence she could command, Winifred set in motion the process of deporting Theodore Kosloff as an undesirable alien.

Her dancing debut thwarted, and her lover accused of statutory rape, Natacha disappeared from Aunt Teresa's apartment and rushed to Kosloff's side. Together they devised a plan that, in fact, had proved successful for her mother fourteen years earlier. Natacha Rambova decided to run away.

With the help of Russian emigrés she was spirited across the Canadian border, where she assumed the identity of a French governess before booking passage on a steamer headed across the war-torn Atlantic. Her destination was Bournemouth, where she would be taken in by Maria Baldina and remain in hiding until the situation in the States improved.

Mrs. de Wolfe's anger was transformed into grief when she learned from her sister that Natacha had disappeared. She thought Kosloff had kidnapped her and had secreted her somewhere in Russia. She sought the help of two American senators and the Russian ambassador in an effort to get Natacha back. Meanwhile, Kosloff pleaded not guilty to the charges that he had treated his student indecently, denied that he had ever molested her or kidnapped her, and counted as ridiculous the accusation that he was now secretly hiding her in Russia. Pinkerton detectives were hired, but it was all to no avail. Months passed without any word. Fall passed into winter, and winter passed into spring.

In Bournemouth, Mrs. Kosloff cooperated in not revealing the true identity of the new "governess" hired to take care of her invalid daughter. Ever since she had retired from the stage, Maria Baldina relied totally on her husband's financial support to take care of Irina and herself. Any danger to her husband's finances in the United States was a danger to her own security. How did she feel about hiding her husband's lover in her home? All evidence suggests that the Kosloff marriage had been reduced to nothing more than a financial arrangement. Baldina's love was now reserved for Irina alone. Natacha, exhausted by the nerve-wracking, heartbreaking ordeal, contracted pneumonia during the English winter. She maintained her charade even in the hospital and returned to Baldina's home for a long recuperation. With each tedious day, she looked forward to receiving from Kosloff the news that the danger had passed and she could be reunited with him in America.

On June 7, 1916, Theodore Kosloff's Imperial Russian Ballet made its long-awaited debut at the Palace Theater in New York City. It proved to be a dazzling success, with the music of Borodin and Stravinsky and costumes and sets derived from Bakst's designs. The company of twelve dancers included Kosloff and his brother Alexis, a Czech dancer by the name of Vlasta Maslova, Vera Fredova, and a brilliant character dancer, Anatole Bourman, and his wife. Their two-week run was extended to three weeks, then four, then five, until finally the troupe concluded its performances after a stay of eight weeks. By the end of its New York engagement, Kosloff's ballet company had broken the box-office record previously established at the theater by Sarah Bernhardt.

The troupe then traveled to San Francisco for a three-week engagement. During this run, a momentous meeting took place between Mrs. de Wolfe and Theodore Kosloff. Natacha's mother was willing to concede defeat. In a tearful plea bargain she agreed to drop all charges against Kosloff, give Natacha permission to dance in his company, and even promised to contribute money to help pay for costumes and sets—if only he would bring her back and facilitate a reconciliation. Kosloff listened quietly. He made no admissions and promised nothing.

After the San Francisco engagement, the troupe moved down to Los Angeles, where it was booked at the Orpheum Theatre for another three-week run. After the opening-night show, Jeanie MacPherson, a former pupil who had danced briefly in the Gertrude Hoffmann–sponsored tour of 1911, rushed backstage to greet Kosloff. She never made a name for herself in dance, but in Hollywood she had attained fame as

the principal scenario writer for Cecil B. DeMille. Kosloff responded warmly when she asked him to have dinner with the director after the following night's performance.

DeMille was extremely impressed with what he saw in Kosloff and his ballet company, and the director studied the dancer with a movie maker's eye. Kosloff's lean and muscular build, his high cheek bones with deep hollows, his energetic spring and expressive grace were just the ingredients DeMille was looking for in a part he was casting for a movie called *The Woman God Forgot.* It was a story about Cortez and the Spanish conquest of the Aztecs in Mexico. So far Wallace Reid and the opera star Geraldine Farrar had been signed for the movie. The role of the Aztec prince, Guatemoco, had not yet been cast, and DeMille asked Kosloff if he might be interested in it. The film was not scheduled for shooting until late summer, when the dance tour would have concluded.

Kosloff was flattered by DeMille, and acting in a motion picture seemed a way to make easy money. As long as the film work would not interfere with his dancing, he saw no reason why he should fail to accept the part. Before leaving Los Angeles he consented to DeMille's offer, thereby launching what would prove to be a long-lasting friendship and professional relationship with the movie director.

After the Los Angeles run, the company moved on to Chicago. Mrs. Winifred de Wolfe was waiting for them there. Shortly after her meeting with Kosloff in San Francisco, she had at long last received word from Natacha agreeing to a reconciliation based on the terms offered to her Russian maestro. Hoping to settle affairs with her mother in time to join the latter part of the ballet tour, Natacha designated Chicago as the place for a summit meeting. The Pinkerton men, however, having been frustrated for so many months without a clue to Natacha's whereabouts, situated themselves on the ledge outside Kosloff's hotel window in order to catch the Russian dancer in a compromising position with his "kidnapped" prey. When he discovered them, Kosloff was furious and demanded their removal. The detectives did abandon their watch, but were soon replaced by federal agents, who had located Natacha elsewhere in the city. Kosloff was then shuttled over to the Chicago office of the Department of Justice, where he was detained for questioning.

In the meantime, Natacha and her mother met in an emotional reunion. Winifred de Wolfe now realized that her daughter's life was entirely her own. She had been lost for nearly a year, and her resolve to follow Kosloff in the world of dance was as strong as ever. It was apparent to her that the compliant child whose life she had tried to model in her own image was no more. Recreated as Natacha Rambova, she had grown into a woman of indomitable will, risking health and enduring a long and painful separation in order to pursue a career and protect the man she loved. After a day-long conversation, Winifred concluded by wishing her daughter success. She dropped all charges against Kosloff, who was promptly released and free to continue with his tour. In a parting gesture of peace, Muzzie gave Natacha money for the ballet costumes and informed her of one other fact, which happily cemented their reconciliation: Mrs. de Wolfe was in the process of divorcing Mr. de Wolfe.

After bidding her mother good-bye, Natacha hurriedly left Chicago in order to join the company in Omaha. She worked through the night on the train, piecing together her costumes for her dance debut. Having brought with her money and her mother's blessings, she was allowed to share top billing with Kosloff.

While her terpsichorean talents were no more than adequate compared to that of the seasoned members of the troupe, she was by far the most striking figure in the company, enthralling audiences with her fascinating attire and clever pantomime. When they reached Kansas City, she and Kosloff posed for a round of publicity photographs, wearing the costumes she had designed. They wore pearl-studded helmets, bejeweled tunics, transparent veils, and body paint. Festooned with garlands and moving through clouds of colored incense, Kosloff and Rambova danced a pas de deux hailed as a triumph of sensuous exoticism.

By the time their performances came to an end that summer, Natacha's energies were necessarily focused more on her art than on her love life. Much to her dismay, she found that her relationship with Kosloff had changed after her return from hiding. Naive to the point of thinking that he would remain faithful to her and to her alone while she suffered exile, she learned a cruel lesson in love: If Kosloff had not been faithful to his wife, why should he be faithful to his mistress? Vera Fredova and other women of the company were sleeping with the insatiable Tartar and had been doing so throughout the tour. "Love comes and goes, my dear," Fredova told Natacha, "but art endures forever."

Like so many in Kosloff's stable of female dancers, Natacha had been at first unable to separate her love of the art from her love for the man. The sexual politics of the Imperial Russian Ballet were such that the maestro controlled all aspects of his lovers' lives. Promising them fame and fortune in return for their unquestioning loyalty, Kosloff was able to form a kind of "family" out of the ambitious women competing for his attention and love. He gave Natacha the affectionate nicknames of "Ila" and "Nina" and called Fredova "Frida" while they cooked, designed, and danced for him without pay. They formed the nucleus of Kosloff's family, even to the point of learning Russian, while other women came and went as their usefulness to his ballet tours dictated. "It became apparent to all of us," Fredova later admitted, "that Kosloff would never be faithful to one woman. He was the type of man who could only be happy if he were surrounded by a harem." Unlike her Mormon ancestors, Natacha found such as arrangement not at all to her liking. But her desire to make a name for herself as an artist stifled her sense of betrayal and disappointment.

In the summer of 1917, Kosloff, Rambova, and Fredova returned to Los Angeles where they rented a house with a large backyard in which they set up a canvas tent to serve as a temporary dance school and studio. Natacha plunged into research on the ancient Aztec culture and designed costumes for DeMille's film as Kosloff prepared himself for his movie debut. The three also served the studio as technical advisors, overseeing the film's choreography and movement. "Wallace Reid had

Theodore Kosloff, Raymond Hatton, Geraldine Farrar, and Wallace Reid in The Woman God Forgot no grace whatsoever," recalled Fredova, "and he spent a lot of time working with Kosloff."

The movie was released in November 1917 to favorable reviews, weekly *Variety* declaring Kosloff's acting the best of the entire cast. Natacha's scenic and costume work were also commended—albeit less directly—in *The Moving Picture World:* "To the student of history the accuracy of the exteriors, interiors, costumes and accessories in *The Woman God Forgot* will make strong appeal." Agnes de Mille remembered her uncle Cecil showing her the sketches for the film, and enthusiastically telling her that a Russian dancer had designed them. But they were not as accurate in their archaeological detail as *The Moving Picture World* led its readers to believe. "In one scene, Geraldine Farrar wore a headdress decorated with Bird of Paradise feathers," recalled Agnes, "which they later found out never existed in Mexico at that time!"

After *The Woman God Forgot,* DeMille offered Kosloff and his assistants work on a number of other film projects. The offer was lucrative, but the dancers, intent on planning their future performances on the

Keith-Orpheum circuit, declined. Movie work was an interesting divertissement, but not worth forfeiting their stage careers.

In the fall of 1917 the Imperial Russian Ballet began its second tour in Los Angeles. The highlight of their program was "The Aztec Dance," performed by Rambova and Kosloff (who wore his costume from De-Mille's film), accompanied by Vera Fredova, Vlasta Maslova, Ivonne Verlainova, and Alex Ivanoff. They displayed themselves most dramatically with exaggerated makeup, partial nudity, copper body paint, and paraphernalia made of leather, metal, and feathers. The presentation incorporated the warlike with the ceremonial. The dance critic for the *Los Angeles Times* praised the performance as one of the best ever seen in the city, but doubted that the Aztec Dance would ever supplant the Hawaiian Hula as a popular craze.

Similar raves followed the troupe around the country, and after thirty-two weeks the second tour ended in New York in the spring of 1918. The dancers then decided to motor down to Florida for a summer holiday. After numerous flat tires and other misadventures, they were received as guests in the seaside villa of a Russian emigré friend of Kosloff's. There they spent the happiest season of their dancing lives together. They swam and sunbathed; they sketched and painted; they formulated plans for the future. It seemed as though the halcyon days would never end.

But end they did.

The Russian Revolution of 1917 had an inevitable effect on Theodore Kosloff's finances. The money Kosloff's troupe had made from the dance tours was being invested in a block of "American style" apartment houses in Moscow. While Kosloff was vacationing in Florida, word reached him that the Bolshevik government had confiscated his property and buildings. This meant the financial collapse of his Imperial Russian Ballet. Vera Fredova recalled that fateful event:

All his earnings and savings had been invested in that American built
apartment complex in Moscow, which was the pride of his heart,
twenty apartment units, and his sister lived in one and managed it.
"Amerikanski arkitect," he would proudly say. Then came that fateful
day. We were resting in our respective rooms when he phoned me to
come immediately to his room. I opened his door and saw him seated in
a chair with an open telegram in his hands, looking very grieved,
oriental, and Tartarish. He said, "Bolsheviks take my apartment house!"

*Rambova and Kosloff
in "The Aztec Dance"*

He told me that he had lost everything, save for the money coming in
that week from our last performance. His wife had deposited her
diamond earrings in a bank in New York, and he told me that they had
been sent to England to help support the child. This situation made him
seriously consider DeMille's offer. He was thirty-five years old and had
devoted his entire life to the ballet. Now he was virtually bankrupt.

A final tour for the 1918–19 season was then planned, during which
auditions would be given across the country for young aspirants who
wanted to enroll in a Los Angeles dance school begun by Kosloff, Rambova, and Fredova. The school would supplement the movie income and
keep all of the instructors rooted in their chosen profession.

Maria Gambarelli of New York's Metropolitan Opera replaced Natacha Rambova as Kosloff's principal dancing partner on the third tour.
Natacha chose to spend more of her time designing the costumes and
sets for new routines revolving around legendary Tartar themes. She was
chagrined by Kosloff's financial collapse and further disappointed by his
decision to work for DeMille. It was apparent to her that their days as
performing artists were numbered, but pride prevented her from leaving
the company and returning home to her mother. She consoled herself by
devoting more of her energies to research and design.

The third and final tour of the Imperial Russian Ballet was well
received across the country, and the Kosloff School of Dance, established
at Trinity Auditorium in Los Angeles, received many applications for
enrollment. One of the students who began classes that summer was the
fourteen-year-old Agnes de Mille, whom Kosloff admitted free of charge
as a courtesy to her uncle Cecil. In her autobiography, *Dance to the Piper,*
Agnes recorded her first impressions of Kosloff and his school:

The studio was an enormous bare room with folding chairs pushed
against the white walls for the mothers to sit on while they watched
their daughters sweat. Across one end of the hall hung a large mirror.
Around the other three sides stretched the traditional barre. I gave my
audition in a bathing suit. Kosloff himself put me through the test. He
did not say how talented I was or how naturally graceful. He said my
knees were weak, my spine curved, that I was heavy for my age and
had "no juice." By this he meant, I came to learn, that my muscles
were dry, stubborn and unresilient. He said I was a bit old to start
training. . . . I looked at him in mild surprise. I hardly knew what

emotion to give way to, the astonishment of hurt vanity or gratitude for professional help.

Vera Fredova remembered the ungainly teenager who appeared twice a week for her dance lessons: "Agnes' appearance was completely incorrect for classical ballet. She had thin legs, a big bosom, and the wrong kind of face. But she was completely dedicated and turned all of these disadvantages into advantages. I was very fond of her, and she of me."

Another student, Flower Hujer, was especially impressed by Rambova and remembered first seeing her when she danced a Victor Herbert number called "The American Fantasy" during the second tour of the Imperial Russian Ballet. So enthusiastic was the eight-year-old that she convinced her mother to let her study with Kosloff while he filmed *The Woman God Forgot*. For Flower, Natacha Rambova was a vision of unconventional beauty: "I remember so well the fascination she held for me when I was a child," she recalled. "I thought she was extraordinarily attractive, with an elegant air about her. I had never seen such an exotic and beautiful woman like her before." But when Flower Hujer returned the following summer to enroll in Kosloff's school at the Trinity Auditorium, she noticed a definite change in Natacha. She was frequently absent from the studio, taught less, and immersed herself in the art of design:

Rambova gave me a few private dance lessons the first time that I was enrolled at Kosloff's studio. I was very entranced with her and preferred her over the others then. The second time she wasn't around much, and when she was she seemed cool and aloof. During this period of tension I remember being invited out to Kosloff's house at 7268 Franklin Avenue where someone asked Rambova how she was doing and she answered, "Oh, I have been weeping all the time."

In addition to her growing estrangement from Kosloff, and subsequent to her bitter disappointment over the end of her touring career, Natacha now harbored a new resentment against the man who exerted complete control over her life. *He* was taking credit for the long hours *she* spent researching and designing in order to further *his* motion-picture career. While he was an avid painter, Kosloff had little interest in designing costumes and sets. Nevertheless, he offered DeMille the services of an assistant—Rambova—who would give her finished sketches to Kosloff for his approval. He would then deliver them to DeMille as if they were wholly his own.

The students and instructors of Kosloff's School of Dance in Los Angeles: in black dresses stand Fredova (left) and Rambova (right); Flower Hujer is at Kosloff's side, holding his hand.

Kosloff also relied on Rambova to design his costumes for the supporting roles he played in DeMille's *Why Change Your Wife?* and *Something to Think About,* both released in 1920. In the following project, *Forbidden Fruit,* DeMille planned to insert a fantasy sequence based on the Cinderella fairy tale. The design of that episode was delegated to Mitchell Leisen and Rambova. It would prove to be the most stunning feature of an otherwise lackluster movie. Mitchell Leisen, who preferred to think of himself more as an architect than a dress designer, later gave full credit to Rambova for her work on the production: "I did some of the clothes for the Cinderella Ball . . . and Natasha [sic] Rambova did the others. One of hers was a black dress for the Fairy Godmother that had little electric lights all over the skirt." Indeed, Rambova studded her Fairy Godmother (patterned after Mater Dolorosa votive statues, which she had seen in European churches) and her Cinderella costumes with tiny electric lights. The shimmering effects of the assembled cast—black trumpeters sporting gold lamé loincloths and page boys encased in onion-shaped silver trousers, ladies-in-waiting wearing colorful butterfly and heart-shaped gowns, attendants with feathered headdresses, glittering tassels, turbans, and bejeweled powdered wigs—all these were dazzlingly reflected in the mirrored black floor. The fantasy sequence exploded in DeMille's film with all the visual delights of an imagination allowed to run wild, and the critics were awed. The *Dramatic Mirror and Theatre World*

Agnes Ayres wears Rambova's electrified ballgown in the fantasy sequence of **Forbidden Fruit** *(top); Rambova's costume design for a lady of the fairy court (bottom)*

observed that "A great many precious shekels have been spent to make this feature one that will not only make a dramatic appeal, but will dazzle everyone who sees it by the gorgeous settings that are inducted into the story in phantasmagoria form." Weekly *Variety* concurred by noting that "In addition to telling his story superbly, DeMille has interpolated, as a sort of pictorial obligato, the story of Cinderella in a fashion probably never attained before. The photography here and all though the picture is flawless, the lighting exquisite."

The highly critical *Photoplay* magazine also marveled at it:

A romance of unbelievable beauty in this fairy-tale translated to the silver-sheet. A stern business-like studio set was transformed into a veritable fairyland. A glass floor was laid on the huge Lasky stage, velvet curtains and dreamlike draperies were hung over ceiling-less walls, and a glittering court came to life under the director's magic wand which he waved after the fashion of the Fairy Godmother. Costly silks and satins and velvets, fine lace and luxurious fur, were used . . . in making the gorgeous gowns for this one episode.

To Rambova's chagrin, *Photoplay* mistakenly credited all this artistry to Claire West, the head of wardrobe at Lasky Studio where DeMille worked. In none of the reviews was the name of Natacha Rambova mentioned, though Kosloff was praised for his role as the crooked butler, and DeMille himself gave him the credit for creating the bizarre costumes of the fantasy sequence.

In the dance studio Kosloff was likewise praised for his innovative teaching and style, but was ultimately resented by those to whom he had broken promises. Flower Hujer, whom the maestro renamed "Kosloff's Flower," recalled him as

a dedicated and extraordinary teacher who developed students to their utmost capability. Unlike so many others who taught only toe work and classicism, he had an open mind. We did all sorts of character work and mime. He did an African dance and an Aztec dance, for instance, and was much more of an artist then a mere teacher of technique. He was very handsome and had a magnetic personality. But he had a bad side to his character as well: his possessiveness and inability to allow people to develop their own careers. He made promises to everyone, telling them that he would make them stars with solo appearances and tours.

Flower Hujer also remembered his violent temper, which could reduce his students to tears—though his fractured English laced even those threatening moments with comedy. When he angrily dismissed a student from class one day he was heard to yell, "Take your make-up and toe shoes and go to home!" The girls in the studio would giggle and imitate his voice when he customarily knocked on their dressing room door after washing his hands and commanded, "Gif me towel!" Frida was continually trying to teach him correct English, but her efforts were met with stubborn resistance. When Kosloff began a sentence saying, "I not vant," she would interrupt him saying, "I don't want," only to be silenced with an ever louder, "I not vant!"

Throughout his life Theodore Kosloff naturally gravitated toward other Russian emigrés, who were mutually supportive of one another. The most famous—and flamboyant—of these was Alla Nazimova, the dramatic stage actress who had signed a contract with Metro and moved to Hollywood in 1918. Impressed with the weather in California, she purchased three and a half acres of lush garden land and a Spanish-styled villa at 8150 Sunset Boulevard. It quickly became a social center for a select group of Russians, actors, and visiting celebrities. Flower Hujer was among those invited to Nazimova's mansion:

Nazimova was taking lessons from Kosloff in preparation for one of her motion pictures. When she came to the studio all the students were expected to leave and clear the room. But I was enthralled with the idea of seeing Nazimova, and made myself so busy at the barre practicing my exercises that they didn't have the heart to make me leave. I remember her wearing this marvelous perfume, something like lemon verbena. She was known in Hollywood to be bisexual, and I found out years later that she had a crush on a few of the girls at the studio. She invited one of my friends, named Virginia, to come and spend an afternoon with her at her house. And Nazimova looked at me and said, "Bring her along too." So I went to what would later be called "The Garden of Allah" and was thrilled to be a guest there. We spent the afternoon painting leaves with iridescent colors. Nothing untoward happened. But at one point she asked Virginia to do some oriental movements. So she had her dance in silhouette before a bright window shade in a room where all the lights were turned off. Then we went home.

Just as he had done with DeMille, Kosloff offered to submit to Nazimova innovative costume and set designs for her movies. As a consequence, Natacha Rambova's artistry found its way into the dream sequences of Nazimova's film *Billions*. Afterwards, she was busy working on designs for the actress's next film, an adaptation of Pierre Louÿs's fantasy *Aphrodite,* when the maestro made a fatal mistake. Instead of delivering Rambova's sketches himself, he asked Rambova to give Nazimova the artwork. When the actress examined the sketches she was pleased with them, but wanted Kosloff to make some slight changes.

Nazimova gazes into a pond in the dream sequence of Billions.

Natacha Rambova dances one of her celebrated pantomimes.

Rambova proudly pointed out that *she* was responsible for the designs, and *she* would be happy to make the changes there and then. Attracted to both the designs and the designer, Nazimova offered Rambova a job on the spot as art director for her films. Natacha accepted and thereafter quietly plotted her break from Kosloff.

She chose a particular weekend as the time to move out of Kosloff's Franklin Avenue house. The Russian had been invited to DeMille's country estate, "Paradise," for a few days of relaxation and hunting. "It wasn't just hunting that was going on up there," observed Agnes de Mille. "There were girls!" Rambova was well aware of this and also knew that Kosloff was now in the habit of sleeping with two of his ten-year-old pupils.

Natacha did not disclose her plan of action to Frida until the morning of her departure. "When Natacha finished packing she sat in the living room and waited for the taxi to arrive," recalled Fredova. "We sat across from each other and exchanged few words. The melancholy air was cut only by the thought that something better would come from all this."

What followed was in fact a scene of unexpected violence and horror. The mournful silence was broken suddenly as the two heard stomping footsteps approach the front door. It swung open with a crash. Theodore Kosloff stood there holding his hunting rifle. He had decided to return home early, only to find Natacha's suitcases lined up on the front porch.

A shower of invectives was followed by an order to unpack. For the first time since they had known each other, she refused him. Then, to the insistent staccato of a taxi horn rising above their shouting, Natacha defiantly seized her purse and attempted to rise from her chair.

Flesh and blood exploded in front of her. A searing pain raced through her leg. Bird shot from Kosloff's gun had ripped into the muscle above her knee.

She fled into the bedroom, with Kosloff in pursuit, firing haphazardly in her direction. Fortunately, Fredova managed to block his advance and wrestle with his gun long enough for Natacha to escape through a window and stumble in her blood-stained dress to the waiting cab. Once inside, she locked the door. As it sped away, she passed out of Theodore Kosloff's life forever.

*M*y friends call me Peter and sometimes Mimi," declared Alla Nazimova in an interview with *Motion Picture* magazine. But behind that facade of disarming informality, the petite actress with the flaring nostrils and upturned nose was a formidable power in Hollywood. In fact, those who worked for her never dared to call her anything but "Madam."

Hers had been a rapid but hard-won road to success. Born of Jewish parents in the Crimea in 1879, she became an accomplished violinist before turning to the stage. She fled Russia during the abortive revolution of 1905, and with other Jewish emigrés she played in Paul Orleneff's Yiddish theater in New York City, where she lived hand-to-mouth in the Bowery until she became Orleneff's mistress, and he showcased her talent. When creditors converged on the impresario and immigration officials began to cast a suspicious eye on his friendship with the Russian-born anarchist Emma Goldman, Orleneff's theater interests in the United States collapsed, and he returned to his homeland. Nazimova, however, remained in New York, perfecting her English and preparing for her Broadway debut in Ibsen's *Hedda Gabler.*

She opened at the Princess Theater on November 13, 1906, to rave reviews that called her another Duse. Her matinee performances were extended to accommodate the crowds. A few months later, she played Nora Helmer in *A Doll's House,* which would prove to be her most famous role, and she was thereafter acclaimed as the definitive interpreter of

Nazimova in Salome

Ibsen. Sponsored by the Shuberts, she toured the United States and loved to titillate the local press with her unconventional views on love, marriage, children, and the arts. Dramatic poses, developed to the point of self-parody by Orleneff, became a trademark on and off the stage.

By 1910 she had a theater named in her honor on 39th Street, and her 1916 film debut in *War Brides* was critically acclaimed, despite a pacifist theme that, on the eve of World War I, was detrimental to box-office appeal. Lured to California by the Metro Studio in 1918, she brought with her the actor Charles Bryant, an Englishman with whom she had shared both bed and stage. Even after the romance cooled, they continued to collaborate and posed as man and wife, although no record of their marriage exists.

Nazimova was known to be a woman of variable passions. In a somewhat cryptic remark to interviewers for *Motion Picture* magazine, she declared that "most of my friends are young girls." Her critics added to the insinuations, often more bluntly, as when one reviewer wrote that "her vogue is based not so much on the perfection of her productions as on her own bizarre personality and artistry, and seemingly an overwhelming appeal for the feminine sex." Paul Ivano, a French-born cameraman of Serbian extraction who found work in Hollywood after the war, befriended Nazimova. Twice his age, she became his lover for six months in 1920. "Alla preferred women most of the time," admitted Ivano, whose combination of strength, sensitivity, and sophistication attracted Nazimova and established a friendship that was to endure for a quarter-century. "Nazimova adored Paul, and he was such a charming young man," recalled the actress Patsy Ruth Miller, who was only sixteen when she became part of their circle and was chosen by Nazimova for a role in the Metro production of *Camille*. "Nazimova was at heart quite respectable," she added. "She would never allow my dress to be too short or tolerate my teenage flirting." Regarding the rumors of lesbianism, the retired actress expressed surprise. "I never noticed anything like that! She had me at her house all the time and never once made a pass. You think that she would have done something other than tease me or scold me for eating too much. She loved men!"

What she loved indisputably was talent. When Madam Nazimova discovered the versatility and depth of Natacha Rambova's artistry, she foresaw in the proud but introverted designer a collaborative relationship that would transform Hollywood filmmaking. Rambova seemed so modern, so intelligent, so elegant. Yet, shaken after her flight from Kosloff,

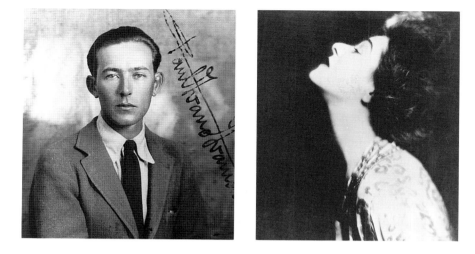

Natacha made a less than auspicious debut at the Metro set, where Nazimova's *Aphrodite* was taking shape.

"She was in tears, nearly hysterical," recalled Paul Ivano, who was hired to photograph the production. "We spent nearly an entire day picking the bird shot out of her leg, as she related how Kosloff had tried to kill her." Despite the shocking nature of the incident, Rambova refused to press charges. The notoriety, she felt, would only cast aspersions on her own reputation and cause her great embarrassment. She did not need a scandal to mark the debut of her career as Nazimova's art director. Instead, she chose to bury that traumatic episode. Later, she would use the excuse that she had been shot and scarred by a jealous ballerina as her alibi for not continuing in dance. For now, she had learned much about life and love, and she made a conscious effort to hide her emotions and her vulnerability behind a shield of aloof detachment. In fact, that cultivated, cold exterior became itself beguiling, a wall of mystery that more than one admirer tried to scale.

Aphrodite was to mark a significant change in the kind of film Nazimova had been doing for Metro. Of late she had been showcased as an exotic adventuress in a number of disappointing vehicles that saw her popularity at the box office wane. When the Hollywood press began to attack her for the stupidity of her most recent productions, it was announced that henceforth Madam Nazimova would star only in films drawn from notable works of literature.

Pierre Louÿs's *Aphrodite,* a controversial novel about ancient Alexandria, had stirred much debate ever since it made its debut in France in 1896. As a story of Greco-Egyptian culture of the first century B.C., it promoted a Parnassian appreciation of beauty and form coupled with an unabashed sensuality. Critics claimed that the work was offensive to public taste because it incorporated elements of sacrilege, torture, murder, nudity, and lesbianism in its tale of a Hebrew courtesan named Chrysis and the ill-fated love she shared with Demetrios, a sculptor and royal favorite. Louÿs deliberately set out to shock conventional morality, condemning in the preface to his book the eighteen "barbarous, hypocritical, and ugly centuries" of Christianity, which had systematically suppressed the pagan freedom of physical expression he extolled. Noting that a little classy controversy might freshen up her own career, Nazimova chose *Aphrodite* as the means by which she might stretch the art of filmmaking and revive her popularity at the same time.

Just a year earlier, in December 1919, *Aphrodite* had been lavishly unveiled in a Broadway stage production engineered by the imperial showman Morris Gest, with a little help from his revered father-in-law, David Belasco. Leon Bakst reportedly contributed to its costuming, and Michel Fokine was called from Europe to choreograph for it a Bacchanalian revel. The highly collaborative spectacle played to overflowing crowds at the Century Theatre, who were eager to believe the advance publicity promising they would be both thrilled and shocked by this flashy pageant of corrupt and degenerate Alexandria. "Compared with the original novel," wrote Alexander Woolcott in his review for the *New York Times,* "it seems as pure as a Barnum and Bailey parade." Nevertheless, he praised it for its mixture of genuine beauty and good circus,

singling out the actress Dorothy Dalton for her riveting performance as Chrysis, the mere mortal who manages to outshine the goddess of love.

Ever since the movie rights to the novel had been purchased, Nazimova had poured over the French text page by page in an effort to interpret for the screen a more faithful version of Louÿs's sumptuous but sordid tale. While Charles Bryant had customarily been credited for the formulation of her film scripts, it was no secret in Hollywood that Madam Nazimova had nearly autocratic control over every aspect of her Metro productions. For her part, Rambova researched the culture of Ptolemaic Egypt and designed a number of striking costumes based on antique prototypes. Several of her updated creations, transparent and sheer in their celebration of the female form, incorporated the shape of the blossoming lotus, the flower of the Nile. For the male actors in the film, Natacha drew heavily upon the togas and tunics of classical statuary, and added to their streamlined linearity dropped pearls and other bejeweled embellishments of an altogether modern idiom.

Before casting had been completed and while photographic tests were still being made of Rambova's costume and set designs, a crisis brought to a halt the entire production. Censorship laws were being passed in a majority of states hard on the heels of a Supreme Court ruling that defined motion pictures as a business and profit-making industry and, therefore, not covered by First Amendment guarantees of freedom of speech. Public charges of obscenity and immorality in the cinema kept movie producers at bay. Metro became increasingly nervous that Nazimova's provocative adaptation of *Aphrodite* might well become the film that would ruin the entire studio. Without warning, the production was closed down. A curt statement was issued to the press claiming that *Aphrodite* was "not suited to the requirements of Madam Nazimova," and in an effort to placate its outraged and difficult star, Metro announced that she would instead be appearing in a new version of the classic *Camille*.

Terribly disappointed herself that work on the historical pageant would cease in favor of a blander modern production, Rambova discarded all but a few of her designs for the film. The mock-ups and sets that had been built were torn down. Some of the costumes were saved for other productions. The collaborative effort of the actress and the designer to capture the essence of Louÿs's *Aphrodite,* a tale of vanity, murder, and frustrated love, might very well have been their masterpiece, had it not miscarried.

Costume sketches by Rambova for Aphrodite; *the costume for the high priest (far left) was later used for the Nazarenes in* Salome.

Camille was to be a "modernized" rendition of *La Dame aux camélias* by Alexandre Dumas *fils*. The updating was meant to set it apart from two unsuccessful film versions of the classic made in 1917. Both Nazimova and Natacha believed that the film should reflect the latest developments in European architectural and fashion design. This was partly an attempt to market the movie and partly a deliberate effort to foster in American film audiences a greater appreciation for art itself. The work on *Camille* also marked the beginning of Natacha's avocation as a teacher; she tutored students in design when she was not working in her Metro office.

Natacha was a gatherer of eclectic inspiration, and in her assiduous research for *Camille* she decided to incorporate derivations from the most recent work of the Parisian designer Emile-Jacques Ruhlmann and the Berlin architect Hans Poelzig. In Camille's apartment Natacha incorporated a semicircular alcove with a beveled glass window, a variation on a Ruhlmann interior that had been published in 1920. For an early scene in the film, set in a theater lobby, Rambova fashioned two enormous torchères with serpentine curves derived from Poelzig's expressionistic column designed for the foyer of Max Reinhardt's *Grosses Schauspielhaus* in 1919. She made the entry to Camille's apartment strikingly austere, decorating it with a cool art deco severity. Double doors of onyx and silver opened to an anteroom with bare gray walls and an arch hung with

Rambova's semicircular alcove in Camille *was inspired by a Ruhlmann sketch.*

*The entry way (top) to
Camille's apartment
(bottom)*

a shimmering, transparent curtain. The main sitting room of the apartment, like the adjoining bedroom, was accented with circular and semicircular lines: arches placed within arches, windows curved like goldfish bowls, a round bed, a rounded fireplace, and global light fixtures hanging from the ceiling and clustered flowerlike around the semicircular alcove. Accenting everything, from the velvet pouffes strewn about the floor to the wall decorations and the ceramic foyer fountain, was the decorative circular ensign of Marguerite Gauthier—also known as Camille—an abstract, rather oriental variation on the camellia blossom.

The circular motif based on the camellia became Rambova's primary symbol in the film. It had nothing to do with a Freudian obsession with orifices, as some critics later implied, nor did the expressionistic angularity of the influential German art film *The Cabinet of Dr. Caligari* have any direct effect on the design of *Camille,* since the former was released in the United States well after Rambova's sketches had been completed, the sets constructed, and the costumes made. Instead, *Camille* reflected Rambova's desire to bring a uniting element into the artistic interpretation of the story. The circle of the camellia blossom reflected not only the heroine of the tale, but was a symbol of the eternal feminine. The circle became the ubiquitous emblem, permeating everything, from the exaggerated moldings Rambova placed around architectural arches to Nazimova's halo of loose curls.

This visual vocabulary was extended further in the design for a scene set in a casino. Scalloped archways radiated from a semicircular stage veiled by a translucent scrim and topped by a semicircular orchestra pit set into the wall. Behind the scrim she placed two dancers performing in silhouette, an entertainment technique she perfected while dancing with Kosloff. To complete the scene a heavy black curtain was drawn to cover the stage. It was highlighted by a gigantic spider web of white, a striking visual element symbolizing the moral web spun by the novelist.

Like *Aphrodite,* the story of *Camille* centers around a courtesan, Dumas's heroine, who becomes part of the fashionable world of Paris. Unlike Louÿs's Chrysis, however, Camille makes a moral choice for the good in favoring the penniless man she loves, Armand Duval, and rejecting the wealthy Count de Varville, whom she does not love, despite the fact that he could pay all her debts and keep her ensconced among the wealthy social set to which she had always aspired. The plot becomes more complicated when, at the urging of his family, Camille must make the ultimate sacrifice in concealing her love for Armand, forcing him to

leave her. She makes him believe that she has tired of their life together and returns to Paris. The story ends with Armand and Camille reunited at her deathbed. The sentimentality of the tale, which reflected many of the moral and social problems of the nineteenth century, made the work popular and prompted its adaptation in two operas. But while Nazimova's distinctively different film version of the story was taking shape, an actor had yet to be chosen for the role of Armand.

"It was a hot winter's day in Hollywood," as Rambova remembered it, when Nazimova knocked on the door of Natacha's office and presented her art director with a fur-clad figure of an actor who had just been filming an Arctic scene on a nearby set.

This, Madam declared, was another possibility for her Armand.

She introduced Rudolph Valentino to Natacha Rambova and asked the designer for her opinion. At first glance, Rambova was not at all impressed. His face was covered with sweat and artificial snow—a wilting contender for the prized role of Armand.

Then he smiled.

"That flash of even white teeth had certainly something very winning about it," she recalled.

The actor stepped forward, shook her hand firmly, and asked her to put in a good word for him with Madam. Then he disappeared to resume shooting.

"Madam" wasn't really interested in Natacha's concurrence this time. Her mind was already made up. Rudolph Valentino would play Armand, and the shooting for *Camille* would be delayed while they waited for him to complete *Uncharted Seas.* "As this day in my office was the first time I had ever seen Rudy," Natacha reminisced, "I personally found it very difficult to understand why so much fuss was being made to get him for Armand. But then, Madam at times had strange ideas."

Rudolph Valentino had been married briefly the previous year to an actress who had once been an intimate friend of Nazimova's. Her name was Jean Acker, and in 1919 her career as a Metro starlet was on the rise. Valentino, an Italian immigrant whose real name was Rodolfo Guglielmi di Valentina d'Antonguolla, had been a tea dancer in New York, an occasional paid escort, and finally a struggling film actor who was usually miscast as the heavy. In an effort to find work, Valentino traveled to California, where he fell victim to the post–World War I influenza epidemic. More bad luck followed his recovery when he received word that his mother, to whom he was very devoted, had died suddenly in Italy. In May, June, and July of 1919 Valentino was unemployed. Lonely and broke, his dreams of fortune in America having come to nothing, the actor jumped at an invitation from his friend, the director Douglas Gerrard, to a party hosted by the actress Pauline Frederick. It was there that he met Jean Acker, who was making two hundred dollars a week in films and living at the prestigious Hollywood Hotel. Both actor and actress were lonely, both were recovering from emotional stress (she from a break-up with a friend), and both were looking for a shoulder to cry on. In their neediness they charmed each other and spent the next several days together. On a whim, really, they decided to get married, procured a license on November 4, and were wed the next day in a quiet ceremony held in the home of the treasurer of Metro.

That night, when Valentino led his bride to her room at the Hollywood Hotel, she abruptly slammed the door in his face, locked it, and wailed that she had made a terrible mistake. One month later, their separation was announced. While Jean Acker's career floundered thereafter, Valentino's was given new hope when a powerful scriptwriter, June Mathis, saw one of his films and insisted that he was the perfect type for the role of Julio Desnoyers in the Metro production of the Blasco-Ibañez novel *The Four Horsemen of the Apocalypse*.

It was just before this big break that Valentino met Paul Ivano for the first time. The two became loyal friends and occasional roommates.

Nazimova's Camille on her deathbed

Ivano had been recuperating in Palm Springs, California, from an illness that followed his having been gassed while serving as a photographer in the French Signal Corps during World War I. Early one morning, Ivano was awakened by Helen Troubetskoy, a longtime friend of his father's, who brought with her a young Italian with whom she had been dancing all night at the Alexandria Hotel in Los Angeles. She asked Ivano if the penniless man could share Paul's bungalow for three days. Ivano consented, and the three days turned into three weeks:

We became good friends. I bought the food, and Rudy would cook it. We went horseback riding. He had done a little acting at Universal, always playing the villain. He had a moustache then. His marriage to Jean Acker lasted one day. She turned out to be a lesbian who wanted to return to her girlfriend. Valentino had originally thought it was a good idea to marry Jean because she knew a lot of people and that could help his career. Now he was planning to go back to New York and earn a living at dancing. On the trip back east he read the novel *The Four Horsemen of the Apocalypse.* When he was in New York he found out that Metro was making a movie out of the novel. He went to the studio's offices there hoping to land a job in the film dancing the tango, but to his surprise he found out that he had been given the lead due to the efforts of June Mathis. She was a tough old dame who always got her way. The director, Rex Ingram, didn't like Rudy, but June Mathis's opinion prevailed.

When Valentino returned to California to make the film, he sent a note to Ivano asking him to come to Hollywood, suggesting that there might be work for him to do on the production:

That's how I became the technical advisor for *The Four Horsemen,* making sure that the French villages and French uniforms made for the film looked authentic. We renewed our friendship and shared an apartment in Hollywood where lots of starlets lived. All the money Valentino made on that film went to pay his tailor back in New York. There were twenty-two costume changes in *The Four Horsemen* and the studio only provided him with one military uniform and the gaucho outfit. Later when we were all working on *Camille,* Rudy, Natacha, Alla, and I became very close.

It took some time, however, for Valentino to scale Rambova's defenses. The two fought when she insisted that Rudy's pomaded hair

was inappropriate for the role of Armand, an unsophisticated Frenchman from the provinces. She ordered that he take a screen test with a more relaxed hairstyle. Furthermore, his self-absorption in approaching the role irritated her; he never seemed to fall out of character. "He was serious about his work," recalled Ivano, who was the technical director of *Camille.* "He would fall into a part and play it all day—it became a nuisance." Finally, in an effort to melt Rambova's icy, businesslike manner, Valentino volleyed an endless barrage of jokes and pranks in an attempt to make her laugh and win her affection. It had the opposite effect. "This continued and forced joviality upset me," she later admitted, "as in those days I took life, work, and myself most terribly seriously."

Natacha's no-nonsense attitude did not endear her to other members of the *Camille* cast, either. Patsy Ruth Miller, who had been given the role of Nichette, was uncomfortable in Rambova's presence: "Her pretensions were too great. She had been a ballerina and would never let you forget it. I was a girl from the midwest, and she had a patronizing attitude toward me. I was not aware that Rudy and Natacha were

becoming romantically involved. In fact he used to make jokes about her, saying 'There goes Pavlova!' whenever she passed by.''

Miss Miller, who would later achieve fame playing Esmeralda opposite Lon Chaney in *The Hunchback of Notre Dame,* found Rambova's art-conscious sets and costumes for *Camille* too avant-garde, even grotesque:

She leaned rather heavily on the bizarre, both in decor and personal appearance. Having been a ballerina, she wore her hair parted in the center and pulled back into the typical ballerina knot. She wore flat shoes, walked with her toes pointed out, and went in heavily for floaty draperies and long beady necklaces. I never saw her dance, but I'm sure it was "interpretive."

Why Rudy fell for her I could never figure out. But then, so did Madam. Perhaps she was an artist after all—a con artist.

The armor Natacha had forged around her heart started to crack as she began to understand what was behind Rudy's tomfoolery: "When I learned to know Rudy better I began to see, underneath all his forced gaiety, the lonely and often sad young man he really was. Being a foreigner and unknown, his way was not the easiest. The same people who then considered him beneath their notice, later after his success, were the first with their attentions and flattery. Long after, this was a source of great amusement to us both."

Valentino touched some maternal instinct in Natacha, and her superior intellect and intuition found satisfaction in his equally fervent love of beauty and culture: "Having both been brought up in Europe, and speaking French and Italian, we soon found a common ground for mutual friendship and understanding. Many were the memories exchanged of our experiences in France and Italy, which always ended in happy plans for our return, although at this time we did not dream of ever revisiting these scenes together."

She had been renting a tiny duplex, which she proudly referred to as a "bungalow," at 6612 Sunset Boulevard. Desiring to live independently and on her own earnings, she had very little extra money to spend on furnishings, so she collected second-hand items and packing crates, which she cleverly transformed into chinoiserie by lacquering them in red and black. Rudy helped her paint and frequently rode home with her from the studio. He would cook elaborate Italian meals, to which they would invite guests like June Mathis, Paul Ivano, and Nazimova.

Nazimova's selection of veteran cameraman—and personal friend —Ray C. Smallwood as the director of *Camille* strengthened the visual impact of the film and ensured Madam's control over the production. Smallwood's wife, Ethel, claimed that she hated to visit the set of *Camille* because there was so much fighting going on all the time. Certainly, Metro Studio heads used such allegations to support the case they were developing against the domineering, temperamental actress, whose contract they planned to terminate after this film. Paul Ivano confirmed the fact that Nazimova, and not Ray Smallwood, actually directed the movie, but he could not recall any discord having taken place during its filming. "It was a happy time for us all," he insisted.

That happy time is reflected in a number of photographs taken on location in the countryside north of Hollywood during the filming of *Camille*. An eighteenth-century dream sequence from Abbé Prevost's *Manon Lescaut* was being inserted into the film script. Snapshots were taken as the company broke for lunch in a nearby apple orchard. There, under the cool shade of the blossoming trees, Nazimova held court with Paul Ivano at her side and Rudy resting his head in Natacha's lap. The puppy love between Valentino and Rambova amused Nazimova. Presumably, Jean Acker found it less entertaining.

When the shooting of *Camille* had been completed, Valentino asked Natacha to accompany him to the West Coast premiere of *The Four Horsemen of the Apocalypse*. The entire film colony turned out to see if this costly Metro production was worth all the ballyhoo that had preceded it. During the screening he held her hand tightly in his own. "I knew he wanted to feel that there was just someone who cared and understood," she recalled. "We were both weeping from mixed emotions—joy at the success which could even now be felt on all sides, and sorrow for the tragedy of the story." Thunderous applause greeted Valentino when the lights went up, but the actor wanted nothing more than to escape from the theater to savor the victory in solitude. His star was rising at last. Silently, as if in a daze, he drove Natacha home and proceeded on alone to his tiny apartment in Hollywood.

Before the release of *Camille,* Nazimova gave several interviews, continuing to titillate the press with her unconventional views. When questioned by *Motion Picture* magazine as to whether she believed in having children, she replied: "Not for creative women. A woman living a creative life is bound necessarily to do things sometimes defiant to convention. In order to fulfill herself, she should live freely. Children bring fear, and in that way arrest personal development." Madam also declared that she would like nothing better than to produce a play or film in which all the characters were women. The director, the writer, even the production staff would all be female, which prompted one newspaper writer to comment that "Mere Man will be as scarce around the forthcoming production as Britons—at a German barbecue."

The release of *Camille* in September 1921 brought Nazimova some of her best reviews, but it also subjected her to biting criticism. *Screenland* applauded "her exotic, dazzling but baffling beauty," and the *Dramatic Mirror* called her performance an "unforgettable portrait." *Variety* praised Nazimova for "the finest acting with which the silver sheet has been graced." But Nazimova's decision to edit out Valentino's presence at her death scene—a scene Rambova had marveled at for Rudy's ability to reduce the film crew to tears—*Variety* castigated as an "arrant misconception." *Photoplay* blasted her for the autocratic control that had become

The film crew went on location for the "Manon Lescaut" sequence of Camille.

Nazimova, Paul Ivano, an unidentified woman, Rudolph Valentino, and Natacha Rambova mug for the camera during their lunch break.

A lovestruck Rudy with Natacha

apparent in her films, rhetorically asking her if she truly believed that "The Queen can do no wrong!" The magazine disparaged her *Camille* as an exercise in artificiality, declaring that "Never once does the picture touch actual humanity, largely because Madam Alla persistently poses rather than acts."

As for Natacha, her art direction was praised for its eye-popping originality. *Picture Play* called it "a haunting succession of mesmeric pictures," while the *Dramatic Mirror* clumsily gushed over the fact that "Camille sees the end of her life drawing near amid surroundings that are so beautiful it is almost worth dying to get to associate with them." *Photoplay* lodged one of the few discordant notes, calling her sets "absurd fabrications of pasteboard" before which Nazimova paraded in "Fiji Island make-up."

Madam—not Rambova—had devised the make-up. As she grew older, Nazimova depended on heavy applications of rice powder to hide the accentuated pock marks of a childhood illness.

Despite the generally favorable reception of her film, both Nazimova and Metro were happy to part company, and her contract was terminated. The actress was now more than ever determined to produce films on her own, works that would elevate the cinema to a fine art. But such independence came at a price: she had to back her artistic ambitions with hard-earned cash.

Nazimova rented space at the Robert A. Brunton Studios on Melrose Avenue amid much publicity. She used the media attention to announce that, henceforth, she would be filming only works of great artistic merit. She further declared her intention to break away from conventional film format; for example, she visualized bringing Oscar Wilde's *Salome* to the screen as a Russian ballet, and she thought that Ibsen's *A Doll's House* should be filmed with nothing but stark theatrical realism. It would be poison at the box office, she had been warned, but she was willing to stake her personal fortune on it.

The influence of Natacha Rambova in this venture should not be underestimated, but even here the two women had their differences. Rambova saw great possibilities in *Salome*, but was not particularly interested in *A Doll's House*, since it was a drab modern tale that left little room for her imagination as art director. Nevertheless, Madam had built her stage reputation as one of the finest interpreters of Ibsen, and, while Natacha was already at work on *Salome*, Nazimova decided to launch *A Doll's House* first. She herself wrote the script, under the pseudonym of

Peter M. Winters, and appointed Charles Bryant as the nominal director of the film. Forced to work within the austerities of Ibsen's bleak tale of an emotionally abused wife who leaves her husband in order to find a life of her own, Rambova combined Norwegian peasant dress with stylized fur costumes that had a distinctively Russian flair.

A subsidiary of United Artists agreed to distribute the production, and it was released in February 1922. It was hailed as an artistic triumph; Nazimova was praised for the seriousness she brought to the role, and Rambova's sets were also cited. Nevertheless, *A Doll's House* failed at the box office. Undaunted, Madam moved ahead with plans to launch what she intended to be her essay in cinematic art, Oscar Wilde's *Salome*.

"I did *Salome* as a purgative," Nazimova later told the journalist Adela Rogers St. Johns. "I wanted something so different, so fanciful, so artistic, that it would take the taste right out of my mouth."

Wilde had originally written his play in French, hoping that Sarah Bernhardt would star in it and hoping as well that its artistic merit might gain him admittance to the French Academy. Owing much of its mood to fin-de-siècle symbolism and decadence, *Salome* is a sordid twist on the biblical account of King Herod's stepdaughter, who danced for him in order to procure for Herodias, her mother, the head of the imprisoned prophet, John the Baptist. Taking his inspiration from Heinrich Heine, Stéphane Mallarmé, and Gustave Flaubert, all of whom had elaborated upon the scriptural passage with much originality, Wilde has his Judæan

Charles Bryant, Natacha Rambova, and Nazimova confer in the planning of Salome.

princess dance before her lustful stepfather, not in obedience to the evil designs of her mother, but out of vengeance for her own unrequited love of the prophet. Unsuccessful in her desire to kiss his lips in life, she demands his death, after which she indulges her unholy passion upon his severed head. Shocked by the sight of Salome's necrophilia, Herod's lust for her is quickly transformed into moral disgust, and he orders his guards to crush her to death with their shields.

Sarah Bernhardt's intention to star in Wilde's *Salome* on the London stage came to nothing after it was banned by the Lord Chamberlain. In defiance, Wilde published his play in French (after consulting several French literary figures, including Pierre Louÿs), and it appeared in 1893, in purple wrappers. The following year, an English translation by Wilde's lover, Lord Alfred Douglas, appeared, illustrated by Aubrey Beardsley, who was ordered by the publisher to redraw some of his illustrations on account of their "obscenity." The subsequent denunciation of Oscar Wilde by Douglas's father, the marquess of Queensbury, and the author's trial and imprisonment for sodomy in 1895, cast a moral pall over *Salome*, which faced various international censorship battles throughout the turn of the century. In 1905 Richard Strauss unveiled his German opera of Wilde's play amid further controversy. Hollywood entered the fray when, in 1919, Theda Bara starred as a celluloid Salome in a film that was banned in many parts of the country. For this reason, Metro had rejected Nazimova's suggestion that she star in yet another film version. Free from Metro now, Nazimova and Rambova schemed to make *Salome* into a film that would prove once and for all that art could come out of a camera.

Left to right: Arthur Jasmina, Nigel De Brulier, Nazimova, Frederick Peters, and Earl Schenck in Salome

*King Herod's court in
Salome—"You have
our warning: this is
bizarre stuff," declared
Photoplay.*

Natacha convinced Madam that the sets and costumes should be derived from the notorious Beardsley illustrations. Nazimova would have a number of costume changes and a variety of wigs to wear, including one *vibrating* headpiece studded with white baubles. Salome's peacock skirt and headdress, found in Beardsley's illustrations, were translated into cinematic versions. His black cape design, part Victorian and part Oriental, became the inspiration for the sandwich board constructions in which Rambova encased Salome's barefooted attendants. Some designs saved from the aborted *Aphrodite* made their way into *Salome* as well, most notably the costume of King Herod, and the ecclesiastical garments worn by the towering Nazarenes.

Rambova's fertile imagination exploded into a stream of exotica. Muscular blacks played slaves, clothed in loincloths of silver lamé grape leaves. Naaman, the executioner, was played by a gigantic white man whom Rambova *painted* black. Dwarfs were hired as an orchestra for the Dance of the Seven Veils. They wore enormous helmets, half their size, from which metallic flames radiated. Three women of the court were, in fact, men in drag, and Rambova adorned them with absurd wigs and exaggerated makeup. The soldiers of Herod were given black leotards

and gigantic beaded necklaces to accompany their armor. The Young Syrian was fitted with a fishnet top stretched over his torso, skimpy enough to reveal his painted nipples. Many of these curious-looking courtiers laced their performances with an effeminacy Nazimova deemed necessary to convey the decadence that surrounded Herod. Whether she was responsible for it or not, the rumor later circulated that the affected and bizarrely dressed cast was made up entirely of homosexuals in deliberate tribute to the author of the play.

The most important costume for *Salome* was for the Dance of the Seven Veils. Rambova originally designed a white, multilayered, diaphanous gown trimmed with pearls. It had an enormous train, an accompanying face veil, or yashmak, and a headdress from which two wirelike antennas radiated, holding an additional veil. Natacha herself modeled this creation and had Edward Weston photograph her in it at his Tropico (now called Glendale) studio. Madam did not approve of this dramatic ensemble, however, because she wished to show off to greater advantage the trim figure of which she was very proud. "Health is like morals," she told a New York newspaper. "It thrives best when thought of least." The forty-three-year old actress was playing a fourteen-year-old princess, and she wanted viewers to marvel at her ability to do so. Her five-foot, three-inch body was kept energetic and youthful, she told the press, by rising everyday at seven, taking only hot water for breakfast, a three-minute egg and dry toast with tea for lunch, and a little meat for dinner. She told Natacha that she desired for her dance scene something more form-fitting and brief. Rambova obliged by giving her a simple rubberized sheath that looked more like a bathing suit, clinging tightly round her body from her breasts to her thighs. Flat slippers and a bejeweled feathered headdress completed the outfit.

Only two sets were constructed for the film in order to preserve the intentionally claustrophobic, tense atmosphere of the play. At the Brunton Studios workers executed Rambova's designs for a banquet hall and a terrace located in Herod's palace. Beardsleyesque decorations covered the walls, the incense pots, and the cagelike canopy that covered the cistern in which the Baptist was incarcerated. As Beardsley's illustrations were black and white, Rambova limited the colors for the sets and costumes to black and white—adding just silver and gold accents. Wilde's play takes place entirely at night; therefore, the film had to be shot indoors with controlled lighting. Engineers worked on an intricate system to give each scene sufficient illumination while creating the illu-

*The Dance of the Seven
Veils (top) and the
abbreviated sheath
Nazimova had
Rambova design for her
in* Salome *(below)*

sion of night. Some of these scenes necessitated seventy spotlights, a certain number of arc lamps, and about twenty-five large mercury-vapor ceiling lights. In order to avoid censorship problems and maintain a high aesthetic tone, it was decided early on that the decapitation and severed head would not be shown on camera. Instead, Salome would receive the shield of the executioner (instead of the traditional silver platter), and the head would be symbolized by a mystical light emanating from the shield. Paul Ivano, the assistant cameraman, recalled how the technicians were constantly being called upon to solve problems both practical and artistic:

One of the most difficult lighting effects for the photographer was the so-called "Shadow of Death," which hovered over Saint John the Baptist and Salome in their most important scene on the terrace of Herod's Palace, and likewise it was raised over John's body in the cistern in which he was held. Several times when we were shooting big scenes, we stayed in the studio until four o'clock in the morning and returned at nine A.M. Since we were shooting during January and February, it wasn't ever very warm at night in that immense studio, especially since most of the actors were naked, or nearly so. Happily our chief electricians invented a heating system and soon fifteen immense electric stoves sufficiently heated the studio.

While *Salome* was being shot, the set was strictly closed to all visitors. The cameramen photographed each scene at least six times, accumulating 300,000 feet of film. Under her pseudonym of Peter M. Winters, Nazimova adapted the scenario from Wilde's text, and Charles Bryant deferred to her during his direction and editing of the production. Charles Van Enger was again hired as the chief photographer. Three negative copies of the film were kept: one for the United States (from which 250 positives were made), one for Europe, and one for South America. The total cost of the film came to $350,000, for that time an exorbitant amount for a movie made on such a small scale. But the costs mounted due to the fact that all of the fabric and accessories were imported from the Maison Lewis in Paris. *Salome* was a labor of love for all who participated in it. "My job obliged me to view the completed film more than four hundred times," Paul Ivano told a journalist during *Salome's* post-production stage, "and I was still not tired of it."

During the time that *Salome* was being filmed and edited, the comedian Fatty Arbuckle was facing three controversial trials for the rape and murder of a young actress during a drunken orgy at the St. Francis Hotel in San Francisco. Even though he was acquitted, public opinion mounted against the wicked excesses of the Hollywood film industry. In an effort to soften the public's perception of *Salome,* the femme fatale whose sexual politics caused a saint to die, Nazimova gave interviews in which she spoke sympathetically of her film character: "She was the one pure creature in a court where sin was abundant. Yet she remained uncontaminated, like a flower in an unfriendly soil. The first time she loved, she asked all, since she was willing and eager to give all. Her capacity for self-sacrifice was rebuked and her love was repudiated scornfully. Since she could not rule, she was impelled to ruin the life that might have saved her. Nowhere about her in the court life of Herod was there any parallel to her encounter with a spiritual influence," Nazimova continued to argue, "and if in her ignorance she destroyed her idol, she was not the first woman to do that, nor the last." Madam then concluded her discourse with a feminist twist that revealed more of Nazimova— and perhaps her protégée—than it told about the little-known princess of Judæa: "The feminine instinct within Salome to command and rule that which she loved persists in the race from the legend of Eve to the newest divorce story in the latest issue of today's newspaper."

While Nazimova exerted her charms over Charles Bryant and Paul Ivano, and Natacha continued to beguile Rudy, they exerted absolutely no control over the Hollywood executives who could ultimately make or break them. On account of a vitriolic dispute with United Artists executive Hiram Abrams, whom Madam claimed wanted a big chunk of her profits from *A Doll's House* and *Salome* before he would market the latter, the production that was being touted as America's first art film sat virtually unseen for a year while distribution was being sought.

In the meantime, Alfred Hertz, conductor of the San Francisco Symphony Orchestra and a personal friend of Charles Bryant and Nazimova, suggested, after he was given a preview of the film in the privacy of their Hollywood home, that music might be written for *Salome.* He recommended Ulderico Marcelli, whom Nazimova hired and who produced a score that drew much of its inspiration from Debussy's *Prélude à l'Après-midi d'un faune.*

Hoping to placate the censors, another private showing was given in New York in July before the National Board of Review. One hundred eighty-two viewers answered a questionnaire on the following: Is Salome an exceptional picture? (one hundred fifty-one replied "yes"). Would legal censorship be justified? (one hundred fifty-four replied "no"). Do you believe it realizes or forecasts the greater possibilities of the motion picture as a medium of art? (one hundred fifty-one replied "yes"). When the press reported that *Salome* had received the Board's approval, the strictures that had long been in place against the performance of Strauss's opera in Chicago and New York suddenly collapsed. Nazimova's film was given credit as the catalyst that legitimated the controversial artistry of Wilde's play. But still the distributors were not impressed, and the film remained in a bank vault, unmarketed.

To counter the notion that moviegoers would not support their film, Nazimova and Charles Bryant held a special preview showing of *Salome* in October 1922 before an audience of thirteen hundred at the Rosemary Theatre in Ocean Park, California. With only a piano available on which to play Marcelli's orchestra score, the movie nevertheless enthralled viewers, who afterwards enthusiastically wrote their opinions on questionnaires provided in the theater lobby. While Charles Bryant took these raves to New York in an effort to convince United Artists to distribute the film, evaluations of *Salome*'s preview performance in California suddenly appeared in newspapers across the country. "Nazimova is great in *Salome*," declared the *Seattle Post-Intelligencer*. "The returns refute the predictions of some critics who, though enthusiastic themselves, doubted . . . whether the public would understand the picture." The *San Francisco Bulletin* reported that "a picture less extraordinary in character and quality would be overwhelmed with music of so high and eloquent a beauty." The *Seattle Times* agreed, saying that Marcelli's score was "the most notable tonal work yet done for any motion picture." The Buffalo *Courier* noted that "money is not the object with this production, but just the satisfaction of an artistic craving." In New Jersey the Newark *Ledger* said, "Critics are agreed that in conjunction with Nazimova and her brilliant protégé [*sic*], Natacha Rambova, designer of the settings, Mr. Bryant has wrought an amazingly fine piece of art on the screen."

Some publications taunted movie industry executives who had seemingly conspired to suppress Nazimova's film. The *New York Herald* pointed out that "members of the film gentry are eloquently silent concerning its present whereabouts, or its ultimate destination. In fact they are apt to duck whenever it is mentioned. What, we repeat, has happened to it? . . . Is it too flagrantly artistic to be profitable?" *Movie Weekly* published a similar indictment. Whether the attempt to keep *Salome* from reaching public theaters was a plot against independent filmmakers like

Nazimova, or whether it was an exercise of good business sense is a topic of conjecture. United Artists finally did agree to distribute it, but the movie failed financially because it was undermarketed. This was disastrous for Nazimova, and toppled her position as an independent power in the film industry. Rambova would suffer a similar fate years later.

Nor were all the reviews for *Salome* sterling on artistic grounds. *Motion Picture* magazine felt that the settings and costumes became more important than the action. *Photoplay* called the film "a hot house orchid of decadent passion," and told its readers, "You have our warning: this is bizarre stuff." The magazine opined that Herod and his queen "savor a bit of Sennet rather than of old Judea [*sic*]," and called Nazimova in the title role "a petulant little princess with a Freudian complex." But the most devastating critique of the film came from the pen of Thomas Craven, writer for the *New Republic,* who called the film "degrading and unintelligent." Nazimova, he wrote, "has attempted a part for which she has no qualifications. She flits hither and thither with the mincing step of a toe-dancer; she has the figure of a boy, and in her absurd costume, a satin bathing suit of recent pattern, she impresses one as the Old

Nazimova, Mitchell Lewis, and Rose Dione in Salome

Tetrarch's cup-bearer. Try as she will she cannot be seductive—the physical handicap is insurmountable; she tosses her head impudently, grimaces repeatedly, and rolls her eyes with a vitreous stare. The effect is comic. The deadly lure of sex, which haunts the Wilde drama like a subtle poison, is dispelled the instant one beholds her puerile form."

Salome may rightfully claim to be America's first art film, but the fact that the stills from the production hold more power and fascination than the motion picture itself is proof that the venture was a triumph of the designer over the actress. *Salome* ended Nazimova's career as an independent producer and sent her flying from Hollywood back to the more secure confines of the Broadway stage. For Rambova, the film meant the beginning of a career as an art director of importance.

While the collaboration of these two women is barely a footnote in the annals of film history, there remains a legacy of innuendo concerning their working relationship.

Madam and her protégée worked well as a female team in a male-dominated industry—so well, in fact, that more than one chronicler of Hollywood history speculated that the pair were lovers. Paul Ivano, who knew both women very well, emphatically reported that they were not. When pressed, in a 1982 interview, to explain his position, Ivano leaned forward and, with a smile, declared: "From the very beginning, she was Rudy's girl, and *nobody* else's."

I n the autumn of 1920 Rudy had been sharing an apartment with Paul Ivano in the Formosa, located at the corner of Hollywood Boulevard and La Brea. In the course of filming *Camille* that following winter, both men moved into Natacha's tiny bungalow on Sunset Boulevard. The three of them believed that by pooling their incomes they could stave off poverty while advancing their careers in the unstable business of making motion pictures. While Ivano slept on a couch in the living room, Rudy shared the bedroom with Natacha.

The attraction between Rambova and Valentino was far more intense than anyone would have guessed from their display of puppy love at the Metro studio. At four o'clock one morning, Valentino awakened Ivano in a wild panic, screaming, "Paul wake up! I have killed Natacha!" As Ivano recalled, "I rubbed my eyes and tried to make sense of what he was telling me." Standing over the couch he could see a shivering and naked Valentino, sparkling in tears and sweat. He had an erection.

"When I saw that, I immediately had a clue to the cause of the problem. I asked him if he and Natacha had been making whoopie. Rudy said yes, but that I should hurry into the bedroom because he thought that Natacha was dead."

Rising from the couch, Ivano calmed Valentino and told him to sit down. He then proceeded to the bathroom. "I took an Italian sponge and soaked it in the sink. Then I went into the bedroom and closed the

Rudolph Valentino

door. There on the bed I saw Natacha lying on her back without a stitch of clothing on. Her hair was unbound and flowing over the bedsheets and pillows."

Ivano vigorously applied the wet sponge to the body of the deceased. In a short while Rudy could hear a moan emanating from the room.

"When I was finished, I returned to the living room and told Rudy that I had revived the corpse, but that he should wait a few minutes before returning because she hadn't completely cooled."

Natacha found Rudy physically overpowering, but it was just as evident that he needed her common sense and intellectual acuity to counterbalance his childlike enthusiasm and naiveté. Making love like tigers did not save them from want. Financial needs inevitably encroached on their passion.

In order to supplement their Metro salaries, Natacha, Rudy, and Paul devised a scheme whereby Valentino's fans who desired to have a photograph of the rising star were asked to enclose twenty-five cents with their requests. Since the fan mail amounted to nearly fifteen sacks a day, the change they collected amounted to a considerable sum. The three were reckless spenders, however, and the Bohemian life-style established in Natacha's bungalow became even more bizarre as Rambova and Valentino purchased one exotic pet after another. They bought a proud and feisty lion cub named Zela, which became inseparable from Rambova, who would spend hours playing with it. The cub learned to perch herself on her hind legs and playfully pat Natacha's face with the pads of her paws. Other pets included a German Shepherd puppy, two Great Danes, a little green moss monkey, and a huge gopher snake. Eventually the menagerie became too much for Ivano to cope with, and he moved out of the bungalow to another home in the Whitley Heights section of Hollywood.

Rudy and Natacha had made their debut together at a costume ball at the Alexandria Hotel in December 1920. They dressed as tango dancers, and their photographs appeared in the local papers. Everyone in Hollywood seemed to remark that they were deeply in love. One who took more particular interest was Jean Acker, Valentino's estranged wife.

Early one morning, as Rudy and Natacha were in bed together, a stranger approached their open bedroom window. As he peered into the room, Zela awoke from her position at the foot of the bed and jumped through the window toward the intruder. She caught hold of the man's

trousers, but the stranger was able to tear himself free. He fled down the driveway, and hopped into a waiting car, and sped away. Rudy and Natacha were to learn later that the stranger was a private detective hired by Jean Acker, and shortly after the incident, Miss Acker filed for divorce, naming "Miss Shaughnessy" as co-respondent. This prompted Rudy to remark about his actress-wife, whose career was in eclipse, "Jean had always claimed that she wanted to be my soul-mate when in fact all she wanted to be was my check-mate."

If Jean Acker thought that she could get a sizeable sum out of Valentino, she overestimated his financial status. Despite the success of *The Four Horsemen of the Apocalypse,* producers did not rush to Valentino with more money. The short-sighted studio was not even convinced that the success of the film was due to its leading man. They turned down Valentino's request for a raise of fifty dollars a week after he had swallowed his pride to ask. Furthermore, since Hollywood actors often had to buy much of the clothing they wore in their films, Valentino, a meticulous dresser, was consistently in debt. In between movie roles, when money was particularly tight, he made the rounds of different studios, looking for better offers, while Natacha took on a few more pupils for private instruction in design. Natacha's advance payment for her work on *Salome* kept the two solvent for a while, but when that money ran out, she had to resort to pawning the jewelry handed down to her from her Mormon grandmother, Phoebe Judd. Rudy also sold Natacha's Buick runabout, which she had bought with her first earnings from Metro. In its stead he purchased a seven-year-old Cadillac roadster, a faster car but, in Natacha's eyes, "an ugly duckling." Valentino made a four-hundred-dollar profit on the deal, but Natacha's reaction was patronizingly bemused: "Rudy was a wonderful salesman, as with his childish enthusiasm and sincerity he could make you see wonders in anything in which he was interested at the moment—wonders which really never existed, except in his own fertile imagination."

With a little ingenuity their meals came free. They would go to the beach at low tide in the early dawn and gather mussels, which they brought home and boiled in garlic and olive oil. When they got tired of mussels, they would get in their roadster and go poaching on the old Robertson Cole Ranch, situated on the outskirts of Santa Monica. Such escapades were exhilarating, but dangerous. Natacha would drive the car through the morning fog and keep an eye out for the police as Rudy sat in the back, with his legs dangling over the side, and his shotgun ready for action.

In later years, Natacha would look back affectionately on these days: "We were both poor, still unknown to the world in general, and glorying in our freedom. They were days of laughter, days of dreams, and of ambitious planning for the future. For myself, I know they were the happiest days I shall ever experience in this life."

Turned down for a raise on his next picture, *The Conquering Power*, and finding no other prospects, Valentino had to accept the studio's humiliating conditions. He knew that he was worth more than the $400 a week he received, but he had no business acumen. Natacha began to work with Rudy in planning a strategy against the studio heads. The film brass considered the foreign-born actor a pushover, but they looked upon his opinionated girlfriend as someone potentially dangerous.

They were right. At her urging, he suddenly broke with Metro. With his pride intact, Rudy found himself out of a job and $4,000 in debt. Natacha was confident, however, that something better would come his way.

Another woman came to Valentino's rescue, his old friend June Mathis, who used her influence as Hollywood's top screenwriter to get Rudy a new contract with Jesse Lasky's studio, Famous Players–Lasky, which had recently united with Adolph Zukor's organization at Paramount. Paramount chose Edith Maude Hull's sensational desert tale, *The*

Sheik, for Valentino's first role under the new contract. Outraged by its low budget, Natacha at first urged Rudy to reject the film. He argued in its favor, however, and eventually won her support. She had to admit, after all, that the costume piece did fit Rudy's personality and capitalized on his love of riding and the outdoor life. For fun, both she and Paul Ivano appeared in the film as extras, playing European socialites. A child actress named Loretta Young was also an extra in *The Sheik,* dressed to look like an Arab. "My siblings and cousins were all in the film," she recalled, "and the studio poured a liquid called Bowlamania over our skin to darken it. In between the shooting, Valentino would give each one of us a ride on his horse. He loved children, and we enjoyed the attention he gave us." Reflecting on the mystique that Rambova created in Hollywood in those days, Miss Young recollected that "her pictures and reputation were *exquisite!"* which was no small compliment from an actress who would herself prove to be one of Hollywood's timeless beauties, as well as a female power in a male-dominated industry.

It was a beauty that sparked the plot of *The Sheik.* "Unfortunately, beautiful women provoke in some men all that is base in their characters," reads one of the film's intertitles, and *The Sheik* is a story of brute force colliding with genteel sophistication. Agnes Ayres, who received top billing in the film, played Lady Diana, who is abducted by the Sheik and raped in his tent. "Why did you bring me here?" she asks him nervously. "Aren't you woman enough to know?" he answers. And Adolphe Menjou, playing the conscientious Dr. Raoul de St. Hubert, asks of Valentino's character, "Does the past mean so little to you that you now steal white women and make love to them like a savage?" The Sheik's answer is curt: "When an Arab sees a woman he wants, he takes her!" Primal in its chemistry, *The Sheik* used Valentino's sex appeal to its greatest advantage. With his dark skin, flashing eyes, broad mouth, straight teeth, chiseled nose, and strong jaw, the actor was capable of unleashing an animal magnetism that women found irresistible. "He was marvelous-looking, more like some sleek jungle creature, a panther, than a man," Myrna Loy would later write in her memoirs. And none of this was lost on Natacha, whose own beauty and sophistication had beguiled Rudy and were in the process of taming him. When the film was completed, she presented Rudy with a portrait she had lovingly drawn of him dressed in the role of Sheik Ahmed Ben Hassan, a portrait he always kept.

Valentino was paid $750 a week for his role in *The Sheik.* But

Paramount, like Metro, was still not fully convinced that Rudy had the makings of a star. Cecil B. DeMille fell asleep while watching the film and bet Jesse Lasky that *The Sheik* would bomb at the box office. Adolphe Menjou remembered the mental torment Rudy had to endure during the production of the movie:

While we were shooting this picture, Valentino kept worrying about the money he owed and about his chances for success in the part he was playing. His Paramount contract was for one picture only, but it included the usual option for a long-term deal. He was sure that the option would not be exercised. . . . He was still worried because of his experience at Metro. And for a time it looked as though he had cause to be. We were almost finished with the picture and nobody at Paramount had even hinted that he liked Valentino.

Convinced of his friend's talent, Menjou himself took out an option on Valentino for thirty days, just in case Paramount did not decide in Rudy's favor. Like Natacha, Menjou felt that the actor needed only the proper vehicle in order to establish himself as a major star in Hollywood. He was convinced that he could raise the money to make a film that would carry Valentino to the top. Paramount, however, did decide to renew Valentino's contract and gave him a small pay raise to boot.

On the domestic front, Rambova and Valentino had to face a growing problem. The lion cub Zela was getting too big for the neighborhood. Being a clever animal, she had discovered how to unlatch the new window screens Natacha had installed in the bungalow, and would walk by herself down Sunset Boulevard, roaring at passers-by. Understandably, this began to alarm the neighbors, who warned Natacha to get rid of the pet or else they would shoot it on sight the next time it managed to escape. Shortly after this warning, Natacha was awakened at dawn by the sound of Zela making yet another escape through a window. Panic-stricken by the thought of the gunshot blast that would surely follow, she dashed out of bed without stopping to grab her robe. Neighbors that morning who happened to gaze out their window caught sight of the lioness racing down Sunset Boulevard with a bare-breasted Amazon in hot pursuit. Rudy and Natacha at last realized that it would not be long before they would have to find another home for their pet.

In the latter months of 1921, after filming on *The Sheik* was completed, Rudy starred in the film version of Frank Norris's novel, *Moran of the Lady Letty,* another slimly financed adventure story, this time set on the docks of San Francisco. As Natacha was preparing for *Salome* at the time, she could not accompany Rudy up the California coast for the location shooting. So Valentino asked Paul Ivano, who was also hired to work on the film, to accompany him on the train to San Francisco, where they took a room at the St. Francis Hotel.

While on location, Valentino and Ivano worked during the day and played at night. They met a friend in the city, the actress Aileen Pringle, who was a native San Franciscan eager to show the actor and cameraman her home town. She owned a large touring car and would pick them up at their hotel several times a week. The three were seen frequenting the Barbary Coast, and partying into the early hours of the morning. This was reported in the newspapers and gossip columns.

One evening, as Rudy was in the shower preparing for such an outing, the phone in their hotel suite rang. Ivano answered; it was Natacha. She asked for Rudy. Ivano responded with the question, "Where are you, darling?" Natacha coldly told him not to call her "darling," that she wasn't phoning from Hollywood, but from her mother's home in San Francisco. Natacha also demanded to know what the two of them were doing at night cavorting with Aileen Pringle. Finally, she told Ivano to bring Rudy to her mother's address at once. Then she slammed down the phone.

Within the hour, Rudy and Paul reached the imposing Nob Hill apartment near the Fairmont Hotel. They rang the doorbell, and were met by a butler who ushered them into a large foyer filled with baroque-framed paintings, mirrors, and Louis xv furniture. Then, at the top of the sweeping staircase, Natacha suddenly appeared in a gown of shimmering gold. As Ivano would later recall, "I looked at Rudy's face, which was filled with wonder and surprise at all that fabulous wealth. At the same time, there was this strange look in his eyes, which told me at that very moment he had decided that this woman would be his wife."

Rambova chose this occasion to reveal to her friends her family background. Her mother's fourth husband, the cosmetic magnate Richard Hudnut, lived in the house and had legally adopted Natacha, who was now formally his stepdaughter. Her parents were away on a tour of Europe, and she decided to use the opportunity to visit Rudy and find out if the reports of his being seen in the company of another woman were true. Valentino was amazed that Rambova had managed to keep from him the secret of her family's wealth. He assured Natacha that his affection for her had not been compromised by his association with Aileen Pringle. The three continued to talk well into the evening, and at midnight Ivano returned to the hotel alone. "It was after that," recalled Ivano, "that Natacha had those sexy pictures taken of Rudy."

The next morning, Natacha decided to commemorate her reunion with Valentino by having a series of photographs taken of her lover in the local studio of an old family friend, Helen MacGregor. Gathering an assortment of cosmetics and bizarre props, she ordered the butler to drive them to the studio at 165 Post Street. Rudy was bewildered, but eager to participate.

When they arrived, Natacha spoke a few words to Helen MacGregor, a bun-faced spinster with blue eyes who dressed in homespun clothing. As the photographer was busy setting up her camera and metering the light, Natacha took Rudy into a dressing room, where she had him remove all of his clothing. Reaching into her prop bag, she handed him a tiny harness with a fig-leaf-covered pouch at one end and a furry short tail at the other. She next opened two jars of body paint, one black and one white, which she brushed in alternate sections up and down his legs, over his buttocks, and around his lower abdomen. As the paint dried, she stuck some putty on the tips of his ears to give them points, and coated the actor's face, arms, and torso with petroleum jelly. Using a fine brush, she painted a single black eyebrow across his forehead, and with a wet comb parted his hair down the middle and coiffed his forelocks into devilish curls.

Rudy had become her replica of the lascivious faun Nijinsky created

Valentino as a lascivious
faun; photograph by
Helen MacGregor, 1921

for Diaghilev's Ballets Russes production of Debussy's *Prélude à l'Après-
midi d'un faune*. It was a production that had captivated Natacha when
she first saw it at Covent Garden in February 1913, and she wanted to
reincarnate that event in Valentino. She handed Rudy a flute and a cluster
of grapes and stood to the side as Helen MacGregor placed him in a
variety of poses and shot picture after picture.

As she stood there gazing at her creation, Natacha knew that Valentino would be her ultimate work of art. She was the new Diaghilev,
and Rudy would be her Nijinsky. He was her lusty faun, a male sex
object fashioned to the dictates of her creative female soul. The photographs would be a visual testimony of their alliance, the wedding of his
body to her mind. And as Natacha stood there frozen with excitement,
Rudy struck yet another pose in an effort to please her.

When they returned to Hollywood, Natacha proudly circulated
some of the photographs and displayed them in her home. What she did
not anticipate was their being used as evidence against her and Rudy in
his divorce trial, commencing in November 1921. On November 30, Jean
Acker's attorney, Neil S. McCarty, called Valentino to the stand and,

while questioning him on the subject of how he spent his money, Mc-Carty withdrew from an envelope a photo of Valentino's faun kneeling at Natacha's feet. It was clearly a maneuver to embarrass Valentino by insinuating that this was the manner in which the irresponsible actor conducted himself with his mistress while neglecting to support his lawful wife. Valentino nimbly dismissed the allegation with the excuse that the photo was merely a study for one of his future film projects. His attorney also objected, reminding the court that Valentino was suing Acker on a cross-complaint, holding that the actress had left *him* and had refused to give *him* his conjugal rights.

In order to substantiate his claims against Jean Acker, Valentino introduced a letter dated November 22, 1919, which had been written shortly after he and his wife had quarreled on their wedding night. It read in part:

My Dear Jean,
I am at a complete loss to understand your conduct toward me, as I cannot receive any satisfactory explanation through telephoning or seeing you. Since I cannot force my presence upon you . . . I guess I'd better give it up. I am always ready to furnish you a home and all the comfort to the best of my moderate means and ability, as well as all the love and care of a husband for his dear little wife. Please, dear Jean, darling, come to your senses and give me an opportunity to prove my sincere love and eternal devotion to you. Your unhappy loving husband,
Rodolfo

The evidence of the letter was further supported by the testimony of a mutual friend in the movie colony, Mrs. Maxwell Karger, who told of her conversation with Mrs. Valentino six hours after the nuptial knot had been tied: "She came to me and said she was sorry they had been married. Miss Acker told me she thought she had made a mistake. She threw herself on the bed and wept."

Despite Jean Acker's pleas of impoverishment and ill health, she herself admitted twice during the trial that she had kept her husband at a distance. The judge ultimately decided in favor of Valentino's cross-complaint of desertion, and on January 10, 1922, granted the actor an interlocutory decree of divorce, which would become final on March 4, 1923. In the interim Jean Acker was to be awarded a one-time alimony payment of $12,000.

Confident of the fact that they would be married as soon as the

legalities of the divorce were behind them, Natacha cabled her parents in Europe informing them of her engagement. A hint of the old mother-daughter conflict is evident in Muzzie's recollection of the cable: "Most modern children have so well trained their parents that they are supposed to sanction every action without question. So we did the expected thing, and forwarded congratulations at once."

When they returned to America, Natacha's mother and stepfather visited Los Angeles to meet their prospective son-in-law. Natacha picked them up at the train station at seven o'clock in the evening and drove them to her bungalow. Muzzie had expected that her daughter would be living in a movie-star mansion; when they pulled up to Natacha's house on Sunset Boulevard, Mrs. Hudnut mistook it for a garage. Escorting her parents to the front of the house, Natacha rang the doorbell, and they were greeted by a uniformed maid hired for the night to make an impression. Her mother later recalled her reactions to Natacha's home. "The front room was quite large enough for four people if you happened to edge in right. The rug, a creation of the most brilliant modern colors and design, was painted on the floor. Four kitchen chairs, lacquered in red, a small comfortable sofa covered in bright modern chintz, two small sofa tables which held lamps with gay paper shades, bookcases which had been originally packing boxes but now transformed by red paint into things of beauty, comprised the unique furnishings of this room." The bedroom was carpeted in black. It had a mirror-topped black table at one end and an oblong casket affair at the other. It reminded Mrs. Hudnut of a morgue chapel. She then moved to investigate the white porcelain bathroom. As she opened the door, she was met by the snarling lioness, Zela, who was sitting in the tub. Mrs. Hudnut gave out a loud scream and slammed the door shut.

After a good laugh, Natacha took the Hudnuts to the adjoining garage to review the rest of the menagerie. When they returned to the living quarters, Rudy had arrived from the studio to join them for dinner. Any reservations Muzzie might have had over her daughter's marriage to an actor vanished when he introduced himself, kissing her on both cheeks. "I saw a slender, boyish, athletic-looking Adonis, with the dark, fervent eyes of romance and a frank, honest smile that completely won my heart." The evening proved to be a total success, and the Hudnuts left Los Angeles pleased with Natacha's fiancé.

Throughout the fall of 1921, *The Sheik* played in theaters across the United States. Valentino's performance would become the signature role of his career. Cecil B. DeMille and even June Mathis had expressed disdain for the project, with its apparent miscegenational love story of a high-born Englishwoman and a dark-skinned nomad. Even though the book and film script both divulged that the sheik's bloodline was not Middle Eastern, but southern European, it made no difference to American women, who were willing to accept that which Natacha already knew: exotic Mediterranean passion could be overwhelming.

While the subsequent *Moran of the Lady Letty* did not garner for Valentino the rave reviews he had hoped for, Natacha consoled him with her firm conviction that his assets demanded a costume drama, not a modern story of dockside brawling, and Lasky's next assignment for Valentino was more to their liking. It was to be a love story featuring scenes with eighteenth-century clothing, and his costar would be the ever-popular actress Gloria Swanson. *Beyond the Rocks* was based on a story by the eminent British authority on sex appeal Elinor Glyn. After meeting Rudy, Glyn declared to the press that he was the greatest lover of the silver screen, an accolade she had previously bestowed on the American actor Wallace Reid. In order to capitalize on his newly acquired title, Valentino wrote an essay for *Photoplay* magazine called "Women and Love," a subject on which he deemed himself an authority, now that his romance with Rambova was in full swing.

Natacha's influence on Rudy and his films was becoming more apparent. Not only was she giving him advice on how he should be lit and photographed for movie scenes, and how he should approach and make love to his leading ladies, but she continued to design all of his costumes and managed his finances as well. In *Beyond the Rocks,* Valentino's eighteenth-century waistcoats betray the distinctive Rambovian touch of mixing modern design with period dress. The stinginess of Lasky's production budget, its cheap sets and costumes, became the more apparent in contrast to Valentino's striking wardrobe.

In December 1921, Rudy and Natacha were just barely able to make a down payment on an eight-room house situated on an acre of land at 6770 Wedgewood Place in the Whitley Heights section of Hollywood. The Spanish-style villa was in disrepair, without gas, hot water, or electricity, and they could not afford to buy new furniture. Two days before Christmas, Rudy and Natacha carted her bungalow belongings up the hill to their new home. A Christmas tree and a chair were the only objects they had to occupy the large living room, so they filled the space with homemade wreaths and other holiday decorations. They poured

their hopes and their happiness into the Christmas spirit, as the house represented a new beginning for them. The only element of sadness was the absence of Zela, who was transported to an animal farm thirty miles outside of Los Angeles and left in the care of Nell Shipman, a trainer of exotic beasts used in the movies. The sight of their pet relegated to a cage broke Natacha's heart. Her tears so moved Rudy that he presented her with a consolation present that Christmas Eve.

At the stroke of midnight, after they had cooked a sumptuous banquet on their tiny portable stove, they lit the candles on the Christmas tree, and prepared to exchange gifts. Suddenly Rudy grabbed Natacha's arm and pulled her upstairs into the bedroom. He told her not to move. He then raced out of the house and down the road to Paul Ivano's house, where he had been keeping most of his personal possessions until his divorce was final. Ten minutes later, Natacha heard him return and rush into the living room. She called downstairs, but there was no answer. The silence was finally broken by a tiny bark, which caused Natacha to rush out of the bedroom, down the stairs, and into the living room. "The head of a Pekingese puppy with two little paws were just visible, peeping out over the top of my stocking hanging in front of the fireplace. Rudy stood beside it, waiting in childish expectation to see my surprise. . . . We opened our packages, laughed, cried, and played with the puppy until the candles on the tree burnt out." They would always remember that Christmas as their happiest, when they were both still poor enough to enjoy the simple pleasures of life, sharing a loving relationship that was as yet unburdened by the fame that would soon engulf them.

In the middle of 1922, Rudy prepared for his next Lasky-Paramount production, *Blood and Sand,* in which he was signed to play the coveted role of the bullfighter, Juan Gallardo. It was the first project in his new three-year contract with Famous Players. Natacha was busy at work on *Salome,* but Jesse Lasky encouraged her to show up on the Paramount set as often as possible in order to mediate conflicts between Rudy and the director, Frank Niblo. Despite Rudy's growing popularity with the public, Lasky never considered Valentino a very popular actor on the lot: "Diffident and reserved, he was always on his dignity and not inclined to mix with studio personnel. I was never on very intimate terms with him and he had very few close friends." By inviting Natacha onto the set, Lasky was inadvertently cutting his own throat; for, as he was later to find out, she was fast becoming the power broker with whom the studio had to deal in order to get any cooperation from its star.

The reasons for Rudy's discontent were many. He had been under the impression that the studio was going to film *Blood and Sand* in Spain; instead, they were shooting it on a Hollywood backlot. Rudy had wanted his friend George Fitzmaurice to direct the film; instead, they assigned the job to Frank Niblo. To add insult to injury, Rudy was not even given a star's well-appointed dressing room, but a tiny room without a private bath. The studio's manager was also being difficult in not allowing Valentino's friends to visit him and in restricting his telephone messages.

Despite such problems, Natacha felt that his role was the best he had yet been given. June Mathis, ever an ally of Rudy's, adapted the story for the screen from the Blasco-Ibañez novel. Costumes were imported from Spain, as well as documentary footage of real bullfights taken in Madrid and Seville. As his reviews for *Beyond the Rocks* had been more favorable than those he had received for *Moran of the Lady Letty,* both he and Natacha were convinced more than ever that costume dramas were what best suited Rudy's Latin character. A dressing scene was incorporated into *Blood and Sand* for Valentino ritualistically to don the embroidered "suit of lights," the costume of a torero. For the role he grew his sideburns long and assumed the character of a bullfighter caught between love for his wife and lust for a vamp.

Nita Naldi played the seductive Doña Sol in the film and became, off-screen, one of the few females in Hollywood with whom Natacha felt

Valentino dressed in the
"suit of lights" for
Blood and Sand
(top); Rudy embraces
Nita Naldi, the film's
vamp (bottom)

comfortable socializing. Born Donna Dooley in New York City, she grew up in a New Jersey convent where her great aunt was the mother superior. After leaving the convent, she became a model and afterward took a fifteen-dollar-a-week job dancing in the chorus line of the Winter Garden Theatre. John Barrymore spotted her there and hired her to play a Spanish dancer in his film *Dr. Jekyll and Mr. Hyde.* He called her his "dumb Duse," as he patiently tried to accustom her to acting before a camera. Thereafter, she attained Hollywood stardom as Nita Naldi, a symbol of sultry, dark passion. In order to hide her real background, her press agent promoted her as a patrician grande dame, the offspring of an Italian diplomat, and (bizarrely enough) a distant relative of Dante's Beatrice.

Critics would later acclaim Rudy's performance as a Spanish matador in *Blood and Sand* as perhaps the finest in his ascending career. Having begun that career playing swarthy villains, Valentino had graduated to an Argentinean gaucho in *The Four Horsemen of the Apocalypse,* an ersatz Arab in *The Sheik,* and now a Spanish bullfighter. In the process, he established once and for all that a leading man need not be from northern European stock. Rudy's image was radically different from that of the boy next door, established by such actors as Wallace Reid and George O'Brien. Nor was he the all-American cowboy, a Tom Mix or William S. Hart, and it was not by chance that Natacha had him pose as a noble Indian brave in another session of photographs bordering on the erotic.

Valentino's olive skin, oiled hair, and Italian grace projected a feline yet virile exoticism that made women swoon. His limpid, heavy-lidded eyes suddenly bulging with sexual passion became his much-caricatured trademark. His posturing, decorative image was focused to seduce the women in the audience, and this made their husbands and boyfriends uncomfortable and envious. The Latin Lover's self-confidence in his own attractiveness was eyed suspiciously by those who had been conditioned to believe that beauty had but one gender, and that was feminine. Valentino was a woman's sex object, he was a woman's actor, and women were his most loyal fans. He could be both menacing and rapine in his characterizations, and at other times exhibit a vulnerability that appealed to the maternal instincts of his female following. The cultural implication of his popularity led many to believe that foreigners make better lovers. Certainly, Natacha thought so, but this seditious idea did not go uncontested by the male writers of the American press. For the remainder of his career, Rudolph Valentino found himself the frequent butt of journalistic jokes that called into question two things: his nationality and his masculinity. A writer for *Photoplay,* for instance, made reference to the Sheik's "wop" heritage, and a few months later in an article that referred to him as a "he-vamp," recorded a litany of reasons why the author, and all men, hated Valentino. "The women are all dizzy over him," the writer mockingly attested. "The men have formed a secret order (of which I am running for president and chief executioner as you may notice) to loathe, hate and despise him for obvious reasons. What! Me jealous!— Oh, no—I just hate him."

Valentino's bond with Natacha became even stronger as he found himself battling with the studio and suffering indignities from the press. She became his anchor and support, as he endured the growing pains of megastar status. This drove them closer together, and they started to look for ways of circumventing the California law that prevented their

Valentino's provocative pose as an Indian brave

marrying before the divorce from Jean Acker was finalized in a year's time. "Only one woman makes a man whole," Valentino told a reporter about of his love for Rambova. "No other woman ever made me touch ecstacy, all the rest were stuffed with sawdust."

The couple believed that if they crossed the border and married in Mexico, as so many other celebrities had done before them, the legality of their union would be recognized when they returned to the United States. Confident that their scheme would work, on Friday, May 12, 1922, they invited three friends, Douglas Gerrard, Paul Ivano, and Nazimova, to accompany them to Palm Springs. There the wedding party spent the night as guests of a friend, Dr. Floretta White, before journeying on to Mexicali the next morning. When they reached their destination, they presented themselves at the house of Mayor Otto Moller, who gathered a string quartet and a military band to play before and after the ceremony. "I shall always love the Mexican people for the happiness they gave us that day," Natacha later wrote. "There was nothing that was too much for them to do."

The entire city seemed to have turned out for the event that quickly developed into a festival. For Paul Ivano, it was a double celebration, since May 13 was also his birthday. Mexican dishes were served, and the

Rudy and Natacha pose on their wedding day in front of the home of the mayor of Mexicali.

festivities lasted until seven o'clock in the evening, when the mayor and the chief of police escorted them back to the border. The weary couple and their friends stopped at the Barbara Worth Hotel in El Centro before motoring on to Palm Springs, where they again took up residence at the bungalow provided for them by Dr. White.

Their honeymoon came to an abrupt end when Rudy received a frantic phone call from the studio warning him that the district attorney's office in Los Angeles was investigating the legality of his Mexicali marriage. As it was possible—even likely—that bigamy charges would be leveled against him, the studio demanded that he and his party return immediately to Hollywood in order to plan a defense. Numb with shock, Rudy and Natacha and their friends left their desert hideaway and, without even bothering to pack their belongings, raced back to the city.

A summit meeting was quietly held between the studio attorneys and W. I. Gilbert, who represented the Valentinos. It became apparent in that discussion that the Los Angeles District Attorney Thomas Lee Woolwine planned to showcase the prosecution of Valentino; he was running for reelection. Not only did he want to portray himself as a champion of law and order, he also needed to distract attention from recent charges brought against *him* by a disgruntled female employee, who claimed that she had had sexual relations with Woolwine over a period of years.

Valentino's lawyers counseled him to submit to the law, explain that he had intended nothing wrong, and rely on the public's sympathy to rescue his image. Natacha, on the other hand, was told to leave the city immediately, if she hoped to save this marriage. The couple must separate while the legal consequences of their rash act were played out in the courts. Reluctantly and with much fear for Rudy's safety, Natacha boarded a train headed for New York where the Hudnuts anxiously awaited her arrival. She took no luggage along with her—only Rudy's present, the Pekingese puppy she called Chucky.

Woolwine's investigators gathered enough evidence in Mexicali, El Centro, and Palm Springs to charge Valentino with two counts of bigamy. The first charge stated that he had contracted an illegal marriage in Mexico, and the second stated that this marriage with Natacha Rambova, also known as Winifred Shaughnessy, was consummated in Palm Springs, California. The penalty for such a crime was one to two years in the state prison and a $5,000 fine.

On Sunday, May 21, 1922, Valentino, accompanied by his lawyer, presented himself to the district attorney's office, where he pleaded guilty to the charges of bigamy. He was told by a justice of the peace that bail would be set at $10,000 in cash. Because it was Sunday and the banks were closed, it became apparent to the star, who did not carry much money on his person, that he would have to spend some hours in jail until somebody came up with the necessary funds to free him. Outraged that the studio heads had not come to his rescue while he was following their advice in pleading guilty in the first place, Rudy was thrown behind bars like a common criminal. No help seemed to be coming from the officials of Lasky-Paramount, so Valentino's friends pooled their re-sources. Later in the day, June Mathis, Douglas Gerrard, and the actor Thomas Meighan presented themselves with the required bail. "Since they had to have cash in order to bail Rudy out, Meighan even handed them his gold coin collection," Paul Ivano recalled. Surrounded by friends, a terribly shaken Rudy was then whisked away to plot his defense.

In the meantime, a scandal-hungry press, which had only half suc-cessfully pieced together some of the details of her true identity, under-took a serio-comic pursuit of Natacha Rambova. Traveling under the name Winifred Shaughnessy, Natacha refused to speak to reporters when she was spotted in Salt Lake City, presumably taking counsel from her relatives there before continuing with the train journey east. As she progressed to Chicago, newspapers across the nation printed her picture, along with the story that Valentino's bride was the daughter of a millionaire, a former dancer, and an art director for Nazimova. Her mother's many marriages were chronicled, the names of Elsie and Edgar de Wolfe appeared, along with the erroneous stories that she had left her mother for South America, where she danced with Kosloff "after some years of popularity in the Basket Ballet [!] at the New York Metropolitan." Her name was also confused with that of Vera Fredova, who had to face reporters back in Hollywood at Kosloff's residence and assure them that she was not Mrs. Rudolph Valentino. In Chicago the real bride learned from reporters, as she stopped to change trains, that her husband had been jailed. Reduced to tears, she pledged her loyalty to her husband and vowed to return to Los Angeles after consulting with her lawyers in New York.

All along the way she had sent telegrams of support and love to Rudy, but the barrage of news writers made it difficult for her to establish any direct contact with him. When she was caught in a vain effort to elude an army of reporters waiting for her at the Newark, New Jersey, station her composure again cracked, this time giving way to the fiery Shaughnessy temper. "Damn!" she shouted, stamping her feet, refusing to answer any of their questions save one. Asked how her trip across the country had been, she snapped back, "Horrid!"

When she finally arrived at Pennsylvania Station in New York, she mutely pushed past the journalists and film fans waiting for her there and took a cab directly to the Hotel Netherlands, in which she barricaded herself. One reporter shared with readers his brief glimpse of Valentino's wife, describing her as one would a prize filly: "She was dressed in form-fitting garments that left little to the imagination. She has a finely tanned complexion, surmounted by flashing brown eyes, and great masses of brown hair. Friends say she will not join the bobbed-hair class. . . . She was deaf to all entreaties as to her wedding plans, but she is wearing a wedding ring."

As the bigamy case against Valentino went to court a few days later, it was apparent to the beleaguered district attorney's office that a clever defense had developed on the part of Rudy's friends. While Woolwine's lawyers had produced everything from diagrams of the position of the beds in the Palm Springs bungalow to the actual pajamas worn by Rudy and Natacha, the entire wedding party testified that Natacha had taken ill after the nuptials and Rudy was forced to make his bed elsewhere in the cabin. If the two had not attempted to consummate their marriage, then no marriage existed, and the bigamy case would have to be dropped.

The defense benefited from the unexpected testimony of an Indian who had passed by the bungalow on horseback one morning. As Paul Ivano later divulged, "Douglas Gerrard had been sleeping on a couch on the porch with a hat over his head, and, when the Indian passed by, Gerrard tipped his hat and spoke to the Indian in Spanish gibberish." The Indian mistook Gerrard for the Italian movie star, and testified in court that it was Valentino he had seen and heard speak to him as he rode past the cabin.

Nazimova was particularly nervous giving her testimony. Swathed in veils and caught in an attempt to leave town, she showed up in court and confirmed, along with the others, that Natacha had been sick and slept in a room by herself. Like Ivano, Nazimova was caught in the difficult position of having to lie in order to save a friend, fearing that if the lie were ever discovered, she might very well be deported as a consequence. Six decades after the wedding party had perjured themselves in Valentino's defense, the truth of that charade still made the French-born Ivano nervous when speaking of it.

While the prosecution made every effort to attack the witnesses' testimony with sarcastic disbelief, their story held. On June 5, the judge dropped the bigamy charge against Valentino on the grounds of insufficient evidence. Much relieved, Rudy issued a statement to the press, apologizing to the public for his apparent miscalculation:

I, of course, regret deeply that I should have done anything that would lower me in the estimation of the American people, who have been so kind to me and have accepted me at every turn for more than I conceive to be my real worth, and who have graciously called me "the lover of the screen." I will say that the love that made me do what I have done, was prompted by the noblest intentions that a man could have. I loved deeply, but in loving I may have erred.

He reconfirmed his intention to marry "Mrs. Valentino" as soon as the required year had expired, adding that "this year's delay will not in any way lessen our love for each other."

For her part, Natacha had pressed the Paramount executives in New York with numerous suggestions on how the studio might come to

Rudy's aid. But because of the notoriety of the trial, they now saw her connection to their errant actor as one big headache. They had no desire to see the couple reunited in the near future, and they resented the active role she had taken in the design of his next scheduled picture, *The Young Rajah.* Both hurt and infuriated by the snubs she received, she began to wonder aloud how the studio could possibly have Rudy's best interests at heart when they allowed their biggest star to go to jail. In frustration, she withdrew from New York and accompanied her parents to Foxlair, her stepfather's spectacular retreat located deep in the Oregon country of the Adirondack Mountains.

Richard Hudnut had begun creating this mountain aerie in 1904. By 1912 he had acquired over twelve hundred acres, including a large lake, a fishing pond, and the once-thriving village of Oregon. This he razed in order to create a wildlife refuge dominated by his two-hundred-fifteen-foot-long mansion, the Big House, Casino, or Tea House, as it was variously known with its subsidiary barns and servants quarters. Elizabeth Hudnut Clarkson, the Hudnut family archivist and historian of Foxlair and its environs, records that it was her great uncle's ambition to develop the wild acres not only for recreational use but for aesthetic value as well. A former superintendant of the estate and a well-known Adirondack writer, Willett Randall, recorded Hudnut's intention for creating the mountain aerie: "For years it had been his dream to find a haven among the high peaks of the Adirondacks, where he might shy away from the maddening crowds and relax in peace and quiet . . . where his fertile mind could reach out and weld together both facts and fancies needed in the perpetuation of his business as manufacturer of the finest perfumes in the world." Over the years he introduced to the estate, with limited success, a variety of animals, including sheep, mute swans, Mexican burros, red setters, and pigeons. All the animals were allowed to roam free in his wilderness kingdom, save one: a red fox that he kept caged in a specially built den.

A self-made millionaire before he was forty, Richard Hudnut was a hard-headed businessman, cold and self-sufficient, imperious and worldly wise. He was a widower when he married Natacha's mother at St. Thomas's Episcopal Church on Fifth Avenue in New York in 1920. Her affable, fun-loving nature helped soften his commanding presence, and together they lived a luxurious, peripatetic life that moved from San Francisco and New York to the wilds of Foxlair, and the glamorous ease of his château on the French Riviera. As he had no children of his own, he delighted in adopting Natacha, especially for the fact that they were in many ways kindred souls, strong-willed, and creators of beauty.

When Natacha went into seclusion with her parents at Foxlair that summer of 1922, it was a time of great tension and unhappiness for her. Herbert Hudnut, Richard's nephew and Mrs. Clarkson's father, visited them there for a short time and remembered that "Natacha's gloom was impenetrable, that the atmosphere was funereal, and he was delighted to get away." Every day she would travel to North Creek to communicate with Rudy via long telegrams or telephone conversations. These communications became the talk of the hill country, as Rudy called Natacha "Babykins," and Natacha referred to her parents as "Muzzie and Uncle Dickie." Their lovesick calls to each other on opposite sides of the continent resulted in Rudy's daring move that August to slip away from the studio's watchful eye, and, in disguise, board a train for New York. Douglas Gerrard helped Valentino carry out his plan, and accompanied the actor on his journey east.

Winifred Hudnut recalled how his arrival brought cheer back to her family, and how his absurd disguise was a memorable sight to behold: "It was the first good laugh Natacha had had for weeks when Rudy arrived at Foxlair. His own mother could hardly have recognized him. His face was covered with a dark heavy beard and his eyes hidden by big dark goggles. He wore a tweed golf suit, with a golf bag slung over his shoulders, and a soft grey cap pulled well over his face. He also wore a smile that reached from ear to ear." Mrs. Hudnut further recalled how Rudy, Natacha, and Douglas Gerrard, whom they nicknamed "Gerry," then spent many carefree days on the estate, occupying their time with swimming, boating, and golfing. "I used to sit up in my boudoir and hear those three screaming and laughing as if no cloud had ever come to shadow their happiness."

The chronicler of Foxlair, however, recorded the testimony of other eyewitnesses to the scene who remembered those days as a little less than halcyon. Katherine Armstrong, whose father was the superintendent of the estate, remembered distinctly "that Rudy's appalling table manners annoyed Uncle Richard immensely—that each meal was a tense affair with everyone making an effort not to notice the incredible sound effects." An impression was also made in the marked difference between the way Natacha and Rudy dressed. "Natacha was always a perfect picture in lovely linen or silk dresses and picturesque leghorn hats. . . . Valentino slouched along beside her, uncouth looking, often in riding breeches that looked as if he had slept in them." Elizabeth Ahoe Piper, the mistress of a nearby farmhouse, remembered the Valentinos bringing her their personal laundry to do, since they were dissatisfied with the way the maid at the Big House handled it. "He was a *beautiful* man, so kind. And she was beautiful, though not so kind. Oh they were a *beautiful* couple."

The Big House became their comfortable and opulent sanctuary in a wilderness that separated them from the problems and intrusions of the outside world. Rising on a shoulder of solid rock at the end of a long valley, the massive edifice was a conglomeration of "balconies, skylights, ornate pillars, eaves, sculptural decorations and protuberances, here an old English chimney of pink brick, there a colonnade with a vaguely Italian look; the effect was intensely personal." Richard Hudnut had filled the mansion with French carpets and Italian chandeliers. A cavernous Norman fireplace dominated the immense living room. Hand-painted murals and rare antiques could be found throughout the house, and in the master bedroom a large Limoges stove burned tiny birch logs. Unlike other Adirondack castles, there was no attempt at Foxlair to incorporate rustic decorations into the fabric of the building. As the historian of the place attests, "Foxlair was a mountain stronghold furnished and fashioned like a provincial Queen Anne chalet. Richard loved the wilderness, but only outdoors."

Rudy and Natacha could only keep the world at bay for a limited

time before they were discovered. One candle-lit night, during a summer storm, when Uncle Richard was away on business and Muzzie was upstairs in her bedroom nursing a "sick headache," the couple entertained themselves by playing poker with Douglas Gerrard. Suddenly, Natacha saw the screen door leading to the verandah slowly pull open. Alarmed, yet cautious, she spoke in a low voice to the others to warn them that someone was watching, for she could see the faint outline of a man in the darkness. She whispered to Gerry that he could find a revolver upstairs in Uncle Dickie's bureau drawer. As Rudy and Natacha played on, Gerrard loudly excused himself under the pretense of getting some drinks. He found the revolver and tiptoed out the back door, creeping around the great stone verandah that encircled the house, until he caught the eavesdropper by surprise. "Damn you, hold up your hands or I'll shoot!" he shouted to the intruder. There was a scuffle. Winifred, who heard the commotion from her bedroom, later recorded what happened:

Catlike the man turned on him and, seizing him with both hands by the back of the neck, pitched Gerry over the porch railing to the ground, twelve feet below. Gerry fell flat on his back, but as the rain luckily softened the earth, no damage was done. Strangely enough, in all this scuffling the revolver was not discharged. The fall quite knocked the wind out of Gerry and it took a few seconds for him to collect himself. Springing to his feet and turning toward the sound of the man's departing footsteps, he fired in rapid succession three shots. Out of the darkness there sounded an agonizing scream. Then dead silence.

Rudy rushed into Winifred's darkened bedroom with Natacha fast behind him. He shouted, "The shotgun, the shotgun—Gerry's been killed!" Terrified by all the excitement, she told him where he could find it. But Natacha, realizing what he planned to do, tried to grab it from him, screaming that he might get himself killed in the process. As they struggled for the gun they knocked over flower bowls and photographs in her room. Trembling as she tried to light a candle, Muzzie followed the couple downstairs, Rudy struggling to get to the front door while Natacha held on to his coat tails.

By the time Winifred reached the living room, it was empty, save for a man covered in mud, standing there and grinning at her in the flickering candle light. She shrieked, throwing her arms up in the air, only to realize seconds later that the figure was Gerry.

"It's Gerry. Don't you know me?" he asked. "I hit him all right, but I can't find him!" The two then went out onto the verandah and shouted into the darkness for Rudy and Natacha to return.

In a little while, Rudy and Natacha came back, soaking wet and muddy. They were unable to find anyone. Grabbing lanterns, the three again went out in search of the victim, but it was to no avail. They returned to the Big House exhausted, drenched, and cold.

Early the next morning, as the others were fast asleep, Muzzie heard the sound of a motor start. She went to the screened balcony leading from her bedroom and saw a Ford automobile race away down the drive and through the front gates. Later, when everyone had awakened, they investigated the scene of the scuffle outside, finding the footprints and broken cigars the intruder had left behind. After breakfast Rudy, Natacha, and Gerry drove to North Creek Station and inquired if any stranger had been seen there that morning. The stationmaster told them that two men had driven into the station very early. One of them seemed to be suffering from an injury to his foot, walking with the aid of two canes. He boarded a train headed for New York City while the other man drove away.

Whether the man was a reporter, a detective, a spy sent from the studio, or a burglar, they would never know. Nor would Rudy and Natacha ever know again the pleasures and freedom of life beyond the public eye.

*S*he is very subtle, is Natacha Rambova.
She is white satin embroidered in gold,
She is absinthe in a crystal glass.
She is a copy of Swinburne bound in scarlet.
She is beauty drugged with sophistication . . .
She is a yellow orchid shining forth from a vase of black onyx.
She is the outward visible sign of Rudolph Valentino's spiritual evolution.
She is the symbol of his culture, she is the crystallization of his success.
She is, she says, absolutely natural.
She is very subtle, is Natacha Rambova.

Such was the dithyramb of praise composed by the journalist Ruth Waterbury for a *Photoplay* article of December 1922, in which she tried to shed some light on the mysterious Natacha Rambova, now also known to the public as Mrs. Rudolph Valentino.

"Whether to call myself Winifred Hudnut or Natacha Rambova or Mrs. Rudolph Valentino, I don't know," she told her interviewer; "Natacha Rambova seems to belong most to me, the individual I think I am."

Reflecting on her courtship with Rudy, Rambova recounted how Valentino's reputation with women at first piqued her interest, but in fact she found him to be a lonely and talented human being whose honesty and simplicity belied such rumors. "There is really nothing

Rudy and Natacha in tango costume for their Mineralava dance tour

sophisticated or seductive about Rudy, whatsoever," she said. "It's like my drawings. I am perfectly willing to admit that they are morbid, yet I am the most prosaic of human beings."

In an attempt to be coldly analytical about her lover, Rambova continued to underscore the gulf between the myth of Valentino and the man she knew: "Rudy has a personality that comes out on the screen which is entirely different from the Rudy I know. Yet I believe it is part of him as the exotic quality in my sketches is part of me." The so-called "Latin Lover," she disclosed, appealed to her maternal instincts, and that had a devastating effect on her feminine resistance to his charm: "Basically he is just a little boy. Things hurt him as they would hurt a child and he is quite as emotional. Also he is just as spontaneous and trustful. Yet with all that there is a remarkable matter-of-factness about him and sincerity. He is the most sincere person I have ever known."

It was the maternal instinct that now convinced her that her place was by his side as he waged war against the Famous-Players Company. After their secret meeting at Foxlair, Rudy and Natacha had returned to New York City and taken up residence in nearby hotels. Now, instead of fleeing from the press, Natacha welcomed journalists like Ruth Waterbury who could report her side of the story. She began by railing against the movie moguls who had tried to separate them:

The company treated Rudy as though he were a criminal. They packed me off East and when I called at the New York offices, by way of being comforting they announced that there was no way of saving Rudy from a prison term and that he would undoubtedly get ten years. I was so excited that I didn't know what to do and because they kept urging it, I nearly went to Europe as they requested. I realize now that they were only trying to get me out of the way as they believed that would improve Rudy's box office value. They declared that I would be the ruin of his career and then finally they told me Rudy had already forgotten me. Then I got mad. I knew Rudy. So, I didn't sail for Europe. I knew my job was right here.

Natacha used the *Photoplay* interview to decry the studio's shoddy treatment of its star during the making of *Blood and Sand,* and to criticize them for deleting most of Rudy's love scenes, which she felt were delightful and reminiscent of old Spain. She reflected on the subject of Latins and love: "With American men love making is merely an annoying preliminary. With a Latin it is like the obligato of a delicate musical motif. It runs softly in and about the creative melody. Beauty like that should not be destroyed."

The studio then rushed Rudy through another film, *The Young Rajah,* Natacha complained. They made him work day and night until they finished the film at three A.M. Although she was responsible for the design of that film, the studio betrayed them both, she said, by putting very little money into the project: "Instead of letting the actor who does fine work go on doing it, they give him cheap material, cheap sets, cheap casts, cheap everything. The idea then is to make as much money from that personality as possible with the least outlay."

While Rambova sought to bring public attention to what the Hollywood film industry called "cheaters," inexpensive films featuring popular stars, Rudy held a press conference to reveal another one of the industry's dirty little secrets: the block-booking system, a policy by which the studios forced exhibitors to show their entire line of films for any given year rather than allow them to pick and choose what they deemed most marketable. Motivated by resentment born of mistreatment, the Valentinos styled themselves advocates of honesty and quality in the cinematic arts. For their part, the studio heads viewed them as ungrateful renegades and spoiled tattletales.

After much legal and journalistic sparring between the film moguls and the offended couple, Valentino decided to break his contract with Lasky, which he claimed was fashioned to take advantage of him at the expense of his trusting nature:

I cannot work for this motion picture corporation. I cannot endure the tyranny, the broken promises, the arrogance or the system of production. I cannot forgive the cruelty of the company to Mrs. Valentino. I cannot look forward to a sure eclipse of what promises to be a lasting career of great success, provided that I am permitted to make productions consistent with my drawing power.

In a last-minute effort to appease their disgruntled star, the studio offered him a salary of $7,000 a week, but with little artistic control over his films. Rudy and Natacha rejected this lucrative offer as nothing more than an attempt to bribe them out of their principles. Further negotiations proving futile, the studio suspended Valentino and secured a court injunction to bar his working as an actor until his original contract should expire on February 7, 1924. With a mounting debt of over $70,000 and money still owed to lawyers and to the workers remodeling their Whitley

Heights home, the Valentinos looked forward to an uncertain future. If need be, Natacha informed Ruth Waterbury, she would go out and find work to support her husband:

Rudy gets horribly excited when I say this, but I do declare that if they keep him from working for two years more, then I will work and support us both. There are many things that I can do. I can dance. I can go back to my designing, but I don't care what it is if it only brings in enough money for him to be able to go on fighting for decent treatment and good material.

Valentino disclosed to the press that the studio had hired detectives to follow him and Natacha, hoping to find them in a compromising position that could then be used to blackmail the couple into submission. In order to thwart such tactics, Natacha invited her Aunt Teresa to live with her. Besides serving the public role of chaperone, Teresa Werner provided welcome company for both Rudy and Natacha. Her affectionate nature and motherly attentiveness were qualities that bonded the older woman to the couple for the remainder of their lives together.

In the months that followed, Rudy and Natacha were able to keep financially afloat by means of an unrestricted loan given to them by a friend, Joe Godsol. Too proud ever to accept money from her parents, Natacha carefully budgeted what remained of her salary from Nazimova and shared costs with Aunt Teresa for their rooms at West 67th Street, while Rudy roomed with an old friend, Frank Menillo, at the Hotel des

Teresa Werner, Valentino, and Rambova enjoy a picnic together.

Artistes close by. During this time of financial and professional crisis, Rudy collaborated with a ghostwriter, Herbert Howe, to present his autobiography in a series of articles for *Photoplay*. That and a radio broadcast called "The Truth about Myself," presented just before Christmas, enabled the actor to keep his image before the public. He also used every chance the media made available to him to praise Natacha and condemn the studio and the films they were forcing him to make: "Every day somebody else comes out to say they discovered me. And the one who actually did discover me—she says nothing at all. And when I think of some of the awful pictures I made, I wonder anybody thinks discovering me an honor to them."

The response to Valentino's public outcries surprised everyone. The offices of *Photoplay* magazine were inundated with letters of support for the suspended film star. This displeased the studio, which had been circulating stories that portrayed Rudy as a temperamental and difficult actor. It was further surprising that, despite the Valentinos' remonstration against *The Young Rajah*, it was doing moderately well at the box office. This might have been due to the number of stills disseminated in its publicity campaign, which showed the actor clothed in little more than a bathing suit or strings of pearls. "Rudy looks best in the nude," Natacha had once confided to one of her relatives, and she had designed the costumes for *The Young Rajah* accordingly. While this story of a Hindu student at Harvard, who exercises clairvoyant powers and has mystical visions of his Indian heritage, did little to impress the critics, scenes of Rudy engaged in athletic events or languishing in exotic settings wearing only baubles and beads generated enough interest to keep the picture solvent and the image of "the great lover" intact.

Coincidentally, around the time of the picture's release, Rudy and Natacha had their first encounter with Spiritualism. The actress Cora Macy and her daughter, Cora McGeachy, a costume designer for film and stage, reported to the Valentinos the multitude of psychic occurrences that took place following the death of a mutual friend. Intrigued by these stories, Rudy and Natacha hosted a number of séances, during which Cora McGeachy demonstrated that she could contact the deceased via "automatic writing." Held in Natacha's apartment, the McGeachy séances had special import for the Valentinos in that encouraging messages were relayed to the couple. As the spirit world purportedly took hold of Cora McGeachy's hand and guided her pencil across a pad of paper, the Valentinos were told that the injunction against Rudy would

"Rudy looks best in the nude," Natacha confided to one of her relatives. She designed his costumes for The Young Rajah accordingly: a string of pearls for his role as a Hindu prince (left); skin-tight bathing trunks for his scenes as an athlete at Harvard (right).

soon be modified and, as a consequence, the couple would be traveling to many cities. These séances confirmed Natacha's belief in an afterlife and planted the seeds of what would later become a scholarly quest for things spiritual: "The more we investigated this remarkable gift of automatic writing, the more convinced we became of the great truth which lay behind it. The truth of life-ever-continuing on its path of progress and evolution and the truth of communication with the so-called dead."

One figure who claimed to have entered the couple's lives upon the recommendation of these spirits was S. George Ullman. Essentially a businessman with a talent for promoting products, Ullman represented a beauty clay, Mineralava, which was in need of a spectacular advertising campaign. The spirit world notwithstanding, it was Ullman who first approached the Valentinos at a time when there was no guarantee that they could even pay him a salary. Yet he succeeded in selling them an ingenious plan whereby they could bypass the studio's injunction against Rudy by having the couple mount a nationwide dance tour on behalf of Mineralava. The injunction, Ullman argued, prohibited Valentino from working as an actor. It made no stipulations against his working as a dancer.

Desperately in need of a solution to their professional and economic woes, and daunted by the fact that their fight with the Lasky-Paramount studio had proven itself more draining than their previous clash with Metro, Rudy and Natacha agreed to a seventeen-week promotional dance tour of forty cities at a salary of seven thousand dollars a week. Little did they realize, however, that by inviting Ullman into their business affairs, they had accepted a Trojan Horse that would ultimately bring them tragedy and defeat. But for now, the dance tour seemed a timely remedy to all of their problems: an opportunity to pay their debts, keep themselves in the public eye, and once again engage in the terpsichorean arts that had been the foundation of both their careers.

The tour was launched late winter in Omaha, Nebraska, where they were greeted with an overwhelming snowstorm that paralyzed the city's public transportation system. Valentino's drawing power overcame this obstacle, however, and the auditorium was packed beyond capacity. After thanking the audience for braving the elements in order to see them dance, Rudy introduced Natacha. She had designed the costumes they wore on the tour: a gaucho's outfit for Rudy, which recalled his role in *The Four Horsemen of the Apocalypse,* and Spanish attire made of black velvet and silk taffeta for herself.

The Valentinos arrive in St. Louis for their dance exhibition.

Inspired by the enthusiasm of the crowd, Rudy and Natacha began a program dominated by Argentine tangos with an additional Spanish-style folk dance they had choreographed. "It was a wonderful thing to see these two exotic and graceful creatures dance," Ullman recalled. "They always appeared to be dancing for and with each other, for the sole joy of being in each other's company." Ullman added what the studios would never admit, that "if Valentino is credited with introducing a new style of love-making, much of it is due to the fact that he dared to be sincere in public and allow all who would into the secret depth of his devotion."

After the performance, Rudy thanked the Mineralava Company for sponsoring the tour and testified that the beauty clay was responsible for his wife's flawless complexion. Natacha then offered some words of her own in favor of the product, and the program concluded with the couple signing hundreds of autographs.

The adulation they received in Omaha was repeated everywhere they went. Crowds even assembled along the railroad tracks of their route to catch a glimpse of the glamorous couple. In Montreal, Rudy and Natacha spoke French to the bilingual crowd, which demonstrated its appreciation with almost hysterical applause. In Wichita, the public schools were closed for the day to enable students to attend the Valentinos' matinee performance. The affability, grace, and good manners

Rudy and Natacha exhibited were noted through the tour, which proved one of the most successful dance exhibitions in American history.

In New York, the writer Mercedes de Acosta watched the Valentinos dance at the Hotel Astor. She called it "an astonishingly beautiful performance," one that would bear consequences later in her life:

Except for the Castles, they were the most striking dance couple I have ever seen. Just by accident . . . I was standing near the exit when they finished their number and paused by it while the audience applauded for an encore. It was certainly not the moment to introduce them to anyone, but Charlie Towne, who was Master of Ceremonies and was standing next to me, in his usual kindly and well-meaning way seized Rambova's hand, swung her around and said, "Natacha, this is Mercedes." Rambova smiled as Valentino dragged her back into the ballroom for the encore. I did not know then that a very great influence would come into my life from this seemingly chance meeting.

Decades later, Mercedes would continue to find herself enchanted by Rambova and would present herself as Natacha's student in an effort to pursue that fascination.

When the tour reached Salt Lake City, the crowds were particularly eager to catch a glimpse of the famous film star and his bride, a native daughter. A stifling heat wave prompted Natacha to suggest that she and Rudy and some of her relatives take a dip in the Great Salt Lake. To do so, however, the police had to cordon off a section of the beach to

Valentino took time to enjoy a swim in the Great Salt Lake with Natacha and her relatives while the dance tour proceeded through Utah.

separate their party from the mob that soon congregated around them. On account of this unscheduled recreation, Rudy and Natacha were late for their evening curtain call at the Saltair auditorium, leaving George Ullman and the orchestra to placate an impatient and overheated crowd. Two hours passed before the couple finally appeared before an audience that was ready to lynch Ullman and wreck the auditorium. But with an aplomb that had miraculous results, Rudy mounted the stage in his street clothes, and apologized for the delay with some remarks that transformed the ugly situation into one of mirth and forgiveness. Quickly the couple donned their costumes and presented a performance that commanded numerous encores.

By March 1923 Rudy and Natacha reached Chicago and were anxiously awaiting word from their lawyer in Los Angeles informing them that the final decree of divorce from Jean Acker had been signed. In the meantime they planned a wedding ceremony to be held in the Blackstone Hotel with Chief Justice Michael McKinley officiating. A reception was scheduled at the Marigold Gardens afterward.

Unfortunately, the full-page advertisement that began appearing in newspapers to promote the dance tour and Mineralava beauty clay began claiming that Rudy himself used the product and the finer barber shops in the country were now stocking it for their customers. This lie enraged Valentino, who suddenly found himself the victim of greedy promoters anxious to cross the gender gap with a product that had always been advertised exclusively as a beauty aid for women. George Ullman claimed to have no hand in the matter. But this false advertising colored the reception Rudy received in Chicago and fueled mocking stories in the *Tribune*.

While the Chicago press was aflutter with the news of Howard Carter's recent discovery of a pharoah's tomb intact in Egypt, and entertainers like Helen Travis were performing in that city their topical "Tut Ankh-Amen Dance," the Valentinos were able to draw all attention to themselves when they made their record-breaking appearance at the Trianon Ballroom. "Sheik of Sheiks Draws Shebas in Sighful Swarms" headlined the *Tribune,* which noted that hundreds of women had lined up to see the film star while their escorts "had come to scoff." By the time the performance was concluded, however, both women and men were applauding for more. A question-and-answer period followed during which one woman in the audience asked Natacha a pointed query:

"Is your husband a real man's man?" she asked.

A Photoplay caricature of the Valentinos campaigning for higher artistic standards in film

"I think so," Natacha reassured her. "A real man from start to finish."

"Like to dance with him?" the woman pressed further.

Natacha brought down the house when she then purred her satisfaction into the microphone.

At last, word reached them from California that the divorce from Jean Acker had been finalized. But much to their surprise and dismay, the Valentinos also discovered that Illinois demanded an additional waiting period of a year before they could legally marry in that state. Exasperated but not defeated, the couple crossed the state line on the evening of March 14 and were officially married at Crown Point, Indiana, with Teresa Werner acting as one of their witnesses. It had been ten months since their controversial Mexicali marriage. Now Rudy and Natacha no longer had to suffer the pretense of wedded lovers living apart.

Throughout the tour the Valentinos missed no chance to condemn the movie studio and the Hollywood film industry in general for venality and dearth of artistic integrity. Occasionally, they were offered an opportunity to express their opinions in print, as Natacha did when she wrote an article for a summer edition of the *Movie Weekly*. Its subject was graft in the motion-picture business and how the unsuspecting public was forced to support corruption by paying higher prices at the box office. Her article had the flavor of a manifesto; indeed, she looked on

the printed word as a useful tool for disseminating truth and correcting false impressions.

Of a less driven nature was Rudy's book of poetry called *Daydreams,* which was marketed near the end of the Mineralava tour. One poem in particular seemed to document the deep affection he felt for his wife:

⁓ YOU ⁓

You are the History of Love and its Justification.
The Symbol of Devotion.
The Blessedness of Womanhood.
The Incentive of Chivalry.
The Reality of Ideals.
The Verity of Joy.
Idolatry's Defence.
The Proof of Goodness.
The Power of Gentleness.
Beauty's Acknowledgement.
Vanity's Excuse.
The Promise of Truth.
The Melody of Life.
The Caress of Romance.
The Dream of Desire.
The Sympathy of Understanding.
My Heart's Home.
The Proof of Faith.
Sanctuary of my Soul.
My Belief of Heaven.
Eternity of all Happiness.
My Prayers.
You.

Valentino's litany of love for Natacha is recorded elsewhere in the book when he describes her eyes as "Mystic pools of beauteous light. Golden brown in color. Deep, yet, amber clear."

Large numbers of Rudy's fans who would never even read poetry let alone buy a volume of it flocked to the bookstores and made the actor a best-selling author. It seemed as though the Valentinos could fail at nothing. Out of the fires of the adversity, from the complications of their marriage to their war with the studio, the couple's popularity only increased. The heads of Lasky-Paramount were dumbfounded.

It had been nearly a year since the studio had suspended Valentino. Besieged by Rudy's fans from all over the country and abroad, they were finally willing to negotiate a new contract with the actor and accede to his demands. On July 18, 1923, Valentino signed a new agreement, committing him to make only two more films for Lasky-Paramount at a salary of $7,500 a week. Furthermore, he would be given substantial control over the stories, the cast, and the directors of his films, and Natacha would have a free hand in the artistic production. It was a major victory for Rudy and Natacha, and a landmark in the history of studio-star conflicts.

But while the symbolic value of this new agreement established the actor and his art-directing wife as real powers in the Hollywood film industry, it also gave them a false sense of security about the very thing that would enable their dreams to come true: money. Clearly, Rudy and Natacha had exhibited a lack of financial savvy in allowing themselves to fall into such debt that George Ullman's readiness to rescue them developed into a contractual bondage that gave him increasing power over their lives. By July 1923 he had graduated from being their dance promoter to their business manager. He hired a new lawyer for them, paid their creditors, and personally guided their new contract with the studio. Relieved of financial burden, the couple relinquished with it much of their financially responsibility as well. From this point onward, neither Rudy nor Natacha would ever again have a clear picture of their net worth. Nor would they particularly care—until it was too late.

Since the Valentinos had not had time for a proper honeymoon, George Ullman suggested that they celebrate their victory by going abroad for a few months of rest. As befitting their new status as monarchs of the American motion picture business, this European vacation would be filmed and documented by Robert Florey, a young Frenchman who had befriended Rudy and Natacha through his association with Paul Ivano. The photographer James Abbe, who had first photographed the stunning couple in 1921 when they were but aspirants to that Hollywood throne and then followed them on their Mineralava tour, would again photograph the Valentinos when they journeyed through France.

In his unpublished memoirs, Abbe recorded the impression Rudy and Natacha made on him when he posed them for the so-called "royal portrait" at his Tin Pan Alley studio in the Romax Building on 47th Street: "No king in history ever wielded more power with the fair sex of the world than did this 'King Rudolph of the Movies.' Natacha, his wife, shone adequately in Rudolph's reflected glory; envied of course by the millions who loved Valentino, vicariously, but didn't get to marry him." It was Abbe's idea to pose the couple in overlapping profile "to suggest an ancient coin upon which a reigning king and queen were more or less immortalized. . . . Their joint popularity at that time was so great, one might imagine the double image appearing on our silver dollars."

On July 23, 1923, the Valentinos, accompanied by Teresa Werner, managed to cut their way through a crowd of adoring fans and eager reporters to board the *Aquitania*. Their journey across the Atlantic was restful, and they enjoyed the company of fellow passengers, including the actor George Arliss and his wife. After docking at Cherbourg, where Aunt Tessie disembarked for her journey to the Hudnut château in the south of France, Rudy and Natacha continued on to the English port of Southampton.

By the time their connecting train arrived in London, a crowd of close to a thousand had formed in the driving rain to greet the film star and his wife. As it was past midnight, there was no public transportation, and a grateful Rudy spent ample time signing autographs before a waiting limousine drove the Valentinos to the Carlton Hotel. For the first three mornings of their stay at the Carlton, photographers and interviewers kept them virtual prisoners inside their hotel suite, but in the afternoons they managed to escape and enjoy the nearby tourist attractions: Westminster Abbey, the Tower of London, Windsor Castle, and Hampton Court. Natacha had visited all of these legendary places during her childhood, but with renewed enthusiasm she now acted as a guide in her husband's first encounter with the architecture of English history.

In the few days they devoted to visiting London, Valentino spent a fortune ordering custom-made suits, hats, shirts, and boots. As Natacha so aptly put it, "London is to men what Paris is to women—the paradise of fashion shops."

The smartly dressed couple was invited to Cumberland Place, the London salon of the brewery magnate Richard Guinness. There they met Lord and Lady Birkenhead and the pianist Artur Rubinstein. Lord Birkenhead had no idea who Valentino was, nor did the Valentinos have any notion of Lord Birkenhead's political stature as a member of Prime Minister Baldwin's cabinet. Mr. and Mrs. Guinness found the mutual ignorance of two worlds very amusing, as did their guests, and the Hollywood celebrities were afterward invited to visit the country estate of Benjamin Guinness at Ascot.

Left: Natacha films Rudy aboard the Aquitania *while Robert Florey peers through the porthole. Right: The Valentinos arrive in London.*

While in London, the Valentinos attended two plays. They saw George du Maurier in *The Dancers,* and Gladys Cooper in *Kiki.* After Miss Cooper's performance, Rudy went backstage, where he collided with the veteran actress's humbling and waspish wit: "Valentino came round after a first night, and when he was going out of the stage-door he found a crowd there. He came back to the dressing-room and said: 'I cannot face those people who are waiting for me. What shall I do?' I am afraid that the answer did not flatter or quite please him. It was: 'Just walk out and take no notice. They aren't waiting for you, and they won't know who you are.'" Years later, when the actress reported that she had thought Valentino was a vain man, she was buried under an avalanche of anger from his fans. A newspaper editor supported her, however, with the observation that "if you want to get hundreds of indignant letters all you have to do is to print something critical about Rudolph Valentino. I cannot understand it; he seems to be a sort of religion with some people, who resent the slightest word that isn't sugary about him."

Before leaving England, Natacha wanted to motor down to Bletchingly in Surrey in order to visit the Pekingese kennels of Mrs. Ashton Cross. Her love for the breed had begun with the years spent at the Villa Trianon, where Elsie de Wolfe's enthusiasm for these regal and decorative dogs quickly spread to her sister-in-law and niece. To the end of her life, Natacha found in such pets a loyalty she missed in human beings. Natacha's almost spiritual obsession with these animals found itself reflected in one of the ditties Rudy collected for *Daydreams*. Dedicated "To Our Little Friend—The Dog," "Faithfulness" begins: "A dog is the nearest approach to the sweet submissive spirit God would have in us, Faithfulness in the highest form."

On the way to Bletchingly, the couple stopped at Leatherhead Court, where Natacha had lived so much of her childhood. The place was deserted for the summer holidays, reminding Natacha of her many years of loneliness there. Little had she imagined then that she would one day return arm in arm with "the world's greatest lover."

The trip to France was made by airplane, and the crowd that met them at Le Bourget airport was considerably smaller than the one that had greeted them in London. Valentino was to discover that the farther south he ventured on the continent, the less he and his pictures were known. The Latin Lover's image was most celebrated in the English-speaking world, where his exoticism was not taken for granted and the roles of sheik, gaucho, and toreador had greater impact. Nevertheless, Rudy and Natacha were fêted in Paris by Jacques Hebertot, owner of the Theatre des Champs Elysées and the editor of such influential magazines as the *Théâtre et Comédie Illustrée*. After they were settled at the Hôtel Plaza-Athenée, they were subjected to the usual round of interviews, but, to their great surprise and relief, the questions focused less on their personal life and habits and more on the art of film and the progress of the industry in America.

In Paris, Natacha's visit to the salon of the couturier Paul Poiret had all the makings of a media event. Robert Florey, in his capacity as the Valentinos' publicist and general manager in Europe, had James Abbe photograph Natacha modeling various Poiret gowns, each creation bearing an exotic name like "Sultana" and "Crimée." These photographs were published in magazines and newspapers around the world. The dresses Poiret designed for the Hollywood celebrity were of such noble simplicity that he called them "paradoxes," and Rambova openly declared Poiret to be her favorite couturier. She began to wear his fashionable turbans as her trademark coronet. Her admiration, however, did not extend to Madame Poiret. As was often the case with Natacha Rambova, the close professional connection to a man of great talent created a subtle barrier between her and his wife. As one of her relatives would aptly put it, "Natacha had the mind of a man in the body of a woman." She saw herself as a man's equal, treated him as such, and had little sympathy for those women whose identity was overshadowed by their husbands' fame.

Rambova models Poiret's creations in his Paris salon. Left: A purple and gold brocade bodice wraps over a skirt of turquoise satin in a creation called "Sultana." Right: A chinchilla fur cloaks a gown of pearl-embroidered satin and white velvet.

While Natacha indulged herself with Poiret gowns, Rudy ordered a custom-built Voison racing car. Her love for clothing and animals was matched by his interest in mechanics and speed. As his car would not be ready for many months, the company loaned them an automobile in which they could continue their journey to the Hudnut château on the Riviera. Neither Rudy nor Natacha had ever motored from Paris to the south of France before, and the experience proved to be the source of their first serious dispute. His reckless driving on unpaved country roads tortured her nerves, upset the dogs, and dirtied her clothes. Her pleas to slow down only encouraged him to speed up. By the time they reached Deauville, their bad humor was evident. They were disappointed with the casino, upset with the food, tired of the wet weather, and disdainful of the fashionable crowd. The push onward through the Alpine thoroughfare brought more screams from Natacha as Rudy tried to pass every car on the highway. One faulty turn at high speed found them precariously hanging over a mountain precipice. "For the first time in my life I felt like having hysterics," Natacha recalled. "Indeed, I would have liked to, to teach Rudy a lesson, but he was so shaken himself by our narrow, miraculous escape, that I merely wilted into silence."

Rudy and Natacha in Deauville, France

It was late at night before they reached the Château Juan-les-Pins, situated on the coast between Cannes and Antibes. Rudy and Natacha were physically and emotionally exhausted, "worn-out, hungry, and beyond recognition," as she described it. "Home and family were never so appreciated. Filthy as we were, we literally fell into the waiting arms of dear Uncle Dickie, Mother and Auntie." With much excitement they toured the rooms of the elegant mansion, built in 1860 by Queen Emily of Saxony, purchased in 1914 by Richard Hudnut, and perfectly appointed in the style of the ancien régime favored by Muzzie. As a surprise, she had decorated Rudy and Natacha's room in bright colors and with the art moderne furniture her daughter preferred.

For ten days the couple relaxed on the seven-acre seashore estate and attended parties at which Muzzie proudly presented them to all her society friends. Rudy felt completely at home in the château and even suggested to Richard Hudnut some improvements that might be made on the property. Natacha's family treated him with great affection, and he would have lingered indefinitely at Juan-les-Pins were it not for his desire to travel on to Italy, where his own relatives awaited him. For this leg of their journey, Aunt Teresa decided to join them.

Valentino's return to Italy after an absence of nearly eleven years was ultimately a deflating experience. Problems began at the border, where the officials tried to extort money from him. His films were

Top: The grand hall of Château Juan-les-Pins. Bottom: Rudy and Natacha stand in the garden at the rear of the château.

practically unknown in his native country, yet his success could be surmised abroad by the expensive car and clothes of his touring party. In Milan they met his sister, Maria, who was overwhelmed with pride that her older brother had done so well in America. But her traditional Italian sensibilities were shaken when she first viewed Natacha:

I am afraid I was a terrible shock to her proprieties. Not only did I use powder, but lip rouge and kohl as well! Not to speak of the brilliant coloring of my clothes and an extensive use of perfume. All of which, according to Maria, was simply not done except by an unmentionable class of persons. She was frightfully concerned over her brother's reputation, and could not refrain from the suggestion that I at least should not wear a glove over my wedding ring.

Although Natacha was eventually successful in introducing Maria to the wonders of modern cosmetics, she failed to convince Rudy to drive more slowly, even for Aunt Tessie's sake. In Genoa she refused to continue on unless Rudy promised to control his reckless driving. No sooner did he agree than he proceeded to crash into a telephone pole.

Valentino visits the Colosseum, Rome

Despite Rudy's driving, they enjoyed taking in the sights, particularly those of Bologna, Siena, and Rome where they were hosted by Baron Fassini and Count Cine, two important figures in the Italian film world. But they were disappointed in not being able to meet Italy's two most celebrated men: Benito Mussolini and Gabriele d'Annunzio. On a visit to the set of *Quo Vadis?*, filming in Rome, they met the actor Emil Jannings, who played Nero, and lunched with him in the Borghese Gardens. The sight of such a grandiose film production made them eager to return to their own careers in America. Finally, when Rudy prepared to motor south to Campo Bazzo to see his brother Alberto, then travel to Castelleneta, his birthplace, Natacha refused to continue. Nearing what could be characterized as a nervous breakdown because of his breakneck driving on the dusty Italian roads, she insisted on returning to France by train. Aunt Teresa, ever comforting in times of stress, volunteered to remain with Rudy. When they returned to the château with Maria two weeks later, Valentino had nothing good to say about his hometown visit. It had been a great disappointment. The people he found there had been rude, even hostile, and were only interested in getting his money.

In November the Valentinos returned to New York for negotiations with Lasky-Paramount regarding Rudy's comeback film. Two projects were being considered: Rafael Sabatini's *Captain Blood* and Booth Tarkington's *Monsieur Beaucaire*. Although the pirate film would underscore Rudy's athleticism, Natacha preferred the eighteenth-century setting of *Beaucaire*, as it would provide her husband with a more magnificent context in which to mark his return to the silver screen. Tarkington's novel needed to be adapted for the cinema, however, and while that work progressed, the Valentinos returned to Europe in order to celebrate the Christmas holidays with her parents.

Both Rudy and Natacha brought with them a trunk full of Christmas-tree decorations, and when a large pine had been procured from a nearby estate, the servants and gardeners erected it in the grand hall of the Hudnut château for the Valentinos and Muzzie to decorate. This took the greater part of Christmas Eve, as they loaded its branches with colorful trinkets, balls of cotton, and wax candles. After dinner, the Hudnuts, the Valentinos, and Aunt Teresa assembled around the tree to revel in its dazzling glory. When the tree was almost completely illuminated, Rudy noticed one unlit candle located deep inside its branches. As he moved to light it, one of the cotton balls caught fire, and in a matter of seconds the entire tree was ablaze. Panic stricken, everyone ran in different directions. Rudy and Natacha ran outside to get the garden hose, Muzzie raced to save her Gobelin tapestry and Saint Cire needlepoint chairs, Uncle Dickie shouted orders to the servants, and Aunt Teresa quietly removed the presents from under the burning tree into an adjoining room. Everyone doused the tree with water, which was carried to the spot in a variety of buckets, pans, tea cups, and glasses. The fire was extinguished, champagne was opened, and the family tore into their salvaged gifts, all the more thankful that they had escaped catastrophe.

On New Year's Eve everyone attended a party honoring the Valentinos, which was given by Mr. and Mrs. John Wheaton at the Negresco Hotel in Nice. Both Rudy and Natacha drank too much that night, and Mrs. Hudnut observed that Rudy had his arms around a dancer, whispering in her ear, while Natacha sat across the bar conducting a monologue on filmmaking for eight amorous men interested only in embracing her. Thinking this strange behavior nothing more than the result of liquor, Mrs. Hudnut was nevertheless relieved when the hosts suggested they move the party to the Perroquet for some early-morning sandwiches and coffee. Wearily, they all piled into a Renault limousine as a tipsy Valentino climbed on the roof of the vehicle and dangled his legs in the chauffeur's face. One day later, Rudy and Natacha, still nursing their headaches, boarded an ocean liner destined for New York City, where they would begin filming *Monsieur Beaucaire*.

*F*amous Players–Lasky, Paramount had arranged for *Monsieur Beaucaire* to be shot at their studio in Astoria, Queens. Even though Valentino had made no films the previous year, every studio he had ever worked for rereleased his old movies during that interim to keep up with the public's demand for images of Rudy. When reports began circulating that the Latin Lover was about to return to work in New York, extra police had to be hired to reinforce the security both at Valentino's hotel and at the movie studio. One New York policeman, Luther Mahoney, was hired to act as Rudy's personal bodyguard. During this tenure, the two men struck up a friendship, and the generous actor told Mahoney that if he ever moved to California and needed a job to look him up. Mahoney found Rudy to be "a regular guy" who was somewhat dumbfounded by his fame. Even the spurious stories that were circulated claiming the actor had syphilis could not deter fans from invading his privacy.

Taking advantage of the heightened expectations of a public looking forward to Valentino's return to the screen, Natacha demanded from the studio everything she desired for *Beaucaire*. And she got it all. Under her command as art director, she had an army of personnel hired, including a scenic artist and two assistants, a costume director, four wardrobe assistants, an art selector, an interior decorator with an assistant, an expert draper, and a supervisor of makeup. The studio management braced itself as she made a number of other demands: André Devan, a

Rambova and Valentino stand silhouetted against the balcony of their Whitley Heights home.

French film critic whom Natacha had discovered as they passed through
Paris, was hired as a technical advisor to make sure that everything in
the film exuded the *dix-huitième siècle*. He was also given a bit part, the
role of the duke of Nemours, brother of Valentino's character, the duke
of Chartres. Rambova would codesign the production with George Barbier, the famous French illustrator and commercial designer. Sixty of the
costumes would be made by Poiret's tailors in Lyon and Paris.

For inspiration in the design of many scenes, Rambova looked to
Elsie de Wolfe's favorite eighteenth-century artist, Fragonard, and to the
wall panels he had painted of courtly love, which had been incorporated
into the decoration of the Frick mansion on Fifth Avenue. Hogarth was
another source of inspiration for scenes set in Bath. Booth Tarkington's
novel tells the tale of a fictitious French nobleman who assumes various
identities and is an expert in the art of lovemaking; the author wove a
number of historical characters into the plot as well, including Louis XV,
Queen Marie, and Madame de Pompadour. These roles were given to
Lowell Sherman, Lois Wilson, and Paulette Duval. The conflation of fact
and fiction paralleled Rambova's own penchant for historical accuracy
mixed with bizarre fancy. In an attempt to portray the world-weary
sophistication and dazzling excess of the era, she gave Pompadour's pet
poodle a set of pearl earrings and a jeweled necklace, and applied enough
beauty marks to the actors' faces to imply that they were suffering from
a terminal case of high-culture pox.

Mrs. Valentino, addressed as "Madam" by the film crew, dominated
the production, controlling even the details of Rudy's personal publicity.

Studio heads were in a bind: to gain their star's cooperation, they had to appease his demanding wife. Neither Adolph Zukor nor Jesse Lasky liked this forced submission to the woman's authority. "Now, as it turned out, we had two Powers to deal with," Zukor declared. "She was the stronger personality of the two, or else her power secured domination over his. It was our custom to give stars a good deal of contractual leeway in their material. Natacha began to insert herself into the smallest details and he backed her in everything." Lasky resented the fact that "if we wanted to see him, we had to make an appointment with Natacha Rambova." He also didn't like the classic or esoteric themes she preferred over action stories: "Our ideas about furthering Rudy's career constantly clashed with his wife's, but she wasn't one to arbitrate. She commanded. When she insisted on his doing perfumed parts like Booth Tarkington's *Monsieur Beaucaire,* in powdered wigs and silk stockings, we had to take him on her terms to have him at all. She designed his costumes herself, and, to give her due credit, they were magnificent. But we hadn't bargained for a dilettante foil for Rambova costumes."

As she had done for Rudy in *The Young Rajah,* Natacha designed the costumes for *Monsieur Beaucaire* to accentuate her husband's physique. The breeches she gave him were absurdly tight, and, as in so many of his films, a dressing scene was included. This time the actor was filmed in a

The extended dressing scene in Beaucaire *made some critics cringe, but Rudy's female fans had no complaint. Here he stands opposite André Devan.*

long sequence stretching and flexing his bare torso while surrounded by a retinue of mincing courtiers. For Rambova, the physical aspects of her lover were best viewed in stasis, as if he were an Apollonian statue ensconced in a museum. The sensuality of the film was not kinetic, but subtle and static, as in the impossibly long and phallic lute Valentino brandishes early in the movie, and in the contrast of bare skin erupting from costumes of shiny satin dripping with lace. Even though a dramatic fencing scene was incorporated at the end of *Beaucaire*, such action was rare, and an episode in which Rudy and Devan wrestle on the ground was cut in the final editing. Like *Salome, Monsieur Beaucaire* unfolds itself primarily as a glorious series of sumptuous settings and poses.

Everyone in the industry was conscious that *Beaucaire* was going to be an important film. It was already garnering more publicity than any other picture in production. The Russian acting theorist Constantin Stanislavski paid a visit to the set and created a photo opportunity for journalists as he posed with several of the actors. "He approved of our costumes," recalled Lois Wilson, "and he was amazed by my ability to cry on command."

Contrary to the rumors coming out of the studio that Rambova stood on the sidelines of the production shouting orders to her compliant husband as he acted, Lois Wilson retorted, "I never saw her on the set, and she didn't boss him around. She was lovely—very dignified and reserved. The costumes she designed were beautiful and needed very

Valentino stands beside the seated Stanislavski, who made a visit to the set. Bebe Daniels and Lois Wilson are seated at left.

little alteration. Valentino seemed to be a happy and humorous person, not at all conceited, and he loved his work."

The actress Doris Kenyon, who played Lady Mary in *Beaucaire,* composed a lyric in honor of Rambova during the film's production. It was later published in *Motion Picture Classic:*

MRS. RUDOLPH VALENTINO

She is an iris, swaying on its stem,
Poised, cool, elusive, in the evening dusk;
Her eyes low-curtained by a veil of mist,
Speak of strange dreams, remembered yesterday
In some far land—as echoes call again;
The lilt of her proud grace and gentle tread
Is like a music played on muted strings;
Out of the beauties of an age-old Greece
Was born her mind, reflecting these today;
Her heart reveals a sheltered garden close,
Where none may enter save he knows the key
That turns the magic lock, but once inside,
Is filled with wonder at the rare perfume.

When *Monsieur Beaucaire* was released in August 1924, the reviews were almost universally ecstatic. The *New York Times* proclaimed it the finest production of its type, one that should not be missed, even by people who didn't usually go to the movies. "Gorgeous is a word we invariably dodge, but this pictorial effort is thoroughly deserving of such an adjective, as never [have] such wondrous settings or beautiful costumes been seen in a photoplay." The *Bioscope* declared: "Pictorially the film is a sparkling delight to the eye—a masterpiece of the united arts of the scene-builder, the decorator, the costumer, and the cameraman." And *Variety* noted that, despite Valentino's two-year absence from the screen, the star had not lost his drawing power, as crowds endured the stifling heat of summer to pack themselves into theaters. It further observed that the film was entirely engineered to showcase the star, relegating "practically the entire cast to the background, so that this feature amounts to nothing less than 100 minutes of Valentino [who] has contributed as neat a piece of work as he has ever done before the camera."

The sterling reviews reflected the more sophisticated centers of public opinion. More generally, the film met with the criticism that there was too much art in the movie and not enough menace, that Rudy's sex appeal had been buried beneath powdered wigs and embroidered clothing. What many people were looking for was a fiercer, less refined role for the actor, one that reflected journalist Adela Rogers St. Johns's opinion that "the lure of Valentino is wholly, entirely, obviously the lure of the flesh." In *Beaucaire,* Natacha had designed a precious jewel of a movie. It was, in fact, more her film than her husband's, and gossip soon circulated in the industry that she dominated the man, and the effete quality of his role in *Beaucaire* was pointed to as proof. Natacha dismissed such criticism with an elitist's disdain. "Some of the farmers of God's Country had taken unkindly to the white wigs," she declared. For now, both she and Rudy basked in the pleasure of knowing that they had begun making what they had so long been crusading for, motion pictures of high quality.

Because of the film's steep production costs, the studio wanted to make their last contractual movie with Valentino as economically as possible. This once again put the couple at odds with their employers, renewing old arguments, gossip, and criticism. Protectively, Natacha blocked all journalists from contacting her husband unless she could be assured of their support. This strategy backfired, reinforcing the studio's claims that Mrs. Valentino completely controlled Rudy.

A Rex Beach story set in South America was chosen for Valentino's last venture with Famous Players–Lasky, Paramount. Given the screen title *A Sainted Devil,* it was the story of a suffering don, a drunkard, whose wife is stolen by bandits. While it was not a typical part for a hero, it did place Rudy back in the kind of Latin role his fans had traditionally appreciated.

To aid her in creating the costumes, Natacha chose another one of her "discoveries," a talented artist who had graduated from the Manhattan and Paris branches of Parson's School of Design, Adolph "Adrian" Greenburg, who was responsible for creating Valentino's Spanish toreador costume, among others, while Natacha concentrated on the gowns for the female players. Jetta Goudal, signed to play the role of Doña Florencia, was a stunning beauty from France who was accustomed to costuming herself in her American-made films. When she dismissed Rambova's sketches as unacceptable, frivolous, and downright bizarre, Natacha acidly countered that "a cinema star has no more use for durable clothes than a subway guard has for a course in etiquette," and Goudal suddenly found herself dropped from the movie. The actress told reporters that Mrs. Valentino had her fired because of jealousy over the amorous advances made toward her by Rudy. Sizzling over this lie and the bad publicity it generated, Rambova replaced Goudal with an old friend, Dagmar Godowsky, who, like costar Nita Naldi, had nothing put praise for Natacha and her designs.

A Sainted Devil was released in November 1924. The *New York Times* said the film was "enhanced by the glamour of picturesque and glistening costumes" and singled out for praise the fine settings of the hacienda and cabaret. "Mr. Valentino is . . . a far better actor in this film than in *Monsieur Beaucaire,*" the paper declared, because "he flings aside all thoughts of good looks and soft smiles, and gives a splendid portrayal of a man seeing red." In contrast, *Photoplay* scored the film for lacking the "force as well as the charm of *Monsieur Beaucaire*" and claimed Valentino was not "real in his stressed emotional moments." George Ullman voiced his own opinion about his client: "Crowds flocked to see him in these two pictures, and both were enormous box office successes."

When the time came for the Valentinos to depart from the studio of Lasky and Zukor, they did so without regret. For some time they had been looking forward to working with a new company, Ritz-Carlton Productions, run by Ullman's friend J. D. Williams. Under this new banner, the Valentinos were promised a say in story selection and given artistic control over film production and a share of the profits. Stretching herself ever further, Natacha won J. D. Williams's approval for a story she was writing under the pseudonym Justice Layne. Slated to be their first film with the new company, it was titled *The Scarlet Power* and recounted the legend of El Cid in the struggle between Christian and Moor in medieval Spain. Clothed once again in Arab costume, Rudy was to play the leader of the Moorish forces, assuming a role with just the right balance of art, adventure, and romance. Unlike *The Sheik,* however, this film would be made on a magnificent scale befitting Hollywood's greatest star. It would be budgeted at a million dollars and filmed on location in Europe. In the meantime, Rudy and Natacha were given $40,000 in advance to finance a research spree in Spain.

In August 1924 Rudy and Natacha found themselves once again in Paris, where they picked up the Voison touring car ordered months before. In it they packed some new gowns ordered from Poiret, a print of the film *Monsieur Beaucaire,* a Doberman given to Rudy by their friend Hebertot, and five more pedigreed Pekingese Natacha had acquired for her menagerie. Without incident, they motored down to the château,

where they were met by Aunt Tessie, Maria, the Hudnuts, and one of
Muzzie's nieces, Margaret Dinwoodey. Using the library as a theater, and
a broken projector transported from Marseilles, which Rudy repaired,
the family gathered for their own private showing of *Beaucaire*. Ten
minutes into the film, however, the projector blew out all the fuses in
the house. When this happened again the following evening—and the
cook threatened to quit if he had to prepare another dinner by candle-
light—Mr. Hudnut called in electricians from Antibes to provide the
château with adequate wiring for Rudy and Natacha to show their film.

During his stay at Juan-les-Pins, Rudy began growing a beard and
basked in the sun to acquire a tan befitting an Arab. Often, he rented a
motor boat and took members of the family out for cruises along the
Riviera. On one such occasion they stopped on the island of St. Lerins at
the site of a ruined medieval castle that jutted out into the sea. There
Valentino revealed his secret desire to buy it from the French government, restore it, and live in it with Natacha—a romantic hideaway far
from the prying eyes of the film industry. It was an unfulfilled wish that
Natacha would never forget.

Rudy's brother Alberto visited them at the château, as did the
photographer James Abbe, who took many pictures of the family gathered together. "Between photographing we indulged in a lot of table
talk," recalled Abbe. "We discussed many phases of life, including love-
life . . . over coffee and liquor." In those discussions there was one point
on which Abbe and Natacha firmly disagreed—the appeal of Rudy's
accent:

While Valentino had acquired an excellent command of English, she would correct him when he fell into his Italo-English accent. I claimed it enhanced Valentino's image; Natacha insisted each language should be spoken as nearly perfect, and without accent, as possible. By the way she spoke French almost like the native upper class. [But] to me, and to Natacha, Valentino was at his articulate best speaking his native Italian, which of course Natacha insisted refuted my argument that people who spoke languages, other than their native tongue, spoke with added charm.

As for Rudy's sex appeal, Abbe found the actor totally without guile: "Valentino was actually naive about his way with women. He seemed to me a bit puzzled by his impact on them. But he liked the idea just the same without boasting of his conquests, which he admitted had been numerous and easy to come by before Natacha harnessed him." Just as Abbe had recorded the image of Rudy and Natacha with his camera, so he jotted down his impressions of their personalities after his sojourn at Juan-les-Pins:

During those Valentino-Rambova days, Natacha was the envy of nearly the entire female population of the United States and Europe. Natacha had as much poise as Valentino. She was reserved, educated, and nicely sophisticated. Valentino never quite got over knowing he had been an immigrant gardener, a part-time gigolo, and a would be actor. By rights he shouldn't have been ashamed of it; he possessed a built-in dignity, was handsome, was never vulgar, never flaunted his overnight fame that never waned, and never appeared ridiculous in the corniest of his movies.

In September, Rudy, Natacha, and Muzzie traveled by rail to Spain to do research and pick up artifacts that would be useful as props in their film, which Natacha had by now renamed *The Hooded Falcon.* Rudy brought along a number of cameras for recording Moorish architectural sites. They photographed the Alcazar and the Alhambra, went shopping in Madrid, and—seated next to King Alfonso XIII and the royal family —they attended a bullfight in Seville, something Natacha reluctantly acceded to for Rudy's sake. This blood sport came to cast an insidious spell of fascination over her.

In the course of buying antique armor and ancient ivories, the Valentinos were sidetracked by personal interests. Natacha made a $10,000 purchase of Spanish shawls, which she planned to retail at a profit in the United States under the Valentino name. Rudy carelessly invested in a number of expensive torero costumes for the sheer pleasure of possessing them. Not only did they buy objects of art for the proposed movie, but also for the decoration of their Hollywood home. By the time they had finished their tour of Spain, the $40,000 allotted for research costs had been spent and an additional $60,000 of debts incurred. The Valentinos finished their European holiday by taking a tour of the châteaus in the Loire valley, accompanied by the actress Nita Naldi, who joined them on the return voyage to New York aboard the *Leviathan*.

Even as J. D. Williams lectured the couple on their unbridled extravagance in Europe, the Valentinos proceeded to lease and furnish, at great expense, an apartment at 270 Park Avenue. From their point of view, *The Hooded Falcon* would prove to be Valentino's greatest film to date, and preliminary expenses would be more than compensated for once the profits of the film were realized. June Mathis had been working on the script, and Rudy and Natacha were anxiously awaiting her finished product so that the production could get under way.

In a matter of weeks, however, the grandiose plans for *The Hooded Falcon* were cut down to size. J. D. Williams informed the Valentinos that his backers would pay no more than $500,000 for the film, that it

Rudy costumed for his projected role in The Hooded Falcon

would be too expensive to shoot in Spain, and that the production would have to be filmed in Hollywood. Williams had just bought the film rights to the successful stage play *Cobra,* and he suggested that Rudy star in that for Ritz-Carlton while the problems of *The Hooded Falcon* were ironed out on the West Coast. Both Rudy and Natacha were stunned by the bad news and, with deflated spirits, packed their bags for their return to Hollywood.

As they journeyed west by train, the Valentinos carefully read June Mathis's script for *The Hooded Falcon,* which had been written in haste, she told them, as a consequence of her having recently severed her ties with the Goldwyn studio in favor of a contract with First National. By the time they reached Hollywood, it was clear to both Rudy and Natacha that the script would have to be rewritten. George Ullman went to see Mathis about this and returned with the news that the scenarist would have nothing further to do with the Valentinos. "What passed at this interview I do not know," Natacha regretfully recorded, adding that as "it was the usual procedure to credit all disagreeable things to my account, this instance was not an exception."

Settling themselves once again in their Whitley Heights home, Natacha took charge of completing its decoration. The European antiques they had acquired were relegated to the private living sections in the upstairs bedrooms. Elsewhere, the house was a paragon of stylish modernity. Over the sunken black marble living-room floor, Natacha placed black velvet rugs and black satin pouffes. She had the walls painted canary yellow and hung them with modern paintings. The furniture was streamlined and highly lacquered in red and black. The bathrooms were fitted with such luxury items as a five-headed shower and a thronelike toilet with a carved seat trimmed in gold. Particularly exotic was a small vanity Natacha had specially made for the dressing room. Electrically wired, it emitted wafts of incense into the air at the press of a button. It may have been inspired by a more grandiose prototype that had fascinated the Valentinos, a perforated floor in a summer palace of the Alhambra, through which perfumed vapors once rose from a subterranean chamber tended by slaves. On the terraced slope outside their home, Natacha planted tropical and semitropical foliage and had a six-sided swimming pool built. The house, nicknamed "The Villa Valentino," also had one of southern California's first barbecue pits constructed in its backyard. An idea inspired by the Middle East, it appealed to Rudy when he was doing research for his role in *The Sheik.*

For the garden, Natacha wanted a birdhouse built in which she could domicile a collection of brightly colored finches. For this she called on the skills of Lou Mahoney, the policeman Valentino had befriended in New York. Mahoney had moved his family to Los Angeles, and, true to his word, Valentino signed him up as a helper at Ritz-Carlton Company. Mahoney built an aviary and a fish pond for Natacha, recalling that "I never saw two people so happy with anything as Mr. and Mrs. Valentino." In a short time, he became not only their handyman, but their confidant.

The Whitley Heights home was fashioned to be a comfortable sanctuary, one in which the Valentinos could enjoy each other's company in splendid isolation. Rarely did they socialize in Hollywood, a town Natacha considered a cultural wasteland where nobodies were trying to become somebodies and stars tried in vain to retain youth and beauty in "a pathetic race after vanishing illusion." Natacha had never been a socialite, preferring honest work to mindless chatter. "Work," she declared, "is the one thing which makes life in Hollywood tolerable."

Despite underlying tensions, Rudy and Natacha were a picture of domestic bliss for photographers admitted into their Hollywood home.

Keeping Rudy happily sequestered from the social circuit, however, alienated her from the film colony, which likened her to a black widow spider feasting on its captured mate.

Just prior to Christmas 1924, Natacha sent Lou to Tiffany's with a sketch she had made for an interlocked chain "slave bracelet" she wanted made in platinum. It was to be Rudy's Christmas present. "It was quite a surprise to me—a man wearing a bracelet. But I did not make any comments at the time," recalled Mahoney. Valentino was overjoyed at receiving it and wore the bracelet faithfully, even as gossips pointed to it as yet another indication of who wore the pants in the family. "Many remarks had been made about the slave bracelet, and Valentino knew them all," Mahoney attested, "but it didn't bother him. A man of his character didn't pay any attention to such comments."

To counter the growing talk in Hollywood that Rudy was a hen-pecked husband, Natacha invited journalists to their home to see for themselves that the Valentinos were a couple enjoying domestic—if not always professional—bliss. Harry Carr, one of those journalists, wrote of Natacha: "There are two things you notice about her the first time you meet her: that she has exceptional powers of concentration and attention; that she gives the impression of a tremendous vital force in a body whose slenderness and strength suggests an archer's bow. She is the only woman I know who can work hard and eat only one meal a day." Valentino was not a henpecked husband, concluded Carr, but he was by his own admission a bad businessman. In handing over such concerns to his wife, Rudy made Rambova the necessary villain in the hard-won negotiations with studio heads.

As Natacha busied herself rewriting the scenario for *The Hooded Falcon,* she set Adrian to work designing its costumes and hired William Cameron Menzies—in her mind "the cleverest dramatic architect in the business"—to create the sets. It was apparent to all that the production would still not be ready to film for several months. Again, J. D. Williams pressed the Valentinos with the proposal that *Cobra,* a relatively small film, be made in the interim. Reluctantly they agreed, but on the condition that it not be released until after *The Hooded Falcon.*

Adrian and Bill Menzies were called upon to interrupt their work on *The Hooded Falcon* to design costumes and sets quickly for the stopgap picture. Natacha took very little interest in *Cobra,* a contemporary story about an Italian antique dealer who finds romance and betrayal in America before returning, a wiser man, to his homeland. "I was far too absorbed in the *Falcon*," she later claimed. But there was another reason: "It was a modern story and modern stories always bored me to tears—I neither cared nor understood anything about them, unless by chance they were fantastical or symbolical, which was rarely the case." While she supervised the work of Adrian and Menzies, and contributed to the brief visionary scenes in *Cobra,* Natacha was willing to relinquish to George Ullman the job of production manager. Later, when *Cobra* was released, it proved to be an embarrassing flop. The *New York Times* declared it "quite absurd." Ullman pointed to Mrs. Valentino as the culprit and wrote that "Natacha had practically full control at the studio during the making of *Cobra.*" Ullman's story was accepted in Hollywood, and the actress Colleen Moore went so far as to claim that Natacha wrote the script by means of invoking the dead: "Every night Natasha [*sic*] would hold a seance, calling forth help from the spirit world in her creative undertaking. Then, pencil and paper in hand, she would go into a trance and start writing. After her outpourings were typed up, they were brought into the set the next day and given to the director." Lou Mahoney, who practically lived at the Whitley Heights house as the Valentinos' trusted factotum, denied that Rudy or Natacha had anything to do with Spiritualism. "As long as I was working with them I never heard them talking about spirits. I never heard them say that they had to first hear from their spirits before making a decision. I *did* hear two Catholics who had fallen away, making a lot of excuses, and giving me sometimes five or ten dollars to put in next Sunday's collection at the church I went to." Mahoney added, with a mixture of sarcasm and regret, that "one of the spirits they may have been looking for—but it never showed up—was one to relieve them of the pressure that was on Mrs. Valentino from Ullman." As Mahoney saw it, there was a power play going on: George Ullman was trying to discredit Rambova in order that he alone might gain full control of Rudolph Valentino's career.

Ullman began his machinations by attacking Natacha's extravagant spending. Here, of course, he was not altogether unjust. He admitted that Rudy was a spendthrift, too, but was only following his wife's lead: "Rudy was not quite as extravagant as she. His sublime confidence in the star of his destiny caused him to spend money like water, and to incur debts which would have appalled a more conservative man. Had his wife spent ten times the amount she did, he would have applauded her judgement and mortgaged his future to gratify her whims."

Mahoney reasoned that the Valentinos' lavish purchasing was due,

This bizarre costume was one of the few Rambova designed for Cobra.

in part, to the financial ignorance in which Ullman kept them. "Do you know where you stand financially?" Lou asked them. Natacha replied, "We don't know anything about the money we have; we don't even sign a check." As they saw it, Rudy was the source of their income, and as long as he continued to work, they felt they would be solvent.

Ullman was also prone to characterizing Rambova as a femme fatale who had an uncanny power over men—particularly Rudy—bending her victim's will to her own insatiable ambitions:

To achieve her artistic success, Mrs. Valentino obtained the services of some of the greatest geniuses in the profession; one and all, I saw those men pass under the spell of her personality and yield up to her the greatest treasures of their art. This brings me to the subject of this woman's amazing fascination. Not only was her taste in dress an eye-arresting thing, Oriental, exotic, sometimes bizarre, but her costumes invariably added to the almost sinister fascination she was able to exert whenever she chose.

Those whom she disliked and ignored, very often hated her. But upon anyone on whom she bent her attention for any length of time, or whose allegiance she desired to secure, to serve her own ambition, or to forward any project of her own, she exercised to the fullest her uncanny ability to charm. Men seemed wholly unable to resist her, but yielded to her spell without a struggle.

Ullman believed that Cleopatra was Rambova's prototype in history: "I could very easily imagine that the soul of Natacha Rambova, with all her physical perfections and her mysterious fascination, had once inhabited the body of Egypt's queen. And that the Nile and its desert sands had once been her natural habitat." Many others would make the same comparison, with Rambova herself finding ancient Egypt the source of her spiritual and intellectual interests in the years to come.

When *Cobra* had been completed, to general dissatisfaction, Rudy and Natacha retired for a few weeks of vacation in Palm Springs at the home of Dr. White. There they swam, went horseback riding, and continued their plans for *The Hooded Falcon*. Their sojourn was interrupted, however, by a telephone call from George Ullman telling them that J. D. Williams had decided to terminate all preparations for the production, realizing that in doing so he was also terminating his contract with the Valentinos. Natacha left Rudy in Palm Springs and immediately returned to Los Angeles for further discussions with Ullman.

J. D. Williams's action did not come to her as a total surprise. Lou Mahoney had acted as her spy at Ritz-Carlton, and she had previously learned from him that Williams had been systematically cutting back the company's staff. His moves to prune the budget of *The Hooded Falcon* had disgruntled her. With their Ritz-Carlton contract now broken, it would only be a matter of time before a new production company could be found to finance Rudy's cinematic epics. On this point George Ullman had promising news. He was in negotiation with Joseph Schenck, the president of United Artists, which was interested in signing Valentino. This thrilled Natacha, for it meant that Rudy could now take his rightful place with other members of Hollywood's royalty. United Artists had been formed to accommodate filmdom's most bankable stars, Mary Pickford, Douglas Fairbanks, Norma Talmadge, and Charlie Chaplin. Filled with new hope, Natacha cheerfully returned to Palm Springs to console Rudy.

"I do think that Mrs. Valentino had a hold over Mr. Valentino," Lou Mahoney attested, "but I think it was a good hold, a progressive hold—something that he needed." It was Natacha, Mahoney believed, who was Rudy's rock of security in the unstable world of Hollywood stardom: "It was from her that Mr. Valentino learned never to be discouraged when something went wrong. He had the same password for dealing with adversity as she had: 'It's over. It's paid for. It's experience. And what experience can you get without paying for it?' They both had the same expression."

Natacha's stoicism in the face of adversity met its greatest challenge, however, when the couple returned to Los Angeles and discovered the details of the contract Ullman negotiated with United Artists. Rudy would be offered $10,000 a week and be expected to make three pictures a year for the studio. He would also receive 42 percent of the profits from his pictures. He would conceivably make a million dollars a year. But these lucrative terms were predicated on one stipulation: that henceforth Natacha Rambova was to exercise no voice, and have no participation, in the making of Rudolph Valentino's pictures. She would not even be allowed to visit the studio set.

At first, Valentino hesitated to agree to such a condition. It was a direct attack on the power Natacha had exercised over his career. Yet Schenck's offer came at a time when the couple found themselves in heaviest debt and their reputation in the industry at an all-time low. After painful deliberation, Valentino signed the contract.

In doing so, he plunged a dagger into the heart of his marriage.

Publically Natacha approved of the transaction and voiced her praise of Mr. Schenck and United Artists. Privately she was devastated, for she saw in Rudy's move the supreme act of betrayal. It also forced to the forefront an unacknowledged issue that had been festering in their marriage. Rudy wanted children as soon as possible, and Natacha was not yet willing to forsake her career in order to accommodate him.

"May a wife deny her husband children?" asked *Liberty* magazine some months later, when the press discovered this sore point between the Valentinos. The author of the question, Elizabeth Redfield, doubted that the majority of American women would answer yes. She challenged Rambova's obstinacy with an unflattering portrait of a woman who loves dogs more than children:

The dog is a noble animal. But, by some uncanny psychology, cold-blooded and self-interested women choose to love tiny, yipping dogs who have the smallest cranial capacity of all the canine family. The Pekingese has become a symbol, in fact, for a certain type of childless wife.

Is Mrs. Rudolph Valentino such a type?

Rambova protested to the interviewer that she was not. Foreign men, she pointed out, are bred to believe that they are more important than women, and while a romance may be filled with marvelous lovemaking, passion, poetry, and adoration, such men never see marriage as a union of equals. She wanted to continue her creative work in movies as Rudy's equal. Her husband suddenly decided otherwise: "And it wasn't as though I had just been working for myself. I have been working for him. It was rather silly for him to say all at once, 'I don't want you to work any more.' I worked harder for him than for anyone, designing nearly all of his productions for four years." Since foreign men look upon their wives as charming subordinates, Rambova reasoned, it would have been a mistake to bring children into the marriage. Rudy was only looking for a son, she said, a mirror image of his own magnificent masculinity. As an American woman, she resented this and felt that girls are just as worth having as boys. Concluding the interview, Rambova proclaimed that she adored children with all her heart and would, in fact, willingly give up her career for them since, she felt, they demanded all the energy and intelligence a mother could give. But she was not willing to give up her career for the love of a husband who did not consider her his equal.

Prior to the signing of the United Artists contract, the Valentinos had decided to move to an eight-acre hillside estate in Beverly Hills they christened Falcon Lair in homage to Natacha's screen project. They had taken out a loan of $100,000 to help finance its purchase and refurbishing, and Natacha had been active in its decoration. After United Artist's debarment of Natacha's participation in Rudy's career and rejection of her *Hooded Falcon* scenario, Falcon Lair became in her eyes the domestic prison to which her husband would have her consigned. She dropped all interest in the sixteen-room mansion and refused to move from their home in Whitley Heights.

"That contract was the breaking point for the Valentinos," said Lou Mahoney. "It was arranged by Mr. Ullman that Mrs. Valentino would have nothing to do with the pictures that were to be made by the Schenck organization. She was entirely shoved out. She was very much upset with Mr. Valentino for signing the contract."

As Natacha's relationship with Rudy deteriorated, he alone negotiated with United Artists to star in *The Eagle,* a story set in Imperial Russia about a Robin Hood character dressed in Cossack clothing. Rambova, in turn, sought to salvage her wounded pride by embarking on her own motion picture production. She took the idea to George Ullman, whose treacherous hand in her affairs she had not yet fully discovered. "I was still somewhat skeptical," Ullman recalled, "and, when Rudy came in, I referred the matter to him. I at once saw that the nerves of both were drawn fine. In fact, I may say that they had begun to pull apart, and it was only by his yielding to her in this matter that an immediate catastrophe was averted."

A sum of $30,000 was budgeted for her production called *What Price Beauty?,* a comic satire she had written on the agonies women undergo in order to make themselves beautiful. Nita Naldi was signed to star in the film, playing a vamp competing with a country girl for the affections of a handsome manager of a beauty parlor. Adrian was placed in charge of designing the costumes. A young dancer name Myrna Loy, whom Rambova had originally hoped to use in *Cobra,* until she failed the screen test, was cast to play a minor but eye-catching role. "She was absolutely beautiful, the most beautiful woman I had ever seen," recalled Loy when she was first presented to Mrs. Valentino. "She always wore turbans and long, very stark dresses, usually velvet or brocade of the same golden brown as her eyes. She was breathtaking and I was scared. 'I know they call me everything from Messalina to a dope fiend,' she

disclosed to calm me, 'but I really don't eat little dancers for breakfast.' "
Rambova put the dancer under the skillful hand of Adrian, and she was
transformed into an exotic vixen:

. . . my only scene, was a futuristic dream sequence depicting various
types of womankind. Natacha dubbed me "the intellectual type of
vampire without race or creed or country." Adrian designed an
extraordinary red velvet pajama outfit for me, with a short blond wig
that came to little points on my forehead, very very snaky. This bizarre
film wasn't released for three years, but Henry Waxman took pictures
of me in that outfit. They appeared in a fan magazine captioned "Who
is she?" and eventually led to my first contract.

Myrna Loy had met Valentino during her audition for *Cobra,* and it
became apparent to her why his wife had assumed such a commanding
presence in his professional life:

It was easy to see why Natacha took charge of his career. He was like a
trusting child who wanted to be liked, agreeing to everything, then
expecting her to get him out of it. Everyone knew Rudy was sweet and
agreeable; therefore, his wife became the villain. "I was a fool," she
maintained after they separated, "young and optimistic and full of fight.

*Top: Myrna Loy
appears in* What
Price Beauty?
*Bottom: Rudy and
Natacha host a
reception for the artist
Federico Beltran-Masses
at the Ambassador
Hotel, Los Angeles.*

I didn't realize the uselessness. Studios don't care about your ideas or you. They want to crowd as many pictures into as little time as possible to collect on you as quickly as they can. What happens to the star is of no concern." It would be a while before I saw the truth of her words firsthand.

When Natacha's movie was completed at a cost of $100,000, more than three times the budget, Valentino was not as sweet and agreeable as Myrna Loy had remembered him. Ullman's complaints to him about the skyrocketing costs of his wife's production made Rudy testy and Natacha increasingly withdrawn. Lou Mahoney remembered how everyone involved in the film tried their best to cut costs, but it simply could not be made for less money. The picture was previewed at a theater on the east side of Pasadena, and Mahoney remembered the audience reaction as positive, but, thereafter, *What Price Beauty?* was consigned to oblivion. Mahoney knew why: "No help came from anyone, no thoughts of trying to get this picture properly released. No help came from Ullman, Schenck, or anybody else. Their whole thought was that if the picture were a success, Mrs. Valentino would be a success. She would then start producing under the Rudolph Valentino Production Company. But this nobody wanted—except herself, and Mr. Valentino."

Disappointed by the lack of enthusiasm her film received from the powers in Hollywood who could have made it a success, Natacha confided to Lou that she wanted to build a boat and sail to some island where she could do what she wanted and get a fresh start. Mahoney counseled her to forget the boat, that what she needed was a vacation, alone, away from Rudy, until he had finished his contract with United Artists and was financially able to produce his own pictures. The boat dream persisted, however, and as soon as Valentino was informed of her wish, he ordered a cabin cruiser built for her.

Hollywood gossip was circulating that the Valentino marriage was in deep trouble, that Natacha was taking drugs to numb the pangs of despair, that she was absenting herself from the Whitley Heights haven, and had taken a lover. To scotch the rumors, Natacha joined Rudy in hosting a reception at the Ambassador Hotel for the Spanish painter Federico Beltran-Masses, who had just completed four paintings for them. Two were portraits of Rudy; one showed him dressed in Moorish garb for his unrealized role in *The Hooded Falcon,* the other wearing a gaucho costume. The third was a portrait of Natacha in Spanish dress, reclining in the manner of Goya's clothed maja. The fourth painting was a sensual portrait called *La Gitana,* a picture of a Spanish gypsy reclining seminude likewise in the attitude of Goya's naked maja. Except for the woman's green eyes, *La Gitana* had the unmistakable features of Natacha. The well-bred Rambova, who was never seen in Hollywood with her hair unbound, brandishing a cigarette, or wearing a short skirt, insisted that Beltran-Masses's naked maja be given a name other than her own. It was Rudy's favorite painting, however, one that he would later place above his bed at Falcon Lair.

Some of Hollywood's biggest names attended the reception: Charlie Chaplin, Mary Pickford, Douglas Fairbanks, Harold Lloyd, Gloria Swanson, Tom Mix, Mae Murray, Bebe Daniels, Marion Davies, Colleen Moore, Barbara LaMarr, John Barrymore, Irving Thalberg, and John Gilbert, among others. The journalist Adela Rogers St. Johns noted that the affair was a social triumph for the Valentinos, but Natacha's attitude, she complained, reduced the dazzling array of stars to nothing more than a royal court. Making her entrance—two hours late—in jeweled turban and Poiret robe, Madam Valentino regally progressed from room to room wearing a Sphinx-like smile and giving barely a nod to her guests, while Rudy trailed behind her, trying to be natural and friendly. When dinner had not yet been served by ten-thirty, the writer left in a huff. Her absence was noted by the hostess. At Rudy's insistence, she later wrote an apology to Natacha for her peasantlike behavior. She was hungry, she protested, and couldn't wait any longer. Rambova did not respond to her apology, but the journalist had the last word by writing an unfavorable review of Natacha's conduct in her syndicated column.

Rambova's disdain for the Hollywood crowd and her growing estrangement from Rudy provided Ullman with a bloodscent, and he unleashed his investigative hounds. Ex-policeman Lou Mahoney knew how to substantiate her suspicion that she was being trailed. He soon discovered that the Burns Detective Agency had been hired to follow her. The detectives had discovered that Natacha was seeing a camera technician who had been working on her film, and that the two sequestered themselves in his studio lab for hours at a time. The exact nature of their relationship could not be determined, but when Ullman presented the evidence to Rudy at his home, the actor flew into a violent rage and grabbed a gun, prepared to kill the man. Ullman wrested the pistol out of Valentino's hand, warning him that violence would only lead to scandal, and scandal would finish his career. Later, when tempers had cooled, Mahoney broached the subject with Natacha: "I asked her about the

Rudy bids farewell to Natacha as she boards the train for New York.

cameraman whom she was supposed to have gotten so familiar with, and she quickly answered, 'He was the only one that seemed to understand my problems, and always had a kind word for me. But that is over now, and at this moment I stand alone.' I told her that I had been on her side, and she answered, 'No Lou, you have been nice to me, but you will always be at Mr. Valentino's side, come rain or shine.' "

Natacha informed Rudy that she needed a "marital vacation," time alone to think things out. On August 13, she would travel to New York with Aunt Teresa and then sail to France to see her mother. George Ullman was going east on business at the same time. Together they would try to find a market for her film. Valentino agreed to all that Natacha desired. It was his ultimate hope that, in this time of separation, both Auntie and Muzzie could help heal the breach that had been created between himself and his wife.

Sadly, Lou Mahoney helped her pack. As they were ready to leave the Whitley Heights home, he found her staring out the window. "Lou, that is some aviary," she told him, "and I had many hours of pleasure with the birds." Mahoney knew how the heart of Natacha Rambova was breaking at that moment, and recalled the sadness of that haunted face: "She looked like a person I had seen in court when the death sentence was pronounced. Everything was lost, and I cried inside."

Mahoney drove the Valentinos to the train depot in Los Angeles. A multitude of reporters were waiting there to record the scene. Both Rudy and Natacha bravely posed for photographs, kissing, smiling, and holding hands. Finally, he assisted her up the steps to her Pullman drawing room and lovingly waved to her as the train withdrew from the station and passed out of sight.

They would never see each other again.

O n opposite sides of the continent, Rudy and Natacha found communication difficult. The press, eager to make a sensational story out of their "marital vacation," forced the couple to a newsprint dialogue while a scandal-hungry public eavesdropped over the numerous publications that charted their estrangement.

Rambova: I am sure this marital holiday will be a good thing for us both. When a husband and wife both are working and both are possessors of temperaments, I think they should have a vacation from each other.

Valentino: For Mrs. Valentino I have the greatest respect and admiration. We have been happy together and may be again. I am sorry that this had to happen, but we cannot always order our lives the way we would like to have them.

Rambova: With butlers and super-butlers, maids and the rest, what work is there for a housewife? I won't be a parasite. I won't sit and twiddle my fingers waiting for a husband who goes on the lot at 5:00 A.M. and gets home at midnight and receives mail from girls in Oshkosh and Kalamazoo.

Valentino: Mrs. Valentino cannot have a career and be my wife at the same time. If she wants her freedom or wants to be a star in pictures, all right. She understood this before she left here.

Rambova launches a new career as dress designer and art collector.

Rambova: Since I've been making my own pictures we have been drawn more or less apart, and I can't find the time to devote to the home that I used to. My husband is a great lover of home life.

Valentino: You know that I am just beginning to feel that I was as well off single as I was married. I love and appreciate beauty. This quality may have given Mrs. Valentino cause for jealousy, and I may have been a very poor husband in that respect. She wanted to isolate me as much as possible. That was her nature. I don't know definitely whether we will be reconciled or divorced. But of one thing I am certain. She cannot come back as my wife as long as she is seeking a career in pictures.

Rambova: He knew what I was when I married him. I have been working since I was seventeen. Homes and babies are all very nice, but you can't have them and a career as well. I intended, and intend, to have a career and Valentino knew it. If he wants a housewife, he'll have to look again.

Natacha did not want to live in the Valentino apartment at 270 Park Avenue, so she established a new residence for herself and Aunt Teresa at 9 West 81st Street. There she pressed Ullman to find a distributor for her picture, and told him that she was now interested in an acting career. During one of his business meetings with her, Ullman asked Natacha outright whether or not she still loved Rudy. Clad in a gold and white negligée, her hair hanging in two long, loose braids, she twisted her hands together nervously and told him in a small voice that she did not know. Her face was pale, he recalled, and she had dark circles under her eyes, testament to sleepless nights. As he continued to question her, she reiterated that she did not know whether to go back to Rudy or whether she should get a divorce. Finally, breaking under the pressure of his interrogation, she burst into tears and told him to leave.

In Hollywood, Rudy did not want to live alone with his memories at Whitley Heights. With Lou Mahoney's help, he moved into Falcon Lair, even though renovation had not yet been completed. Beltran-Masses kept him company there and gave him painting lessons. The work the actor chose to reproduce in these lessons was *La Gitana*. Obsessed with the picture, he painted it over and over again.

Valentino's attempts to telephone Natacha consistently failed. She

Left behind in Hollywood, Rudy paints a copy of the Beltran-Masses portrait of Natacha.

did not want to talk to him. The letters that he received from her were accusatory and bitter. Ullman returned from New York with news that Natacha had landed an acting role in a film based on a Laura Jean Libbey story, and she was preparing for a trip to Paris with the excuse that she needed to purchase her wardrobe there. In reality, she was going to France to obtain a divorce.

Grieving over his crumbling marriage, Rudy became increasingly reckless. He declined to use a double for some of the dangerous stunts required in the filming of *The Eagle*, needlessly submitting himself to being battered and beaten. Santa Monica police stopped him for speeding and reckless driving. The following week, on a trip to San Pedro to see the boat he had made for Natacha, he spun his car out of control and crashed into a telephone pole. Beltran-Masses found him a short time later, sitting alone in the library of Falcon Lair with a gun pointed at his head. The painter quietly approached Valentino's chair from behind and knocked the pistol from his hand. The actor collapsed into a fit of tears.

While Valentino contemplated suicide, Rambova took solace in things spiritual. Before leaving for Paris, she was consoled in New York by her mother, who had become a recent convert to the teachings of Helena Petrovna Blavatsky, the controversial nineteenth-century founder of the Theosophical Society. Ann Wollen, Rambova's cousin, recalled how Mrs. Hudnut's spiritual journey had taken a circuitous route: "Aunt Winifred was born a Mormon. When she married the Colonel she was a Catholic. When she married Uncle Edgar she turned to Christian Science. Then she married Richard Hudnut in the Episcopal church. But she ventured into Theosophy on her own, and got her husband and Natacha to follow her."

Natacha learned from her mother the basic tenets of theosophical belief: that a divine intelligence guides the cosmos and is a part of every creature, the evolution of the soul takes place through repeated incarnations, and in its progress from materialism to pure intelligence, the soul finally passes to the emotional world of the astral plane at the body's death, whereupon it awaits forgetfulness and rebirth before entering into a state of Nirvana in heaven. Borrowing heavily from Buddhism, Blavatsky's doctrines were purportedly the spiritual fruit gained from a pilgrimage she made to Tibet before 1875. Her 1877 book, *Isis Unveiled,* a collection of Eastern religion and philosophy that she ascribed to her Tibetan masters, was followed in 1888 by *The Secret Doctrine,* which placed greater emphasis on the occult and esotericism. Standing on the shoulders of Spiritualism, which, at the end of the nineteenth century, was given serious attention by intellectuals and artists, Blavatsky claimed that communication with the Masters, or Mahatmas, was possible for the spiritually advanced, and that revelations could be received through telepathic amanuensis.

Despite the protests of her critics that she was a hashish-smoking charlatan, a plagiarist, and a mediumistic trickster, a multitude of followers embraced Blavatsky's doctrines in the United States, Europe, and India. Mystical, otherworldly, ritualistic, and elitist, Theosophy clearly appealed to Winifred Hudnut and her receptive daughter, whose Mormon ancestors had also claimed adherence to latter-day revelations about ancient truths. The spiritualist branch of the Theosophical Society, which had been galvanized in America by the medium Katherine Tingley, was the splinter group to which Winifred Hudnut pledged her allegiance, and here Natacha found her own inclinations satisfied, having already flirted with séance phenomena three years earlier in New York.

While Muzzie and Natacha discussed spiritual subjects, they decided to fortify their beliefs by inviting a medium into their midst. George Wehner, sometime musician, composer, and actor, was the seer recommended to them. Arriving at Rambova's penthouse apartment, he was charmed by its chic atmosphere: "The floors were carpeted in jet black. The walls were a soft gray and the woodwork, silver. Across the front of the large living-room a long step led up through vermilion-curtained French windows into a glass veranda from which the myriad lights of Central Park and the city beyond could be seen."

Seated at a table awaiting the medium was an assembly of invited guests. Besides Mrs. Hudnut, Wehner was introduced to the director of Rambova's upcoming film, and Clive Brooks, her costar. The vivacious American singer Donna Shinn Russell sat next to Natacha Rambova, who captivated Wehner:

Tall, slender, and strikingly beautiful in an exotic way, clad in a long graceful gown of purple satin over which she wore a long Persian coat of gold and silver lamé lined with red, and on her head one of her famous turbans, of lacquer-red, she seemed like a princess just stepped out of some Oriental fantasy. Her ancient Oriental jewels accentuated this idea.

Her movements were lithe and graceful and her dark eyes filled with the smoldering light which mediums at once recognize as belonging to the psychic personality. But what struck me most about this picturesque personage was the unusual quality of her beautifully modulated voice. In that voice I read pathos, sympathetic understanding, and great depth of feeling.

The séance that evening was successful, with everyone receiving messages from beyond the grave, except for Mrs. Hudnut. Wehner noticed that the eyes of the participants were wet with tears: "The important point of this séance was that it wrought a great change in the mind of Miss Rambova, upsetting many of her materialistic viewpoints and creating the desire in her for the more spiritual."

Hungry for more experiences, Rambova hired George Wehner to conduct séances twice a week in her apartment, and before she returned to France, Winifred Hudnut invited the medium to visit them at the Château Juan-les-Pins.

In November Rudy attended the premiere of *The Eagle* at the Mark Strand Theatre in New York City. He escorted United Artists press agent Beulah Livingston to the event and was greeted by an unprecedented mob. The film was receiving critical acclaim across the nation, with *Variety* voicing the popular opinion that Valentino's career was back on track with this "he-man" role, forsaking the "ladies' man" image of his previous movie ventures. This poured salt into Natacha's emotional and professional wounds, and the coincidental timing of Rudy's triumph in New York with her return from France on the *Leviathan* confirmed in her mind that she had done the right thing in initiating divorce proceedings. Rudy had chosen the studio over her; let him now savor these glory days promised by his new "bride."

The couple made no attempt to see each other, and shortly thereafter Rudy took the same ocean liner on its return trip to Europe in order to market his film and establish residency in Paris to comply with French divorce requirements. Reporters observed how tired Valentino looked when he boarded the *Leviathan*. His face was lined, and his hair was beginning to thin. What reporters did not know, however, was that the actor's health was deteriorating. He was already experiencing sharp stomach pains.

The crowds of women who greeted Rudy in London and Paris were several times larger than those that had met him there before. Even while his marriage was sound, Natacha deliberately kept her name off of his cinematic productions in order that his wedded status not interfere with the public's perception of him as a lover on the prowl. Now that his pending divorce was public knowledge, women were throwing themselves before him, hoping to become Rambova's successor. The press assumed that any actress with whom he had established a professional or social relationship was a lover. Candidates included Vilma Banky and Mae Murray. After attending a number of well-publicized parties and premieres, Valentino made one last visit to the place where he had spent some of the happiest days of his life, the Hudnut château. Muzzie was there to greet him: "In January he came back to us, the same sweet, loving boy of old. It was impossible for him to remain many days, as his sadness was too great. He often went to Natacha's room to sit there awhile by himself, and when he came out he would kneel beside me and bury his head in my lap and cry like a baby. I was heartbroken."

Reporters for the *New York Times* mistook Winifred Hudnut for Natacha Rambova when Rudy was seen escorting her to a restaurant in Nice. They also presumed that the couple had been discussing a property settlement, a conversation that never took place. When the divorce decree was granted on grounds of desertion and announced in Paris on January 19, 1926, Natacha's birthday, Rudy was in Cherbourg preparing to return to the United States, and Rambova was in Connecticut preparing to appear in a one-act suspense drama on the vaudeville stage. She had been horrified to learn after completing her film that the distributors of the movie decided to call it *When Love Grows Cold,* capitalizing on her marital woes. The first intertitle of the film, in which Rambova tearfully plays Margaret Benson, a shunted wife, summarized its theme, which did strike close to home: "A powerful heart stirring story of a woman's supreme devotion and sacrifice for a man who paid the penalty of 'forgetting' when success came to him." That she was being billed as "Mrs. Rudolph Valentino" proved to be the last straw, and Rambova swore that she was finished with the film industry once and for all.

She turned to the stage, and her manager, Daniel Goodman, found her a role playing a beautiful Russian woman who cunningly battles a poisonously cruel general in a one-act Grand Guignol sketch called *The Purple Vial.* The play was to open on the vaudeville circuit in Bridgeport, Connecticut, where the managers of the theater wanted to couple it with a Rudolph Valentino film. Rambova adamantly refused to cooperate, thereby postponing the play's debut until after the Valentino movie had completed its run. When *The Purple Vial* opened on February 8 at the Palace Theatre in New York, the reviewer for *Variety* was amazed to discover that she could act: "Natacha Rambova was surprisingly adequate as the girl outwitting the fiendish general. Playing with expression and

The billing that infuriated Natacha (left), and a scene from When Love Grows Cold, in which Clive Brooks was her costar (right)

running gamuts that would have taxed some of our better known emotional actresses, she gave a performance that was a revelation for one coming out of silent drama for her first speaking role. Her interpretation was perfect at all times. . . . Miss Rambova has demonstrated sparks of an emotional actress that may ride further in either vaudeville or legit."

While Natacha appeared onstage in New York, Rudy commenced filming *The Son of the Sheik* in California. It was United Artists' blatant attempt to capitalize on his previous success in the same role. The depression over the failure of his marriage now took a new course, as he tried to ease the loss of Natacha by engaging in a number of sexual liaisons with eager Hollywood actresses, including Nita Naldi. Valentino's makeup artist, Mont Westmore, steered the cabin cruiser Rudy had commissioned for Natacha while the actor made love to Naldi below deck. Mont's brother, Frank Westmore, recounted the scene: "Often, while Mont stood on the bridge with his eyes peeled for the treacherous reefs off Catalina, he could hear Nita's melodious voice extolling Rudy's capabilities. Mont always was especially amused when she would comment on his soft, sweet-smelling hair."

It was not the first time that a presumed friend had bedded Rambova's man in her absence. Worse, Nita Naldi savaged what was left of Rambova's reputation in Hollywood by circulating the story that Natacha had procured no fewer than three abortions during her years with Valentino. Naldi also claimed that she had unwittingly accompanied Natacha

Despite their separation and divorce, Rudy continued to wear Natacha's slave bracelet, visible here in The Son of the Sheik.

to the doctor when she had her second one, not knowing what had taken place until she came out of surgery. The third operation, the actress declared, took place in Europe, with Rambova blaming Valentino for a "miscarriage" caused by his reckless driving.

Naldi's story is quite suspect; for she used it to gain leverage with her former friend's ex-husband, who desperately wanted a child. Such allegations do lend support, however, to the position Rambova's detractors took, that Valentino's wife would stop at nothing to satisfy her career ambitions. Could it be that Rambova, contemplative, brooding, saturnine, and solitary, destroyed her unborn progeny rather than let motherhood deter her from becoming the greatest artist in the Hollywood film industry? Ann Wollen, Rambova's cousin, disputes such claims, noting that her family would have been aware of the reputed pregnancies and abortions had they taken place: "Aunt Teresa was living with them most of the time, and she would have known of such things. She rode in the car with them to Rome. If Natacha had indeed been pregnant then, she would have accompanied her back to France. Instead, she continued south with Rudy. Teresa's maternal instincts were such that no sign of pregnancy could have gone by her undetected." Furthermore, had Valentino known that Natacha was pregnant, it is extremely doubtful that he would have driven so recklessly in Europe. Whether or not there was any truth to the stories Naldi circulated, Rudy tired of her quickly and turned his attention to Pola Negri.

Paul Ivano, who saw more of the actor now that he was free of Natacha, introduced Rudy to Pola Negri at a party given by Marion

Davies in July 1926. After they spoke, Negri left the party around mid-night, claiming she must go to bed because she had to appear at the studio early the next morning. Valentino then announced that he also had to leave for the same reason. Ivano knew that Rudy was not telling the truth and was well aware of what the actor had planned for the evening: "Rudy went home and changed out of his formal attire and into some regular clothes. He drove to Pola Negri's, and rang the doorbell. A servant answered the door. Without any exchange of words, he handed the man his hat and cane and proceeded upstairs. He went directly to the first big door, which he correctly guessed was Negri's bedroom. Without knocking he walked in. Pola was in bed. Rudy took his clothes off and joined her. The next morning he said to me, 'Thanks for the introduction, Paul. She wasn't bad, wasn't bad!' " Although the romance with Negri was real, Ivano claimed that the much-publicized announcement of marriage plans was a total fabrication.

Throughout his post-Rambovian sexual wanderings, Valentino continued to wear Natacha's platinum slave bracelet. Luther Mahoney claimed that the actor never gave up the hope that he and Natacha would be reunited. After his contract with United Artists expired, Valentino planned to finance an independent "Rudolph Valentino Production Company," which would allow Rambova to rejoin him in the art of filmmaking. The actor had even picked out the vehicle for their next venture, a book he kept in his library, *The Silver Stallion* by James Branch Cabell, a medieval fantasy set in thirteenth-century Europe. But Mahoney, mindful of the stranglehold Ullman and Schenck had on the actor, knew that independence would be hard won, and he told Rudy, "You are a gold mine, but they know that the end of the rainbow is near. The greedy are shooting to control and pick off of you all that they can before you start on an independent outlook." He reminded Valentino of Natacha's frustration in trying to distribute her film and noted that the actor received no encouragement from Ullman or Schenck whenever he mentioned plans for *The Silver Stallion.*

As his thoughts turned toward Natacha in the seven months following the divorce, Rudy had ample time to rethink the reasons for their break-up. Before embarking on a cross-country tour to promote *The Son of the Sheik,* he penned for publication his own story explaining why his marriage had failed. He had not beaten her, he claimed, nor had he objected to her having a career—her *own* career. He had not even demanded that she bear children and keep house. Money was an aggravating factor. The more they made, the more it seemed to enslave them. But the major cause of their split, he concluded, was the change in Natacha's temperament. She had first guided his career out of selfless love, but then her own ambitions took over: "She gives up her career . . . to better and more completely aid him in his. Almost imperceptibly, but slowly and surely, her attitude changes. It gradually dawns on him that, while she has given up her particular career, she has not given up A career. She has started on a new one, which is to 'manage' and make a success of him. Now, you will say, a man should be deeply grateful for that." Valentino was not. Natacha's calculating brain brought him success, he admitted, but that success, and the perception it created, ensnared him. She subjected him to social and professional restrictions for the sake of his image. When he finally took the management of his career away from her, she had to make a choice between love and pride: "If her love is greater than her pride, she will surrender gracefully and make the adjustments which will enable them to start all over again on a new basis. If her pride is paramount, she will probably slap him across the face with a bill of divorcement."

Valentino hesitated to allow the *New York American* to publish his essay until he had an opportunity to discuss it further with his literary agent. After the fatal turn of events that took place in the summer of 1926, the newspaper went ahead and published it anyway in September of that year.

On July 18, the *Chicago Tribune* leveled an editorial attack on Valentino that dealt him psychological—as well as gastric—pain. The anonymous writer claimed that the actor was responsible for the feminization of American males. On account of the image he had popularized in films, the newspaper declared, face-powder dispensers and pink powder puffs could now be found in men's lavatories.

The bigotry and xenophobia behind the attack on the dark-skinned actor were lost in the aspersion cast on his masculinity. To imply that the actor was effeminate or gay was an easy and cowardly journalistic subterfuge that masked the unsettling fact that the thief of hearts in America was a foreign-born Italian. While the *Tribune* had a history of anti-Valentino rhetoric, this latest assault may have been provoked by the actor's application for United States citizenship some months earlier, a move that disgruntled Mussolini as much as it did some American men.

In a letter published in a rival Chicago newspaper, the inflamed actor challenged the anonymous writer of the editorial to a boxing match. No one came forth, but Valentino used the media attention to prove to the American public that he was no "powder puff." Photographed in boxing shorts, he flexed his muscles and skillfully participated in a one-round exhibition bout with Frank "Buck" O'Neil, a sportswriter for the *New York Evening Journal.*

While Rudy boxed in New York to defend his image, Rambova immersed herself in Spiritualism in France. In early May she had boarded the *Homeric* with Aunt Teresa, George Wehner, five Pekingese, and a monkey. In the course of their storm-tossed journey across the Atlantic, the dogs got seasick, the monkey jumped in and out of portholes, and the medium saw deep-sea "elementals" and "air-beings" materialize on deck. In Paris they were joined by Mrs. Hudnut, who was accompanied by her own medium, Blanche Wheaton, and the retinue conducted psychic readings in the galleries, museums, and historical monuments of the city. They continued their search for earth-bound souls and memory pictures in the astral light of the palaces and châteaus of Versailles, Fontainebleau, the Loire district, and the French Riviera. As Wehner psychically observed the great moments in history that had taken place in these fabled locales, Natacha made copious notes. In the meantime, Mrs. Wheaton's extrasensory skills were focused primarily on the discovery of valuable antiques and art objects hidden away in little shops located throughout France and the Mediterranean, from Paris to Taormina in Sicily.

At the Hudnut château, Natacha learned that Uncle Dickie, heretofore a scoffer and a skeptic, had become president of a group formed by Madam Blavatsky called "Legion de Service Spirituelle." One of the

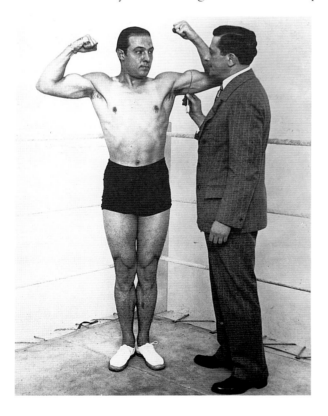

Fighting for his reputation, Valentino flexed his muscles before engaging in an exhibition boxing match.

mansion's salons had been set up for séances, with a portrait of Blavatsky —painted by Paul Ivanovitch, a Serbian court painter—placed over the Italian mantelpiece. The salon was referred to as the "H.P.B. room," after Blavatsky's initials, and her portrait cast its spell over Wehner: "The eyes of this picture follow one about with a mysterious persistency as if seeking to pierce one's very soul with the light of understanding. On many a night we have sat there in our circle room while that strange three-day wind, the Mistral, howled down the chimneys, and the roar of the Mediterranean swept up through the Court of Palms."

The diminutive Ivanovitch had also painted a full-length portrait of Natacha gliding down the stairs of the Grand Hall of the château wearing an imaginary outfit gleaned from an assortment of fashion photographs Mrs. Hudnut had given him. Rambova hated the picture. Since she had not even posed for it, she found it to be false and artificial.

The painter came under attack from another critic. The novelist Ford Madox Ford introduced Jean Rhys to the Hudnuts in response to Winifred's request for a writer to help her produce a book on psychic therapy and reincarnation. Mrs. Hudnut wanted to expound her own theory, which held that if one acquired furniture dating from the periods of one's previous lives, the spirit of those earlier incarnations could rest in peace. Rhys privately viewed the assignment as comic, until she arrived at the château that summer and found herself given a relatively unimportant room on the third floor of the mansion while Ivanovitch was entrenched in a sumptuous boudoir on the second floor. In the weeks that followed, Winifred dictated to Rhys detailed memories of her dreams and past lives. She suspected that she had once been a courtier in an eighteenth-century French salon. Unable to continue transcribing what she thought was nonsense, and angry that the artist had been given preferential treatment over a writer, Rhys left Château Juan-les-Pins, and satirized her experience there in a sketch titled "At the Villa D'Or," which was later included in her collection of stories called *The Left Bank*. She subtly mocked the safe and shallow Riviera life of the rich and glamorous Hudnuts, calling them Mr. and Mrs. "Valentine," whose daughter was a famous movie star in California. Ivanovitch was transformed into a Bulgarian named "Mr. Ivan Pauloff," and in one passage Mr. Valentine cautions the artist as to the propriety of some nudes:

He added in a lower tone: "Yes nood, but not too nood, Mr. Pauloff."

"There will be drapery," the Bulgarian assured him.

Mr. Pauloff had painted Mrs. Valentine two years ago surrounded by her Pekinese, and made her incredibly beautiful. Then he had painted Mr. Valentine with exquisite trousers and the rest, brown boots and alert blue eye.

He was now decorating the panels of Mr. Valentine's bedroom door with figures of little ladies. And a tactful drapery was to float round the little ladies' waists. After all he had been a court painter and he had learned to be miraculously tactful. A polite smile was always carved—as it were—on his ugly little face; in his brown, somewhat pathetic eyes was a look of strained attention.

Rhys was unsparing toward her characters: Pauloff requests that old newspaper reviews of his exhibitions be read aloud as he works; Mr. Valentine, a bald "cheerful insect with long thin legs," frets over such major decisions as the menu for the day, while Mrs. Valentine babbles on about art, music, furniture, the Russian character, secret agents, victrolaphobia, Spiritualism, and automatic writing. These absurdities are set against the blue-jeweled beauty of the Mediterranean Sea, a warm starry night with music drifting through the air from the distant casino below, and the magnificent "Villa D'Or," the Hudnut House of Gold that Natacha now called home.

On Monday, August 16, 1926, Rambova received—at Valentino's request—an unexpected cable from George Ullman. It disclosed the shocking news of Rudy's burst ulcer, his hospitalization, and the emergency operation that had been undertaken to save his life.

The anger and resentment that had hardened Natacha during the past year suddenly melted away, and the disagreements that had separated her from Rudy seemed unimportant now. Filled with anxiety, she turned to her mother and Aunt Teresa for support. They had never stopped harboring the hope that someday the couple would reunite. Perhaps this illness would be the crisis that would bring the lovers back together. That afternoon Natacha and Teresa Werner sent Rudy a cablegram, reassuring him of their prayers and love. Muzzie and Uncle Dickie also sent cables.

As the week progressed and no more news was received from Polyclinic Hospital in New York, Natacha retreated into nervous introspection. What her thoughts may have been, no one knows. Perhaps she recalled those earlier days when a young Italian actor at Metro tried so hard to break her cool reserve with his silly jokes; how he helped lacquer her furniture and cooked scavenged mussels and pasta in her tiny bungalow, and shared in her poverty, her dreams, and her ambitions. George Wehner provided some consolation. During the family séance on Wednesday evening in the H.P.B. room, the medium was able to contact Rudy's spirit, which reached out to both Natacha and Aunt Tessie, but in a rather incoherent way. He seemed to think that they were there in New York comforting him. An astral spirit named Jenny took over to describe Rudy's rush to the hospital, and how his thoughts turned to his wife and her beloved aunt.

Relief came to them all on Friday, August 20, when Natacha received another cable from Ullman stating that Rudy was much better and on the road to complete recovery. That night they held another séance in which two spirit guides, an Indian named Black Feather and an Egyptian named Mesolope, spoke to Natacha of Rudy's insights and character traits. At this séance the love that Natacha and her family still felt for Rudy gushed forth in an array of tears.

The next morning, Natacha again cabled Ullman, hoping that he would have more good news. But no response came on Sunday or

Monday. Then, on Tuesday morning the long-awaited word from Ullman reached them. Natacha opened the cablegram eagerly.

Rudy was dead.

Pleurisy had weakened him, and he died of endocarditis and septicemia on Monday, August 23, at 12:10 P.M.

Rambova was prostrate with grief. For three days and nights she refused to leave her room or eat. When at last she opened her door, her eyes were hollow, and her face swollen from sobbing. She wanted more news from Ullman. Had Rudy called for her when the end came? Had thoughts of Natacha occupied his last moments of consciousness? But no words of comfort were to come from the man, only a terse negative response to her request that Rudy be buried in the Hudnut family vault.

While Rudy's body was but an empty shell, she felt there was no point in going to his funeral. It was his spirit that Natacha desired to communicate with, and beginning that Friday evening, August 27, she called upon Wehner to make almost daily contact with Valentino's wandering ghost. This was an absolution for Natacha, a desperate attempt to communicate in death with the husband whom she had cut off in life.

Valentino's last photographic portrait

Wehner was skillful in easing Natacha's torment. Had not Black Feather and Mesolope predicted Rudy's death in their loving exposition of the spiritual insights he had gained in this life? Was not the perfume of tuberoses that Natacha noticed filling her room that warm morning earlier in the week a clear sign from Rudy telling her that he had passed on to a higher plane? In Wehner's séances, the conjured spirit of Valentino seemed at first confused and upset that death had taken him at the height of his career. Then Madam Blavatsky's spirit spoke through the medium, explaining that such behavior was due to the sorrow of his fans. As the sessions continued, Rudy began to express delight in his newborn existence on the astral plane, thus confirming the group's theosophical beliefs.

In California, Lou Mahoney, upon hearing of Valentino's death in New York, raced to Falcon Lair to carry out two tasks. First, he removed the jewelry that Valentino had hidden in a secret compartment in the mansion's stairway. He wanted the jewels to be inventoried among Rudy's belongings and not hidden away for some future owner to discover. Secondly, he removed all of Pola Negri's negligées from the premises and took them home to his wife and daughter. Better they wear them, he concluded, than have reporters discover that Miss Negri had been living with Valentino in his Beverly Hills love nest. Mahoney knew that his days of employment at Falcon Lair were numbered, since George Ullman was now in complete control of the actor's estate.

Ullman was also in charge of the funeral arrangements and the transport of the body to the West Coast after memorial services were held in New York. Even though Valentino's estate was said to be worth nearly three million dollars, the executor accepted from a bereaved June Mathis her offer to have Rudy's body laid to rest in a mausoleum vault she owned in Hollywood. As the cortège made its way from the Church of the Good Shepherd in Beverly Hills to the cemetery, Lou Mahoney, as a final gesture to the man he knew and admired, hired a biplane to fly overhead and drop rose petals.

Soon after the burial in Hollywood, the Hudnuts and George Wehner were sitting in the château watching the sunset, "like a bright glimpse of some celestial plane fading behind the Esterals." Suddenly, the spirit of Madam Blavatsky appeared to the medium, ordering him to tell Natacha that she must write the story of her life with Rudy. In her sorrow she did not seem responsive to the idea until Wehner informed her that the book was to have an additional part to it, in which Rudy's revelations of the astral plane would be published for the benefit of the public. Seeing the good that would result from it, Natacha began recording her memoirs with help from her mother. Wehner, for his part, began receiving detailed impressions from Valentino as his spirit continued to journey beyond the grave.

Rambova had originally threatened to write a book on Rudy while he lived, and had been photographed by journalists on August 24, 1925, as she assembled his love letters and other data before her typewriter. It could have been on account of this that Valentino decided to change his will on September 1, 1925. His estate was to be equally divided between Alberto Guglielmi, Maria Guglielmi, and Teresa Werner. Natacha Rambova was to receive the total sum of one dollar.

"I loved Rudy like a son, and he loved me," a trembling Teresa Werner told the crowd of excited journalists who had invaded the front steps of the château, eager for a statement. Gaining her composure, she continued, "And, of course, I worship Natacha. Isn't it possible for Natacha to share in it? It comes to me because of her after all."

Alberto, Rudy's brother and an equal heir, did not see it that way. In his own reply to reporters he declared, "Since she divorced Rudolph, she has no right to more than one dollar which he left her in his will." That divorce, he later claimed, was something that killed Rudy even before his actual physical death. Alberto told the journalists that he intended to monitor the disposition of Valentino's bequest closely. While the executor, George Ullman, had not divulged all the document's details, he was already making all sorts of claims on the estate for debts reportedly unpaid by the actor.

In the weeks following Valentino's death, Richard Hudnut found his home invaded by reporters and ghosts. Fearing that his château had become a house of the dead rather than the living, he called a halt to the séances in November. As a consequence, Natacha and her medium decided to return to America to complete their work. On their journey to Cherbourg to board the *Homeric,* they stopped in Paris to see the Louvre and attend the opera. They also visited the dancer Loïe Fuller at her home in Neuilly. Fuller was an occasional participant in the Hudnuts' clairvoyant exercises, but on this visit she could speak to Natacha and Wehner of nothing else but the American journey of her friend, the queen of Rumania.

During their voyage across the Atlantic, Rambova and Wehner conducted séances daily, and they received many messages from Rudy, which Natacha later transcribed for her book. When the *Homeric* docked in New York on November 25, Thanksgiving Day, a throng of reporters was there to greet them. Natacha announced to the journalists that she had been receiving spirit messages from Valentino, who was in the astral plane. Asked whether any of the messages were intended for Pola Negri, Rambova snapped, "No! He spoke only of significant things and those subjects that mean something."

The startling news that Valentino was communicating with Rambova in spiritualist séances resulted in her being besieged by requests for interviews and lectures. Photographs were published of her gazing into the light of a crystal ball. From some church pulpits, however, she was denounced for dabbling in things unholy. On this point, her great-grandfather, Heber C. Kimball, would have agreed. Although he himself spoke in tongues, prophesized, had visions, and healed the sick with a magic rod, the Mormon patriarch saw no point in contacting invisible spirits: "The invisible world are in trouble; they are knocking and rapping, and muttering; and the people are inquiring of them to know concerning things of God, and there is not a soul of them can tell them

Natacha gazes into the crystal ball.

anything about the end of the world. . . . I have a brother-in-law [in Rochester, New York] who is a Presbyterian priest; he couldn't inquire of God about future things, so he inquired of the spirits; but they could not tell him anything about the dead nor the living." Rudy's revelations came to Natacha's defense. Although he appreciated the fact that the last sacraments had given his soul a peaceful passing to the next life, no one but Blavatsky could have prepared him for the shock he received when he found himself a disembodied spirit on the streets of New York: "With all their preaching about the rewards of the next life and eternal salvation, and all the rest of it, of what avail was it if it left me standing there on Broadway being refused recognition? I felt anything but kindly toward the Churches. Here I was, dead to the world, and all because the Churches had inbred in people's consciousness the false idea that spirits cannot reach back through the veil."

When Natacha's manuscript was completed, it first appeared in installments in the *Graphic,* which pandered to sensationalism by adding composite photographs of Valentino meeting Blavatsky on the astral plane. Later, it was issued in book form by London's Hutchinson and Company as *Rudy: An Intimate Portrait Of Rudolph Valentino By His Wife Natacha Rambova.* An American edition soon followed. Two thirds of the book charted her life with Rudy, recalling situations that had been recast to show him in the best possible light. Ann Wollen points to one instance in the book where her cousin turned the story completely around:

When Rudy and Natacha drove to the lion farm to see Zela for the last time, the keeper warned Natacha not to go near the animal as it had grown far too big and was dangerous. But Natacha knew that the lioness would not have forgotten her, and entered the cage against everybody's protestations. When she was inside, the fierce looking animal perched itself on its hind legs like it did when it was a pup, and gently took its paws and patted Natacha's face the way it used to in her bungalow. It brought tears to Natacha everytime she recounted this.

In her book, it was Rudy who entered the cage with Zela. Elsewhere, he was portrayed as a paragon of clairvoyant power. As she was in his life, so she continued in the telling of his story after death: the unseen manipulator of the myth. For Rambova the work was a catharsis and a vindication. She condemned Hollywood as a "gilded hell" and "that fatal capital of Filmdom," where corruption is all consuming. But her experience there, she admitted, taught her a lesson in seeking worthwhile values in life: "It has been said that this earth life is the schoolroom in which we learn our lessons. In Hollywood, like many others, I was given a test to pass and like many others I failed in it. We are also told that we learn our lessons by bitter experience; I think next time I shall pass the test. Rudy is more fortunate; he has already passed into a higher grade."

Her book was a bestseller, particularly among Spiritualists, and Sir Arthur Conan Doyle wrote her to say that he had difficulty keeping the work in stock at his Psychic Bookshop. But George Ullman's own story, *Valentino As I Knew Him*, beat Natacha's work to publication. Whitewashing his own role in their affairs, he portrayed the Latin Lover as the sacrificial victim of his wife's egotistical ambitions, thus laying the foundation for yet another myth that has perdured alongside Rambova's own recollections of Rudy.

In New York Natacha continued to pursue her psychic interests and joined a group of Spiritualists known as "the Bamberger circle," or "the Saturday Nighters," a group that met every weekend to conduct séances and study theosophy and the various branches of what was referred to as the "Wisdom Religion." George Wehner participated in this group until May 1927, when he left the United States for a year-long excursion through Europe with his homosexual lover. In the course of that same year, Natacha embarked on a number of theatrical, literary, and fashion enterprises.

In January she was in Boston appearing onstage in a complicated murder mystery called *The Triple Cross*. Playing the part of Anne Dowling, a beautiful Slavic heiress who becomes distraught over the arrest of her fiancé for murder, Rambova received lukewarm reviews. The *Boston Evening Transcript* declared: "The part of the granddaughter suits her somewhat limited range. She has a picturesque way with costume. Her light voice, not too well placed, hampers her only slightly." By the time the play opened at the Empire Theatre in New York on February 21, it had undergone some last-minute rewrites, including a new title, *Set A Thief*. This time press reaction was more favorable, with *Variety* proclaiming it a hit. The thriller, which included such characters as an alcoholic grandmother, a comic black maid, an ex-convict, and a dubious private investigator, was replete with shots ringing in the dark and corpses branded on the forehead with the mysterious letters "S.Q.V." Despite the script renovation, Rambova's performance was only noted for its striking "mannequin" presence.

While she spent her evenings at the theater, Natacha occupied her

days writing a seriocomic play, a three-act thinly veiled indictment of Hollywood and her marriage to Rudolph Valentino. Titled *All That Glitters,* the work opened old wounds with such merciless, surgical precision that Muzzie wept when she read it. A cavalcade of film personalities made their appearance under Rambova's aliases: Max Schwartz (Joseph Schenck), William Kendall (George Ullman), Floris MacGillacudy (June Mathis), Marcelle Marson and her spouse Count Jean de Linsky (Gloria Swanson and her husband Henri, Marquis de la Falaise de la Coudraye), Morris Goldberg (Robert Florey), Agnes Drake (Marion Davies), Mary Elizabeth Binter and her mother Mrs. Binter (a combination of Mary Pickford and Mary Miles Minter and their stage mothers), and "Curly" Pike (Tom Mix). The main characters, Henry Warwick and his wife, Alice Warwick, were transparently identifiable as Rudolph Valentino and Natacha Rambova.

Henry and Alice begin the play as nobodies, working on the fringes of the movie industry. He is a ticket taker at a theater, and she is an usherette. When a female scenario writer discovers Henry and he is catapulted to stardom, the couple's marital troubles begin. The childlike, athletic Henry is quickly carried away by the glamour of being a star. He treats his new status as a "delightful game," becomes a clotheshorse, spends far beyond his means, collects expensive cars, and breaks movie contracts in fits of pique. Alice's severe beauty becomes weathered and worn in the course of looking after her boyish and enthusiastic husband. She becomes a "combination mother, nursemaid, and private secretary," only to have outsiders protest that she "wears the pants in the family." Withdrawing from her husband in an attempt to make him mature and stop taking her for granted, Alice is accused of carrying on a secret romance, which prompts the infuriated Henry to search for his revolver. Finally, when Henry's creditors have picked him clean, and he comes to realize that he was living in a fool's paradise, Alice returns to him and reveals that she had secretly squirreled away some of their profits and invested in a flourishing dry-cleaning business. The curtain closes with the reconciled couple happier for the fact that they survived the beguilement of filmdom's glitter, and wiser in the knowledge that Hollywood is "just a lot of make-believe," where everyone is so busy creating fantasy that they "haven't time to be real until it's too late . . . and [they have] forgotten how."

All That Glitters was never produced on stage. It may have been too risky a venture in that so many of its characters were uncomplimentary depictions of powerful celebrities. Nevertheless, writing it was therapeutic for Natacha, who portrayed her marriage to Rudy as vindicated and saved—if only in the make-believe realm her own play attacked.

Besides her play, Rambova told an interviewer, she was writing a novel, covering the sensational Snyder-Gray murder trial for a newspaper, designing the wardrobe for an upcoming Broadway production called *These Few Ashes,* and writing a history of costume and decoration throughout the ages, commencing with the year 4,000 B.C. "I am illustrating the costume book too, so, all in all, I haven't much time to throw away." She declared a preference for the stage over film because of "the personal contact with audiences" the legitimate theater afforded, and stated that she wanted to play foreign roles rather than sweet American heroines: "I want character parts, such as soiled ladies, half-caste or Oriental parts, Russian ladies, French ladies, etc. I also like costume plays, and I'd love to enact a 'dirty crook' role. You might call me the Irish lady with the Russian name, who wants to play Oriental parts." The reporter for the *Portland Express* left the enthusiastic Rambova with the comment that "[she] is carrying out a program of industry in different arts that is probably unrivaled among actresses on Broadway today."

In September 1927 Rambova appeared in another play, "a romantic comedy drama" called *Creoles,* which opened at the Klaw Theatre. Despite a spectacular New Orleans set designed by Norman Bel Geddes, the plot of *Creoles*—which focused on a convent-bred girl, Jacinta, and her infatuation with a Caribbean pirate—left the critics cold. Rambova was cast as Gonlondrina, Jacinta's older, more experienced friend, and received good reviews for her minor role. But neither Helen Chandler, who played Jacinta, nor Princess Matchabelli, who played her mother, could rise above the mediocre script. Rambova and Princess Matchabelli were kindred spirits insofar as both women were related to magnates in the cosmetics industry, and both were students of theosophy and metaphysics. Matchabelli's spiritualist theories, however, were allied primarily to her thespian interests, a vocation Natacha decided to abandon for a more ambitious career.

That summer, Rambova moved to an apartment above a storefront at 58 West 55th Street near 5th Avenue. In the store below, she opened an exclusive dress-designing studio dedicated to "helping . . . women express their individuality in clothes that emphasize character and personality." She was quick to point out to reporters that "I'm in business, not exactly because I need the money, but because it enables me to give vent to an artistic urge." When asked at the same time whether or not she intended to remarry, she replied, "That's hard to say—emotion is such an uncertain thing. But I certainly am not thinking of marriage now."

Her line of clothes and cosmetics capitalized on her noted taste for the unusual and the exotic. Her philosophy as a couturiere stressed that women need not dress alike, and they should not blindly follow the mandates of France: "I loathe fashion. I want to dress in a way that is becoming to me, whether it is the style of the hour or not. So it should be with all women, in my opinion. All women should not wear knee length skirts, even if that is the prevailing fashion; clothes that are becoming to the tall, languid type, would not do at all for a short girl of the staccato type, who has to have sharp clothes to express her personality."

Rambova's own ankle-length skirts, which had become as much her trademark as had her turbans, were worn not only to proclaim her individuality, but to hide what she considered her worst feature—her legs. The family called them "Kimball legs," thick-ankled and shapeless appendages that appeared in every generation, from Muzzie and Aunt Tessie to Natacha, who felt that her career in dance had only made her legs bigger and out of proportion to the rest of her svelte physique.

Rambova's dress shop proved to be such a success in the first few months that she even contemplated expanding from a retail business to a wholesale establishment. Celebrities—actresses, in particular—patronized the store, and her generosity was noted by her friends. "I went there to ask her about some costumes I was making," recalled her former

Natacha models one of her own creations.

student Agnes de Mille, who had moved to New York to pursue a career in dance. "She gave me a lot of blue velvet material from which I made a Tyrolean costume that I wore for years." The stage actress Beulah Bondi, who was on her way to Hollywood and had ordered a new wardrobe from Rambova, remembered also receiving from her some words of hackneyed but valuable advice on surviving in the film capital: "Always keep your sense of humor." But the actress Mae Murray, who had ordered a Jahan black coat, black turban, and jewelry from Rambova and then neglected to pay for them when they were delivered C.O.D. to her Venice beach house in California, felt the full fury of Shaughnessy temper when Rambova slapped her with a fifteen-hundred dollar lawsuit. "Oh, that suit," barked Murray when questioned by reporters. "I suppose it is advertising for Miss Rambova. She's a modiste you know. . . . People are always trying to get something out of me."

In May 1928, George Wehner returned to America and was hospitalized soon afterward for a "nervous condition." The Hudnuts were visiting Natacha in New York at the same time, and when Wehner was sufficiently recovered, Mrs. Hudnut treated him to a tour of the West Coast, where he conducted a number of séances for society figures in Los Angeles and San Francisco. In Los Angeles, they stayed with Teresa Werner, who had returned to California to protect her interests in the Valentino estate and reclaim some of the property that had been owned by Natacha. Executor George Ullman had dragged the settlement through a number of legal delays, which provoked Alberto and Maria Guglielmi to file charges against him for fraud and mismanagement. "I could have sent that man to jail," Teresa Werner said of Ullman, "but I would have felt responsible to raise his kids."

The soft-hearted Mrs. Werner decided to accompany her sister and the psychic on their continuing journey to Salt Lake City. There they held a séance in the Mormon Tabernacle while a cousin, Edward P. Kimball, gave them a private recital on the world-famous organ. The powerful strains of music echoing throughout the chamber enabled Wehner to receive messages from the Mormon religion's founder, Joseph Smith, and from Brigham Young, the Mormon pioneer patriarch, as well as such relatives as Heber C. Kimball, Uncle William Kimball, Aunt Margaret Judd Clauson, and Phoebe Judd Kimball, the mother of Winifred and Tessie. Afterward, when these spirits faded away, Wehner claimed to see a most remarkable vision: "I saw the whole interior of the Tabernacle shimmering in a glorious blaze of golden light, in the midst of which appeared in the air above the organ, the figure of a young man in blue robes holding a long trumpet of gold. From my clairvoyant description of this radiant being my friends recognized the spirit as that of the Angel Moroni . . . who led his people across the plains and deserts to ultimate safety . . . as a beacon light of faith and love."

In June 1928, Natacha was visited in her dress shop by an old acquaintance, the British adventure writer and theosophist Talbot Mundy. Their paths had crossed in Hollywood, where some of his work had been translated into film. Estranged from his wife, Mundy brought with him the new love in his life, Theda Conkey Webber, who was twenty-four years his junior. He wanted her to meet Natacha, who was busy designing a cover for his latest book, *Queen Cleopatra.* The young woman, who had seen Natacha tango with Valentino when the Minera-lava tour passed through Connecticut, was enthralled. Not only did she buy a new wardrobe, but, like her couturiere, she changed her name to fit her personality. Theda Webber became Dawn Allen. She also became Natacha's lifelong friend.

When George Wehner returned to New York with Mrs. Hudnut, Talbot Mundy invited him to join Dawn and Natacha in some investigative psychic research in his 9th Street Greenwich Village apartment. Together with a hired court stenographer, the group of five tried to discover what lay beyond the trance state. Regularly throughout the fall and winter evenings, the group assembled around a refectory table in Mundy's darkened apartment while light from the fireplace danced across a gold sari stretched along one wall. Their meetings inspired many intellectual discussions on the subject of life after death, and at one séance they felt they had brought healing to an ailing friend by invoking the spirit of Christian Science founder Mary Baker Eddy.

Spiritualist therapy was not accorded to Richard Hudnut, whose death in October of 1928 took everyone by surprise. Winifred and Natacha mourned his loss, and the fact that he felt closer to them than anyone else was made manifest in his will. He left all but $4,000 of his estate to his wife and adopted daughter. Muzzie put Natacha on a regular allowance thereafter, one that would enable her daughter to pursue spiritual, artistic, and intellectual interest without financial worry.

Despite Wehner's inability to predict Mr. Hudnut's death, Talbot Mundy had great admiration for his psychic powers, and he wrote an introduction to the medium's 1929 autobiography, *A Curious Life,* calling him "a gentleman *sans peur et sans raproche,* whose acquaintances respect him and whose friends love him. He is in need of no apologies and no advertisement." Wehner was also asked to accompany Talbot and Dawn on a European vacation they took in the spring of 1929. When the three returned in September, they joined Natacha in a new cultural movement with religious overtones that had been spearheaded by Nicholas Roerich, a Russian artist, philosopher, explorer, and visionary.

Trained at St. Petersburg's Imperial Academy of the Arts at the end of the nineteenth century, Roerich was awed by the cultural triumphs of the West and at the same time captivated by the philosophical and spiritual teachings of the East. He cultivated a great reverence for the fine arts, crafts, religious myth, and history. As director of the school of the Society for the Encouragement of the Arts, Roerich taught his students that the pursuit of beauty would advance the evolution of humanity and bring peace to the world. Roerich was involved in the revival of the applied arts in Russia, and was instrumental in bringing about a renaissance in ecclesiastical art, designing icons, murals, and mosaics for church interiors. In the broader history of art, however, his name is most often associated with designs for operas and ballets. He collaborated with Nijinsky, Stravinsky, and Diaghilev on the design of sets and costumes, most notably in the 1913 production of *Le Sacre du Printemps.* As a writer, lecturer, painter, and world traveler, Roerich became well known to the international community, particularly for his efforts to induce the nations of the world to sign a peace pact that would preserve cultural monuments in times of war. In March 1929, he was nominated for a Nobel Peace Prize on this account, the first time an artist had ever been nominated for the award.

Natacha convinced Talbot Mundy, Dawn Allen, and George Wehner to move into the Roerich-sponsored Master Building, a newly erected twenty-nine-story skyscraper with low-rent apartments available to artists, singers, actors, musicians, and scholars interested in the pursuit of universal harmony through art and culture. Dawn and Talbot occupied apartments on the eighteenth floor, while Natacha rented a suite on the twenty-first. The first three floors of the building were reserved for the Roerich Museum, which housed the artist's thousands of canvases, mostly of a religious or romantic nature. Lecture and concert halls were also included in the complex, as was a library.

Because Nicholas Roerich seldom visited New York, it cannot be said that Natacha and her friends were his disciples. They did, however, hold him in high esteem. Dawn Allen remembered him at the opening of the Master Building as "a small man with an exceptionally quiet voice, who exuded an air of mystery—a personification of one of his own paintings of a Tibetan mystic." They befriended Roerich's son, Svetoslav, who occupied the top floor of the building. A few years younger than Natacha and Dawn, a man of striking good looks and impeccable dress, Svetoslav, or "Svetie," as they nicknamed him, had studied architecture and painting at Columbia University, and was an accomplished portraitist in his own right. He found Natacha a fascinating woman with a broad scope of interests. They were often seen together at social functions, and he captured her beauty in several portraits from 1931.

Svetoslav, Natacha, Talbot Mundy, and Dawn Allen joined R.T.M. Scott and his wife, Leslie Grant, in founding a Museum of Religion and Philosophy headquartered in the Master Building. Its purpose was to show the basic unity of all faiths and religions, a scholarly and artistic endeavor on a much higher plane than the Spiritualist investigations that had previously preoccupied them in Greenwich Village. George Wehner continued to conduct his séances for the group, but his nervous condition started to affect him as a medium, causing his friends to lose faith in his psychic abilities. On two occasions, Wehner contacted the spirit of Mundy's long-lost brother, an English brigadier general, who told Talbot of his death in Egypt. The morning after the second appearance, Dawn recalled a sobering incident: "The medium stopped at Talbot's apartment with the morning mail, and handed him a thick letter with English postage. As he left, Talbot plumped into a chair, a quizzical expression on his face. 'Haven't seen the handwriting in fifteen years, but I'd recognize it anywhere. My brother Harold's . . . very *much* alive!' "

In the séances that followed, Wehner's behavior became quite alarming, and at one sitting he tried to commit suicide by jumping off the balcony of Mundy's apartment. Dawn Allen threw herself in front of him, foiling his attempt, but as she complained later, "his strength was so great, he nearly took me with him!" Soon afterward, Wehner claimed to have contacted the spirit of a dead musician, and during his séance he would whistle original tunes composed by the musician on the astral plane. Dawn, whose own musical training provided her with an ear for perfect pitch, transcribed the melodies. So excited was the group with their discovery that they planned a concert of the celestial harmonies with Dawn at the piano and Donna Shinn Russell singing. But when an infuriated Wehner suddenly attacked Dawn for stealing "his" music, the group severed all ties with the unbalanced medium, who, as a consequence of these scandals, left Spiritualism behind and returned to the stage as an actor. Mundy would later admit in his novel *I Say Sunrise* that Spiritualism can be deceptive, and that one does not need a medium in order to contact the dead.

By 1931 the frightening momentum of the Great Depression alarmed Natacha, who felt that a revolution in the United States was unavoidable. She contemplated moving to France and shared her concerns with Dawn and Talbot. The Roerich Museum was unable to pay the mortgage on its new building, and, much to Rambova's sorrow, Svetoslav was called to join his father in India. With everything around them collapsing, Natacha decided to accompany some friends on a cruise to the Greek islands, while Talbot and Dawn traveled south to Mexico with plans to get married.

Returning from Europe on the *Ile de France* that August, Natacha saw the face of an old friend from the past, Vera Fredova. She and Flower Hujer had booked passage on the same ship, and Fredova visited Natacha's first-class cabin for an evening of reminiscences. Kosloff and Cecil B. DeMille were traveling together through Russia, Fredova told Natacha. Kosloff's wife, Maria Baldina, had at last been permitted to bring her invalid daughter to live in the United States. Vera was returning from a visit with her family in England to run Kosloff's new dance studio in Dallas, Texas, while Flower was planning to teach at the studio in Hollywood. Vera's patience with Kosloff was wearing thin, however, since he had not yet made good his promise to divorce his wife and marry her. To end the evening with some wicked fun, Rambova and Fredova composed a cablegram and sent it to Kosloff's hotel in Moscow: "Having a wonderful reunion aboard ship. Don't you wish *you* were here?"

While Talbot and Dawn spent the winter of 1932 enjoying a postnuptial vacation on a Florida beach, they received a surprising note from Natacha. It announced that she had left the United States and taken up residence in the town of Genova on the island of Mallorca, where she was modernizing old villas and renting them to tourists. "Come on over," the letter read. "I've got just the place for you." Intrigued, they packed their bags and headed for Spain, where Natacha had an even bigger surprise waiting for them.

I want you to meet my husband, Alvaro de Urzáiz," Natacha cheerfully told Dawn and Talbot when they disembarked from the ferry that had brought them overnight from Barcelona to Palma de Mallorca.

The man standing next to Natacha greeted the Mundys, and Dawn recalled how perfectly he complemented Rambova: "Slim, black-haired and charming—Natacha more beautiful than ever—they made a striking couple."

Natacha recounted how her trip to Greece and Crete had been punctuated by an excursion to Mallorca, where she decided to join a yacht cruise around the Balearic Islands. Alvaro had captained the yacht, and Natacha discovered that the handsome Spaniard was suffering from deep depression, a feeling that he had wasted his life. He came from a noble Basque family; his mother, Maria de Silva, had been a lady-in-waiting to the queen. She had sent him to be educated in England, preparing him for a career as a Spanish naval officer, but the recent fall of the monarchy and the political turmoil in Spain ended these ambitions. He was miserably resigned to living his life as a tour guide. Natacha, having herself recovered from a similar depression, consoled and encouraged Alvaro. This led to a whirlwind romance, and Natacha never reached the Hellenes. Instead, she returned to America to close her dress shop and immediately sailed back to France, where she rejoined Alvaro in Paris, and they were married in a civil ceremony. Since Alvaro was a

Left to right: Talbot Mundy, Natacha, and Alvaro de Urzáiz on the rocky shores of Mallorca

count, Rambova's marriage to him rendered her the title of countess. But she shied away from using it, especially since titles were no longer popular in the Spanish Republic. Nor did they pursue the life-style of idle aristocrats. They went into business together, buying and modernizing old houses for tourists who had discovered the beauty and charm of the picturesque island of Mallorca.

Natacha installed the Mundys in one of her renovated villas perched high on a mountaintop overlooking the Mediterranean. The broad-terraced, gleaming white structure was located in the village of Genova, just three miles outside the capital of Palma. It was in this village that Natacha and Alvaro had decided to settle. To help her lure tourists to Genova, Natacha negotiated a lease on the fabled caves there, one of the natural wonders of the island. She installed electrical illumination throughout the rock forest of stalactites and stalagmites, and constructed diverse paths along which visitors could wander through a geological fantasy land.

Alvaro de Urzáiz

These enterprises of renewal and theater were financed in part by her inheritance. While the stock market crash of 1929 had some deleterious effects on the size of the Hudnut fortune, there was enough money tied up in land holdings to make life comfortable for Winifred and Natacha. Since Richard's death, Muzzie discovered how lonely the château had become, and she preferred to spend much of the year living close to her daughter. Therefore, she too invested with Natacha and Alvaro and bought one of their renovated villas for herself.

The Mundys found life on the island restful, if primitive. There were few paved roads to accommodate their imported Cadillac, there was no refrigeration, goats populated the mountainside and were milked directly into the household pitcher, septic tanks often backed up, and water had to be trucked in from Palma. But the remoteness allowed Talbot to concentrate on his writing, and the island provided a number of recreations. One could swim in the numerous rocky coves, or "calas," as the Mallorcans called them, and explore the diverse scenery of the island, from its sandy beaches to its craggy mountaintops. Mallorca had been the site of numerous civilizations, each of which left its mark on the land. Prehistoric peoples left behind their mysterious stone monoliths, or "talayots," as they were called; the Romans left a theater and a bridge; the Moors built baths; the medieval townspeople erected castles and a cathedral; and monks built monasteries. Modern Mallorca added cafes and fashionable hotels to attract tourists. Meanwhile, the peasantry of every age relied on fishing or farming to make a living on an island noted for its warm weather and brilliant sunlight.

Natacha, Alvaro, and the Mundys enjoyed exploring all these things together, and frequently they visited the Charterhouse of Valldemosa, the remnant of a fourteenth-century Carthusian monastery, to which Madame Dudevant, better known as George Sand, brought her ailing lover, Frédéric Chopin, during the winter of 1838. Mallorca was steeped in romance, history, and natural beauty, a place that attracted artists and writers from around the world.

During the eight months they spent on this island of calm, the Mundys discovered that politics and religion were two subjects on which Alvaro and Talbot could never agree. Inevitably, Natacha found herself acting as mediator in their disputes. Though he and Natacha had not been married in a church, Alvaro considered himself a staunch Catholic. His father was a wealthy lawyer, and his aristocratic family was monarchist and anti-Republican. Mundy, on the other hand, distrusted all right-wing organizations, avidly supported the Republican government of Spain, and disliked lawyers and Catholicism. While their arguments were civil, even friendly, many of their discussions became the basis for the rhetoric found in Mundy's book, *Thus Spake the Devil,* which was later rewritten and published under the title *I Say Sunrise.*

In December 1932, the Spanish government threatened to tax all foreign cars on their original cost—in gold. This was a sign to Talbot and Dawn that it was prudent to move on. After spending Christmas with Alvaro and Natacha, the Mundys packed all their belongings into their Cadillac and headed for England. They left in good time, and not just on account of taxes. Storm clouds of revolution were beginning to gather.

In January there were riots in Barcelona and Cadiz. Farmers were up in arms. While the left-wing government in Madrid found itself increasingly factionalized, a confederation of right-wing Catholic parties began to unite under the figure of Gil Robles. In May, a religious reform bill was passed that sought to eliminate the role of the church in education, causing the rightists to organize more aggressively against what they feared would be the triumph of nineteenth-century secular liberalism. In October, the authoritarian Falange party was founded under the leadership of an Andalusian lawyer, José Antonio Primo de Rivera, the son of General Miguel Primo de Rivera, who ruled Spain in the previous decade as a monarchist dictator. The continuing struggle between the left and the right in a nation facing general elections had less impact in Mallorca, where, during the lazy spring days of March, Francisco Franco was appointed commander of the military forces of the Balearic Islands, a position that led to his elevation to major general a year later.

Alvaro and Natacha came to know Franco during his tenure as the island's chief military officer, and the three grew to be close friends. Later, after he became the leader of the Nationalist forces, Rambova would write down her reasons for supporting him: "In the hands of General Franco, who is a disciplinarian . . . Spain may have a great future; she may rise again to reclaim her position of past grandeur. These hopes of the future are voiced in his words, 'All citizens of the New Spain must work, there will be no place for the idle or for those who have lost their pride of race in the pursuits of foreign amusements.' " The virtues of discipline and industry were qualities Rambova treasured—for herself, and for the country in which she now lived. Franco's vision of Spain invoked the past glories of Ferdinand and Isabella, and the mystique of power and style he cultivated was no doubt attractive to a woman who had aspired to lofty heights in the image factory of Hollywood. Better to promote an atavistic pride in the trappings of empire, she reasoned, than allow the country to be manipulated by outside forces agitating for class warfare. While Rambova was not uncritical of the Falangists, she saw them as a bulwark capable of challenging what she most detested: communism and Moscow's influence in Spanish affairs.

If Franco found the former Mrs. Rudolph Valentino beguiling, this was certainly not the case with Alvaro's family. They looked upon his civil marriage with dismay, and the fact that she was a Hollywood personality added to their grief. More to their liking would have been a union like that of his brother, Mariano. He married the duchess of Villahermosa, who also bore the additional title of duchess-countess of Luna. In the family chill caused by his marriage to an American show-business celebrity, Alvaro and Natacha were happy to live on the island of Mallorca, away from the aristocratic mansions of the Urzáiz dynasty in Madrid and San Sebastián. Their happiness was increased by the stunning villa they built for themselves in the village of Paguera on the western coast of the island. Natacha had designed the modern white multiterraced mansion rising from the Mediterranean on the rocky cliffs of Cala Fornells. Nearly ten years after Valentino had expressed his dream one day to buy the deserted fortress on the island of St. Lerins, Natacha had her castle by the sea.

Natacha and Alvaro's terraced villa on the cliffs of Cala Fornells

The year 1934 witnessed the resurgence of right-wing parties everywhere in Spain, except in Catalonia. Uprisings, insurrections, and strikes were common. Against this background of political strife, Alvaro and Natacha decided to make peace with the Urzáiz family by having their marriage blessed by the Church. Although Natacha had been baptized a Catholic, she had never been raised as one. In her opinion, all religions were but various cultural manifestations of a primordial Divine Wisdom. Like her mother, Rambova was ambivalent toward her religious roots; unlike her, she was loath to join groups—religious, political, or social. It was in deference to Alvaro and his family's wishes that she finally consented to the religious ceremony performed on August 6, 1934, in the Oratory of St. Peter and St. Bernard.

The ceremony caught the attention of the worldwide press, as newspapers proclaimed, "Rambova Re-wed in Palma Church." Natacha was amused by the feverish coverage, and sent one of the notices to Lou Mahoney, who had always wanted her to be a more observant Catholic. Many of the reporters, however, saw in Alvaro something that may have been buried in Rambova's subconscious when she first met her groom. As one article bluntly put it, "Don Alvaro bears a striking resemblance to Valentino, having the same Latin type of good looks that characterized the popular film star."

As a consequence of the Church-sanctioned nuptials, the Urzáiz family now accepted Natacha Rambova into their family circle. Alvaro was allowed to offer his bride a variety of the family jewels as a wedding present, but she chose only two items from the large and dazzling collection. The first was a ring that had been made by the Elizabethan alchemist John Dee, by order of Emperor Maximillian II of Austria. It was a large, dark cabochon sapphire set in what was purportedly alchemical gold. The second piece she chose was a small alchemical vase made of alabaster and decorated with carvings of a phoenix and planetary symbols. It had also belonged to John Dee and at one time supposedly contained a red powder used in his alchemical rites. That Natacha chose these occult objects over a variety of more costly jewels is evidence of her symbolic rather than sumptuous turn of mind. As she later wrote, wealth was at the core of Spain's political turmoil: "Wealth centered in the hands of indolence and indifference does not tend toward national strength or progress. That has been the tragedy of Spain. With wealth goes responsibility; those who have refused to take their responsibilities have had to pay bitterly for their short-sighted idleness."

Alvaro and Natacha's visit with the Urzáiz family in Madrid proved to be a stifling affair of formal luncheons and cocktail parties, and Spain's capital struck Natacha as having something in common with Hollywood: "Madrid, I discovered, was in reality but a very small Main Street. Everyone knew everyone else, knew what everyone else was doing. This latter required little ingenuity as no one did anything that was not done by everyone else. No one dared brave ridicule or criticism by an original thought or action."

They lunched at two-thirty and took siesta until six. Afterward, they indulged in golf or the cinema. Natacha noticed how the city was filled with expensive cars, streamlined Chryslers and LaSalles. The women wore expensive Parisian fashions, and the popular cafes and restaurants, Bakanik, Chicote's, and the Bar Club, were packed with the smart and affluent. While the right wing currently had the upper hand in the political conflict, Natacha noticed that "wealth was cautiously emerging from its seclusion," but she added, "it kept one eye ever on its refuge for a hasty retreat at any loud rumbles from the Left." Since the establishment of the Republic, she observed, no one dressed for dinner unless for a very special occasion. Usually, it was scheduled at ten in the evening, but they rarely sat down before eleven, with the "tedious affair ending about one in the morning."

Conversation at these family gatherings centered on the aristocrats' hope that Gil Robles would set Spain back on the right track. Some of them condemned the exiled king for having lost his position as a consequence of his own "democratic innovations," including driving *himself* around in a Ford, attending the public cinema, and establishing University City for the education of his people. "If everyone became educated, who was going to do the manual labor?" she recalled them asking. The conversation was always the same, and Natacha found it boring and out of touch with reality. The older aristocrats were living in the past, she observed, and their younger generation was blindly and indolently lost in the present.

In January 1936, Natacha and Alvaro traveled to the Middle East in company with Muzzie and Mariano de Urzáiz and his wife. Natacha was particularly excited to visit what she called "the fountainhead of the world's great cultures." They traveled through Greece and Turkey, then on to Damascus and Baghdad, Jerusalem, and finally Egypt, where they met Howard Carter. His archaeological discoveries had long fascinated Natacha, who believed that she had lived in the Nile kingdom in some past life: "I felt as if I had at last returned home. The first few days I was there I couldn't stop the tears streaming from my eyes. It was not sadness, but some emotional impact from the past—a returning to a place once loved after too long a time." They visited the ancient monuments of Memphis, Thebes, and Luxor. They explored the temples of Karnak and Edfu, and the funerary pile of Queen Hatshepsut. Natacha was spellbound. It was with great sadness that she departed the land of the Pharoahs for the return trip to Spain with her in-laws. Muzzie returned to the château.

Natacha, on her first visit to Egypt

Madrid in 1936 was vastly changed from the year before. The Left was now in power again, and the Popular Front victory at the polls resulted in street fighting and church sackings. The Falange party had been banned and Primo de Rivera arrested. Francisco Franco found himself banished to the Canary Islands. The streets of the capital were no longer filled with limousines; second-hand cars had taken their place. The fashionable restaurants and bars were no longer fashionable. The moneyed classes were in retreat. Rambova recorded the tension she felt in Madrid, capital of a nation on the brink of explosion: "Anxiety, fear, and class hatred hung like a pestilence in the air. The proletariat glowered and waited. Confidence had gone. Money beat a hasty retreat to its underground refuge. The sidewalks were no longer crowded; there were now no women in smart Paris clothes. Everyone this year was economizing—whether one needed to or not."

The political situation was on everyone's mind. But Alvaro and Natacha, being "country cousins from Mallorca," still made an attempt to enjoy the cinema and the bars. Yet a visit to the Capitol Theatre for a viewing of *A Tale of Two Cities* proved sobering to the two. "It was so unwise to show such a picture at such a time!" Natacha reflected. "Such obvious revolutionary propaganda . . . [with] such awful Spanish [sub]titles, just written to incite the people to more fury!" In an attempt afterward to visit a bar called the Aquarium, they were stopped by the Guardia Civil. A bomb had been thrown into the place, the result of a dispute between two waiters' unions.

Fearful now of venturing outside at night, Natacha and Alvaro dined with his family at their home. The sound of explosions was routine, sometimes so close as to rock the great house. Arrests were made daily. The family butler, who seemed to have contacts everywhere, reported to the Urzáiz family over their morning coffee the names of their Falangist friends who could now be found behind bars. In the evening, the family gathered in the drawing room where the political situation was again the main topic of conversation. The women of the family discussed with horror the burning of the churches and the hideous atrocities inflicted on religious orders. Alvaro's mother had supported an orphanage run by nuns. It had recently been attacked, and the government now was going to close it. What would happen to the children? Natacha sympathetically recorded their concern:

Would they be turned into the streets? Many of them had been brought into the world by the nuns, had been cared for by them while their mothers worked; many had known no other mothers. These same nuns who nursed the poor without reward, who cared for their children, were the ones who had just been attacked and beaten. One had her face and teeth crushed in by the boot of an infuriated communist mother. And the government allowed such things, apparently encouraged them. To what, they asked, was this going to lead?

Stones were occasionally thrown through the windows of the Urzáiz home. The men of the family collected guns, for fear that they might be murdered in bed. Natacha noticed how the younger members of the family were rising from their lethargy and disappearing at all hours of the day and night. Mysterious whisperings and meetings were going on. There was talk that the military would support the Falangists, with a Nationalist uprising planned for September. All their hopes and expectations rested with the politician Calvo Sotelo and his upper-class conservative followers. In the midst of the family's renewed anxieties, Natacha and Alvaro returned to Mallorca.

"Life settled again into its lazy, peaceful routine," Natacha recalled. "The fresh, sweet-smelling ozone of our Island of Calm, soon banished from our nostrils the nauseating odor of pestilential class hatred which permeated the streets of distant Madrid. Those alarming incidents of our visit now seemed like scenes from an improbable nightmare."

Yet the nightmare came to invade even their island sanctuary. One of their servants brought them tales of the burning of churches on Mallorca. In Esporlas an angry mob of leftists were superstitious enough carefully to remove the statues of the Madonna and saints, depositing them reverentially in the padre's house, before torching the church to the shouts of "Viva Rusia." Even in Paguera, Natacha and Alvaro knew of many communists who parroted slogans they did not understand and could not explain. They seemed harmless enough, she admitted, adding that "we refused to take seriously their rather childish, illiterate enthusiasm." Natacha loved to point out that the leading communist in the town was a fat cafe owner, made rich by his farming properties, and the father of a large and, by all appearances, "overfed" family.

On July 15, 1936, Alvaro went to the village to pick up the daily mail and newspaper. He unfolded the newspaper to the headlines: CALVO SOTELO ASSASSINATED!

The leader of the right-wing monarchists had been killed in retaliation for the assassination of an officer of the Republican Assault Guards the day before. What would become of the *Renovacion Española* now?

Natacha and Alvaro nervously asked themselves. They jumped into their car and raced to Palma, where everyone was congregating in quiet, anxious groups, asking the same question.

The following Saturday, July 18, Alvaro and Natacha again motored to Palma to attend a Requiem Mass for Calvo Sotelo in the Church of San Francisco. At the memorial in Madrid some days before there had been a demonstration; many were expecting one here. The church was packed with people, women in black mantillas, men wearing Falangist and Carlist insignias. Every available space was occupied by the crowd, which overflowed through the Gothic portals into the square outside. At a given moment during the ceremony, the congregation lit long slender candles. Rambova recorded her memory of the scene: "My husband whispered that this ritual was unknown on the peninsula, it was a custom individual to Mallorca. The musical chants, the incense, the muttered prayers, vibrant with emotion in the soft glow of thousands of small flickering lights, contrasted strangely, I thought, with the almost suffocating atmosphere of strained explosive tension and watchful glances that darted from side to side."

As the ceremony concluded, the crowd emptied out into the plaza. There was whispering everywhere and hands stole cautiously to weapons concealed within clothing. Would there be a riot? Would a bomb be thrown into their midst? As the crowd dispersed, Natacha felt the tension slowly let up. For the moment, nothing would happen. But Natacha and Alvaro were made aware of one thing: there were more Falangists living in Mallorca than they had thought.

In the days that followed, news reached the island that a major rebellion was in the making. General Franco had left the Canary Islands to lead the forces stationed in Spanish Morocco. Seville, Cadiz, Algeciras, and Jerez had already gone over to the rebels. Granada would soon follow.

In the Balearics the civil governor had been put in detention while the military took control. All imprisoned Falangists were freed. Communication between Mállorca and the mainland had been cut off. Trucks and cars filled with soldiers now circulated through the city streets and country roads. "The next few days were filled with anxiety, absurd surprises, and moments of humor," Rambova recalled. "People we had never suspected of any political interest suddenly blossomed forth in full Falange regalia." One poor woman about to give birth was rushed to a local clinic only to discover that her doctor was being arrested as a communist. She pleaded for the soldiers to let him stay until after the delivery. The soldiers replied that they could not release him until they had checked with higher authorities. By the time they returned from headquarters, the woman had given birth on her own. "The new arrival showed her independence and disdain of a communist doctor," Natacha wryly commented, adding that it was "another incident to confirm my belief that doctors and priests should refrain from politics."

In August the bombing began. Republican forces had captured the nearby islands of Ibiza and Fromentera. Their planes showered the city of Palma with propaganda leaflets. When the city did not surrender, the planes returned, this time to drop hand grenades on the defenseless civilian population.

Mallorcan contempt then turned into fury. The islanders heard radio broadcasts from Barcelona proclaim to the world that Republican forces had been victorious and that the rebel city of Palma now lay in smoking ruins. "Palma laughed scornfully," Rambova declared, "except those who had members of their family abroad who realized the agonizing heartaches such lies would cause." Her thoughts turned to Muzzie in France, and to Aunt Teresa in California.

The bombing of Mallorca became a daily occurrence, with a shower of larger bombs hitting the island every morning around eleven-thirty, and every afternoon at five-thirty. During one morning attack, Natacha and Alvaro were buying cigarettes for the soldiers when they heard the hum of planes overhead. Before they could pay for their packages, a deafening crash exploded outside the store. As Alvaro rushed out into the street, Natacha recollected how her body reacted as she fumbled to complete the transaction: "The shop owner and her two children had disappeared below the counter. As I tried to count out the money I was surprised to find that my hands were shaky. I was not conscious, however, of fear, but of a suffocating excitement, intense exhileration. That same dreaded, quivering excitement—near to nausea—one experienced at a bullfight!" Together, Natacha and Alvaro jumped into their car and sped down the highway in an attempt to deliver their goods. "I craned my neck and looked up from the side of the car; a huge flying monster seemed perversely to be following us," Natacha recalled. They slowed down and let the plane pass. "At any other time we would have been filled with admiration for their beauty," Natacha said of the planes circling overhead. "Now their grace meant death! And it was repaid with resentful hatred."

The Mallorcans were not equipped with antiaircraft guns, leaving the people defenseless against the deadly raids. Commerce in the city of Palma came to a standstill after eight o'clock every morning, as citizens braced themselves for the next shower of bombs. "The terror of the people was pathetic," Rambova wrote of these islanders getting their first taste of modern warfare. With dismay she watched more and more of them flee the city for the uncertain safety of the countryside:

After the first bombing, the roads leading out of the city were crowded with people lugging mattresses, bird cages, baskets of food, followed by straggling children and dogs. Every cart and car that the city possessed was heaped with white-faced, trembling human bundles. In one cave, in the hills back of Palma, seventy people remained in terror without food for three days and nights. Senseless panic ruled the stricken city.

Foreign warships and steamers crowded the harbor of Palma, evacuating English, French, German, and American residents. The radio, newspapers, and posters warned all foreigners to leave. The American consul and a British naval officer came personally to aid their fleeing countrymen. But Rambova would not depart with them. She decided to stay by her husband and suffer the consequences. With Shaughnessy determination, she held her ground: "I watched the heavily laden tenders going back and forth, back and forth, from the landing to the ships. When the last one left, carrying all my foreign friends and acquaintances, I watched it go with uncertain feelings. For the first time it occurred to me that possibly an island was not the most comfortable spot from which to watch a revolution. Once the last boat left there was no escape."

The defense of Mallorca demanded that all able-bodied men take their place at strategic military stations. This left Natacha alone with her maid and cook at the villa in Paguera. Those two were hysterical, fearing that local communists would rape them and cut their throats. To calm them, Rambova decided to have a heart-to-heart talk with the cafe owner in the village.

Her discussion with the town's leading communist opened on the topic of the economic crisis behind the present conflict. "Here on the island your children have never gone hungry," she pointed out to him, "but you must see that you cannot ask for double wages when the farmers have no market for their crops." The farm crisis could only be solved slowly, she argued, with the government changing its custom restrictions, creating new markets, and putting hoarded money back into circulation for the benefit of the country. But she soon realized that her listener did not understand a word of what she was saying. His only answer to her reasoning was, "No, no, Señora, you will see, soon we will take the *fincas* [farms] and we shall have everything." She rejoined: "And what are we going to see? You are surely not thinking of doing the same dreadful things that the communists have done on the peninsula?" The cafe owner paused, and then slowly nodded his head. "Come now, Juan," Natacha reacted, somewhat excitedly, "we have always been friends; you cannot tell me that you would actually come to our house to kill us! You can't think such things seriously?" Juan's response was ominous and chilling—"Well, Señora, maybe I wouldn't, but there are many who would."

Rambova left the cafe, shocked by the lesson *she* had received. "I could only marvel at the power that could, with such devilish efficiency, transform kindly loveable peasants into instruments of death and destruction." As she would soon discover, such blind fervor was also shared by many of the island's Falangists. Ironically, the side she now allied herself with in this sad chapter of Spanish history would ultimately be the one to place her life in jeopardy.

The following week, Alvaro was appointed naval commander of the southern coasts of Mallorca. Natacha closed down the villa and let her servants return to their villages. She then joined her husband in the southern port town of Campos, where she took up residence with her white Pekingese, Bimbo, in a tiny shack on the beach facing the Republican-held island of Cabrera. "We are quite elegant," Natacha wrote her cousin Katherine Peterson, in America. "We have two beds, a table, two wash-stands, and a couple of chairs." Included in the letter were some photographs Rambova had taken of their humble surroundings. One showed a broken-down privy located behind the shack. "Our magnificent W.C.," Natacha wrote in the letter, "known, I believe, in the time of your parents as the 'back-house.' Only ours has not a door. They probably thought the odor was quite sufficient to keep away all intruders. They were right!"

Since Alvaro was gone most of the day and night patroling the coast, Rambova found herself alone on the beach with her dog. "Bimbo and I are leading the quiet life," she wrote her cousin. "I write until I can't think of another word, and then we swim or read. Believe it or not, I am thoroughly enjoying it. We run up to Palma twice a week to exchange news and have a change of diet."

One of Natacha's projects in Palma was to design overalls for the farming women of the island whose husbands had been inducted into the local army. With no men available to harvest the crops, the women were taking it upon themselves to do the job. Natacha's heavy-duty pantaloons provided them with working clothes more practical than dresses.

While returning from one of their jaunts to Palma, Natacha and Bimbo were trailed by Republican aircraft. As her car sped down the road, the plane descended behind them dropping bombs in their wake. Realizing it was useless to try to outmaneuver the approaching plane, Natacha grabbed the dog with one hand and opened the car door with the other. She leaped from the automobile and rolled with Bimbo off the side of the road to the cover of a tree. Her car ended up in a ditch, unscathed by the pursuing bomber.

The Mallorcans were frustrated by their inability to fight off the Republican air attack. The Nationalist planes that had been promised to aid them never materialized. A young Mallorcan by the name of Crespi who owned an ancient biplane took it upon himself to defend the island with his decrepit aircraft. Using the beach at Campos for a runway, Crespi marked as his target a Republican submarine that skulked in the waters between Mallorca and Cabrera. Swooping over the sub and dropping his bombs by hand, Crespi harassed the vessel as the villagers of Campos stood on the beach cheering.

"We watched our hero proudly," Rambova recalled. "His maneuvers were repeated several times before we realized something was wrong. Suddenly the motor stopped and to our horror we saw the plane dive, crash on its nose, and turn slowly on its back." Before the villagers could reach him, Crespi had swum to shore, holding a live bomb in his hand. Why it had not exploded in the plane crash was a mystery. "Providence works in strange ways," Rambova concluded.

The next morning Republican planes circled the village of Campos in retaliation. The first bomb fell with a deafening explosion sixty feet from Natacha's beach house. Rambova recalled the frenzy of the attack:

The astonished and terrified villagers scuttled indoors, hysterical with fright. I made for the thickest wall I could find, collecting a sobbing old woman and a young girl on the way. We flattened ourselves on the wall and waited. Crash! Another bomb fell on the other side of the house. We could hear the shrapnel hit the walls, one bit splintering the shutters on the window. For more than a half an hour bombs rained around us.

Ironically, the only casualties of the air raid were two Republican spies from Cabrera who had been hiding in an abandoned house. While most of the villagers fled from the bombing of Campos, Rambova remained with Alvaro and the soldiers, sharing their meager diet made up of a few abandoned chickens and the contents of some old tins. After more than a week of enemy fire, Natacha's resolve began to crack. "I made the unpleasant personal discovery," she wrote, "that eight days of continuous bomb dodging had an effect on my nerves."

When word reached them that the Republican forces had captured the nearby island of Ibiza, Mallorcans braced themselves for the invasion of their own island. Since it was expected that Campos would be the site of their arrival, Natacha was ordered to evacuate to Palma.

She found the city to be calm on the surface, but she sensed a turmoil of human emotion underneath. When the sirens screamed a warning of approaching planes, the townspeople automatically disappeared into the bunkers marked *Refugio*. The Mallorcans were extremely generous in responding to the military commander's appeal for gold. Since they were completely cut off from the mainland, basic supplies had to be purchased from foreign nations, and gold was needed for these transactions:

My throat tightened with emotion as I noticed the quantity of peasants, the tranquil resignation on their weather-worn faces; for the salvation of their country they had come to offer their few gold pieces, the gold buttons from the sleeves of their regional costumes, the trinkets that had been treasured and handed down for generations, the gold that represented the dowries of their daughters. Looking at the preponderance of the peasantry in the waiting line, I wondered if the wealthier classes would respond with equal sacrifice.

In the early morning of Sunday, August 16, Republican forces landed at Porto Cristo on the southeastern coast of Mallorca. "The news came as a relief," Rambova recalled. "There was now something to fight, something on which to vent pent up emotions." The Mallorcan forces knew that they were outnumbered, and the fighting would be hard. Every able-bodied male was inducted into the army to halt the Republicans' approach. Old men and young boys—the *segunda fila*—were left behind to defend the capital. All supplies were strictly rationed. Women patched together uniforms with rags.

Rambova drove back and forth from Palma to Manacor, on the

eastern side of the island, carrying biscuits, *anis, herez,* cigarettes, and clothing to the soldiers serving in Alvaro's unit. On her journeys she picked up news detailing the horrors of the battle, and of the many bloody ambushes that contributed to the mounting death toll. Reports went from bad to worse when it was discovered that the Republicans had just landed a large number of reinforcements from a hospital ship, the *Marqués de Gomilla.* Thereafter, the dreaded planes dropped leaflets over Palma giving the city twenty-four hours to surrender. If it failed to do so by noon the next day, it would face a massive onslaught from air and sea.

By one hour before the deadline, all ships in the harbor had left for safer ports. A little before noon, Rambova, along with the American consul and his entourage, took their seats at the lookout of a fort high in the hills above Palma. They were expecting a decisive spectacle, which, Rambova surmised, "might mean anything from the destruction of our city to the sinking of the Red [Republican] fleet by our fortress guns." Anxiously, they peered upward, looking for the first sign of invading aircraft. By 12:20 they could hear the whirr of engines; the planes were coming, discernable now as white specks in the distance. Breathlessly, they watched as the large white fighter-bombers grew in size. They began to descend lower and lower, circling over the helpless city. With nerves taut, they waited for the bombs to fall.

But none fell.

Suddenly, a shout went up, as one man in their company began waving his arms yelling, "Nuestros aviones! Nuestros aviones!" They were Franco's planes. As Rambova commented, "They could hardly have chosen a more dramatic moment for their arrival."

Natacha descended from her mountain perch to find the city delirious with joy. Church bells rang, and people danced in the streets with joyous relief. By one o'clock there was no sign of the Republican approach, either by sea or air. As more Nationalist planes arrived, with accompanying soldiers, morale in Palma surged. The island could now launch a major attack on its enemy.

In the following days, Radio Barcelona was heard calling for volunteers in the battle of Mallorca. Frantic radio calls had been intercepted from the leader of the Republican forces on the island, complaining of heavy losses and demoralization among his men. The Nationalist reinforcement of fighter planes and twelve thousand soldiers had turned the tide against them. Even the Republican fleet was scattering in confusion.

The Falangists planned a concentrated offensive. The night before the attack intended to rid the island of its invaders, Natacha drove Alvaro from Manacor to the front lines. He had returned to the capital to commandeer some much-needed supplies and missed the last military truck leaving the city. The road from Manacor to Porto Cristo sloped gently to the sea, but the drive was harrowing, as Rambova recalled: "Once beyond the village we drove without lights; our route lay in full view of the Red lines and within range of their guns. We crept through the stillness. Tree stumps and boundary posts emerged from the dim light to make my heart thump—each one an imagined Red. Some, I knew, had filtered through our lines."

After arriving at their destination, they whispered the password and took a position in the battery located on a small hill rising above the port. "The sea was glimmering silver in the moonlight. There was not a sound to be heard; surely this was not war!" Natacha exclaimed. She was led to a lookout, where she could see the enemy lines below. Both sides were eating their dinner, she was told. As soon as they were finished, someone would fire in the air and the battle would recommence. Rambova was then escorted to safety behind the lines, carrying the company's mascot, a puppy from an abandoned farmhouse.

By September 4, the Nationalists' incessant shelling and bombing forced the withdrawal of Republican forces from the island. "The disordered haste of their departure," Rambova recalled, "was such that quantities of guns, rifles, munitions, cars, an armored truck, and valuable medical supplies had been abandoned. Even their loot in gold, jewelry, and church ornaments, mostly stolen from the rich peasantry of Ibiza, had been left behind." Among the prisoners captured were French and Russian communists, but the most formidable prisoners, as Rambova recounted, were five machine-gun operating Republican women: "They were the sans-culottes of our Spanish revolution. When ordered to surrender, they had all raised clenched fists in the communist salute and shouted 'Viva Rusia!' They were not cowards like many of their men who had given themselves up with cries of 'Arriba España!'"

Two days after the victory, Alvaro took Natacha on a tour of the battleground. In Porto Cristo the sanitary units were still cleaning up. "The air reeked with the fumes of burning bodies heaped here and there on smouldering piles," Rambova recounted. The Red losses had been heavy, over a thousand dead. Natacha recorded the devastation with her camera: "The streets were littered with debris and the decaying carcasses

Rambova's snapshots of the war in Mallorca: men firing from behind street barricades in Porto Cristo (top); one of many corpses left lying in the street (middle); houses destroyed by bombs (bottom)

of mules and horses. Corners and crossings were barricaded with stacked furniture and mattresses." The houses were perforated with holes from shell fire. Many of them held grim discoveries. "In one house there were twenty-seven dead," Natacha wrote. "It was curious how callous one soon became to death."

Rambova resented how the international press portrayed the Nationalists as aggressors in the civil war, and the editorial call for the necessity to uphold the legal government of Spain. "A 'legal' government," she bitterly commented, "that was Russian—a government whose apparent idea of law and order was to allow and encourage senseless slaughter, the burning alive of priests and helpless nuns, the violation of women, the mutilation of innocent children, the destruction of priceless treasures of history and art." Never at a loss for rhetoric, in response to a rally held at New York's Madison Square Garden, which raised $50,000 for the Spanish Republican cause, Rambova wrote a forty-page essay of her own first-hand experience of the war. She hoped to show that the so-called rebels and insurgents were "men who were giving their lives to save not only their own country, but civilization from the contagion of class hatred turned to madness, from an epidemic of such brutality and cruelty that it made the most hideous episodes of the French and Russian revolutions pale in comparison." Had her essay been written a few months later—after Franco had invited Nazi planes to bomb the Basque town of Guernica—the moral indignation of her argument might have been muzzled. For now, as she saw it, the only martyrs in Spain were those whose lives were sacrificed in a war against communism. As fate would have it, the essay never reached publication. Shortly after she finished her account, an ironic chain of incidents caused her to flee the island.

The Nationalist victory in Mallorca was celebrated by a triumphant march into Palma, and a Mass of Thanksgiving held in the city square. "We witnessed a proud display," Rambova recounted. "For hours we watched them pass: infantry, machine gunners, Carlists with bright red berets, blue shirted Falangists, captured enemy cannon and planes, dozens of Communists and Catalan flags dragged in dishonor through the mud. Many of the men had their mascots—pet roosters, rabbits, goats, dogs, one carried three small kittens in his cape."

But during a subsequent church ceremony celebrating the victory, Natacha's sense of justice was outraged. The former civil governor of the island had been deposed and arrested as a consequence of his having

The Nationalist forces make their victory march before the cathedral in Palma.

embraced the leftist policies of the Republican government in Madrid. With the right-wing victory in Mallorca, more leftist sympathizers were being arrested; many of them were being shot. The governor's wife and children, fearful for their lives, sought protection from the bishop of Palma. Rambova was the woman's friend, and knew that she was a devout daughter of the Church. When the bishop refused to grant the women sanctuary, Rambova raced to the cathedral where the prelate was conducting a Te Deum, and she denounced him to his face, in front of the congregation. "When will you stop the slaughter?" she screamed as she was dragged out of the sanctuary.

Suddenly it appeared to the right-wing victors that this foreign woman could no longer be trusted. Her denunciation seemed to be calculated to stir up sympathy for the vanquished Left. Her rash action placed her under suspicion, and Rambova realized that within hours she would have to make an escape from the island or face arrest herself. Alvaro, still on duty at Porto Cristo, could not help her.

"It was Franco who got Natacha out of Mallorca," recalled her cousin, Ann Wollen. The surreptitious escape was arranged for her on a coal freighter that was leaving Palma for Nice. Carrying only Bimbo, her white Pekingese, Rambova became a political stowaway, hiding in the coal bunkers of the massive ship.

"Aunt Winifred was standing on the garden terrace of the Château Juan-les-Pins," Ann Wollen continued, "when she saw an empty dinghy floating in the surf below her. And walking up the hill on the drive leading to the mansion was a filthy character carrying a black dog." To her shock and delight, the soot-covered creatures were Natacha and Bimbo.

Rambova did not return to Spain for the duration of the war. Her reputation was too controversial. Alvaro, on the other hand, proved indispensible to Franco, and by necessity he continued to serve in the Nationalist forces. This placed a strain on their marriage and frayed Natacha's already taut nerves. The tension she had been living under finally took its toll on her body. A short time after her dramatic flight, she suffered a heart attack.

*N*atacha's collapse at the end of 1936 signaled the start of a physical decline that would plague her for the remaining thirty years of her life. While she had been known in Hollywood as a hard worker who was able to labor long hours without food or rest, the physical fitness she inherited from her father was tested to the breaking point by the cumulative stress of the Spanish Civil War, separation from her husband, and the fact that she was aging. Nearly forty, she could no longer bend her body to her will as she had done in her youth. Her heart gave out, and she was confined to recuperative bed rest at the château. The forced inactivity moved her to self-reflection and to investigate, for the first time, the relationship among mental, physical, and emotional well-being.

Both before and after her heart attack, Alvaro managed to visit Natacha at Juan-les-Pins while on military leave. On one occasion, she and Alvaro reunited with his brother and sister-in-law in Rome. Mariano and his wife had been smuggled out of San Sebastián through the quiet diplomacy of the English consul. Other friends and relatives, however, had not been so fortunate, and the reports of their torture and murder haunted the survivors. The Condé de Torre-Arias had been accosted on a street in Madrid, dragged away, and his mutilated body was discovered a few days later in a cemetery. The beheaded body of another relative was found there also, his identification papers having been tied to his leg. While in Italy, the exiled aristocrats celebrated their rescue by paying a visit to their aged ex-king, Alfonso XIII. Rambova later wrote to her

Natacha at the Hudnut château, recuperating from her heart attack

cousin telling of their ride along the coast to Amalfi: "I remember driving there one afternoon with Alfonso, my husband, and sister-in-law. We stopped for tea at one of the cafes—everyone in great form, and we sang old Spanish songs in the car, there and on the way back. He loved all the old military songs and sang them well. He was quite a dear with a great sense of fun."

The war, which lasted until April 1939, took its toll not only on Natacha's physical health, but on the health of her marriage. The long separation from Alvaro undoubtedly contributed to this, but one might rightly assume that there were underlying tensions as well. As with her marriage to Valentino, Natacha enjoyed being Alvaro's wife, but she was not disposed to becoming a mother. Furthermore, the controversy surrounding her flight from Mallorca must have caused the Urzáiz family some grief. Alvaro himself must have had a change of heart, for the message that he brought her revealed the weakness of his conjugal commitment. On what would be his last visit to Juan-les-Pins, Alvaro disclosed to Natacha that he had fallen in love with another woman. Ill as she was, the news came as a terrible blow. She broke off all communication with him and privately nursed her grief. The failure of this second marriage soured her on matrimony, and she would never marry again. In fact, it became her outspoken opinion that professional women seeking to develop their creative talents should avoid marriage altogether.

Yet Rambova would not allow self-pity. Viewing all experiences in life, whether good or bad, as opportunities for inner growth, she embarked on a program of rehabilitation.

For the first time she cut her hair. Her waist-length locks, which had been elaborately braided and coiled for decades, now became, in middle-age, a simple chignon. In an effort to improve her circulation, she discarded her tight-fitting turbans. She started to eat regularly and took more time to rest and read. She studied world religions and symbolism, from ancient Egypt and Greece to Hinduism and Buddhism, taking notice of those elements that seemed to link them, particularly the science of numbers and the zodiac.

Rambova's renewed passion for finding a meaningful life was played out against the background of a world arming for combat. The debacle in Spain proved but a prelude to world war. In the short interval between the lightning and the thunder, Rambova strove to attain equilibrium.

She found the key to self-renewal in the philosophy of George Ivanovich Gurdjieff. Having always had a predilection for sages who were

able to bridge the gulf between East and West, Rambova found in the
teachings of Gurdjieff the wisdom of the Orient systematized into a
program for Occidental understanding. Gurdjieff's personal history, like
Blavatsky's, was shrouded in mystery. Born to a Greek father and an
Armenian mother around the year 1872 in Alexandropol, at the foot of
Mount Ararat in the Caucasus, Gurdjieff was educated at an Orthodox
cathedral school. Planning for a vocation as a physician and priest, the
young man took great interest in the physical and spiritual evolution of
human life. After having witnessed a variety of paranormal phenomena,
such as table-tapping at séances, inexplicable physical cures at holy
shrines, and the accurate predictions of seers, Gurdjieff set out to find
the answers to questions that were not addressed in his scientific or
theological books. Wandering through the nomadic territory between
the Black and Caspian seas, Gurdjieff made contact with a number of
hermetic groups that had, over the centuries, grown out of the intermin-
gling of Christian, Islamic, Assyrian, and Zoroastrian societies. He
searched for human beings who were somehow directly connected,
through their traditions, to an unchanging source of true wisdom. His
quest led him to travel extensively throughout Europe, Egypt, and Asia.
Everywhere he went, he picked up knowledge and techniques deemed
useful for self-realization and spiritual fulfillment. From the Orthodox
monks he learned contemplative prayer and the meaning behind the
ancient symbolism of the liturgy. From the Sufis he learned the ways of
the Dervish and an understanding of the enneagram. From the Tibetan
lamas he gained a knowledge of ritual movement and energy control.

Like Blavatsky, Gurdjieff had his detractors, who claimed that the
would-be sage engaged in charlatanism, thievery, black magic, and even
espionage. He did seem to supply some communicating link between the
czarist government and the Dalai Lama at a time when Tibetan borders

were being threatened by British and Chinese forces. Gurdjieff himself became a member of the Imperial Court of Nicholas II when he married the Countess Ostrofska, and he tried unsuccessfully to counteract the influence of Rasputin. During the Russian Revolution, he fled with a number of his disciples to Constantinople, Berlin, and finally Paris. In time, he was able to raise enough money to purchase the Château d'Avon, known as the Prieuré des Basses Loges, near Fontainebleau, where he set up his Institute for the Harmonious Development of Man.

Whether Rambova ever personally met Gurdjieff when he lectured in France or in New York is not recorded. Her friends do, however, attest to her indebtedness to his teachings. The physical and mental exercises she undertook—and later promoted—can be traced directly to Gurdjieff's work. His use of art, music, posture, and gesture to transform human consciousness became her abiding interest. His psychic connection to the ancient civilizations, his study of the lost continent of Atlantis, and his elevation of symbol and myth were allied to her own beliefs. Eschewing the reputed dark side of Gurdjieff, including his predilection for magic, Rambova took from the sage what seemed most positive and practical.

After three years of intensive study at the Hudnut château, Rambova was ready for a change of environment. Her life had become more steadily ascetic, a progression away from physical conceits toward a preoccupation with matters of the mind and spirit. She no longer painted her face, and she exchanged her exotic robes and jewelry for simple tweed suits. In her pursuit of esoteric knowledge, she read voraciously in several languages. In contrast, Muzzie continued to express her fun-loving temperament. She was always addicted to luxury, and she enjoyed living the life of a grande dame. "I remember seeing her arrive at a hotel once in her limousine," an acquaintance recalled. "She was wearing a beige gown over her hourglass figure, a choker around her neck, a hat with egret feathers, gloves and a cane. She looked like an empress, a queen. She was a very elegant lady—but from a different era." Her behavior seemed sometimes comic, as when she discovered that one of her Pekingese was constipated so she gave her entire kennel enemas, wielding a syringe and a bucket of water while dressed in negligée and jewels. Yet she was also practical to a fault. The presents she gave her closest friends were often assortments of mops and other cleaning utensils. Winifred Hudnut was certainly more sensible than Natacha when it came to management of money. Rambova felt that money had been created for one purpose: to be spent. If she went broke, she always knew that she could swallow her pride and rely on her mother for security. Mrs. Hudnut, who had worked hard to amass her fortune, was a shrewd businesswoman, and she kept Natacha on a regular allowance from the Hudnut estate. "I should have been a crook," Muzzie often said of herself, "because I have the mind of a crook." While mother and daughter were markedly different in personality and taste, they agreed on one thing: neither was willing to marry again. With her self-deprecating humor, Winifred Butts Shaughnessy de Wolfe Hudnut commented, "I have made three men miserable in my life, and I'm not going to do it again." Obviously, her short-lived marriage to husband number one had either been forgotten, or just didn't count.

Ann Wollen recalled that "Natacha was an avid naturalist, loving beauty as it was found in nature—untampered with. Aunt Winifred, on the other hand, always seemed to think that she could improve nature's beauty by tying a big bow onto it." This comparison suggests why Natacha at last decided to leave the château and make a new home for herself in the Arizona desert. She had already designed the house she planned to build. It would incorporate symbolic architecture and include a five-sided living room with a brilliant red door.

In the summer of 1939, Rambova visited Britain before leaving for America. She booked passage on the *Athenia,* which left Glasgow at noon on September 1. The political situation in Europe had become very tense. Hitler had attacked Poland; England and France issued a joint ultimatum to Germany. After docking in Liverpool and Belfast, the *Athenia* proceeded across the Atlantic Ocean with 1,400 passengers on board, over 300 of whom were Americans. When Germany failed to respond to their ultimatum, England and France declared war on September 3. On that very day, at 4:00 P.M., two torpedoes from a German U-boat struck the unarmed and unescorted *Athenia,* sinking the ship within twenty minutes, drowning more than one hundred passengers, including some Americans. A gossip columnist reported that Natacha Rambova was among those missing. This sent Winifred Hudnut into a state of shock. Soon after, however, the report was discovered to be false. Natacha had decided against sailing on the *Athenia* because it did not provide a run for her pet.

On October 12, 1939, the scene was played out again in Bordeaux. Rambova walked up the gangplank of the United States liner *Manhattan,* with Bimbo in her arms. An hour later, just before the ship's departure, she walked down the gangplank. The ship's officers would not allow her to keep the dog in her cabin. He would have to be kept in a cage in the ship's hold, she was informed. Reporters were there when she tearfully cancelled her passage. "The Peke would never live to set foot on home soil," she told them, as she caressed her faithful, but aging, companion. She then boarded a train for the Mediterranean, where she hoped to find more liberal-minded ship's masters.

Rambova did finally sail to America and settled in Phoenix, Arizona, with her dog. She found in the American Southwest a serenity and beauty compatible with her new outlook on life. "Dearest Auntie," she wrote Teresa Werner in a 1940 Christmas letter sent to Los Angeles, "I love the desert here with its peace and marvelous coloring. We have been enjoying the sun and warmth until the last few days—but the rain is good for the farmers. And I expect to be a farmer soon." She signed her letter "Wink." But the desert sands where she felt so at home were not to be hers much longer. The Nazi invasion of France in June sent Muzzie fleeing from the Riviera. Even though the collaborationist Vichy Government issued orders that no artworks were to leave French soil, Natacha's mother managed to smuggle out the château's most valuable pieces and get them into storage in New York, where she herself took up residence at 30 West 56th Street. Feeling the need to be close to family in such perilous times, Natacha abandoned her plans for a home and ranch lands in the desert, and returned to the East Coast. She took a small apartment close to her mother's, at 140 West 55th Street.

By situating herself in New York, Natacha was able to communicate more easily with those who shared her enthusiasm for the psychic and healing arts. With an instructor of physical posture, James H. Smith, Rambova coauthored a number of articles on mental and physical exercises, which appeared in *Harper's Bazaar* and *Town and Country* magazines. Containing simple illustrations by Mildred Orrick, these articles promoted a technique for combating nervous tension. The authors took physical movements, derived from yoga and Gurdjieff, and combined them with a philosophy of positive thinking. This was expanded into book form in 1944 and published under the title *Technique for Living.* Self-control and self-government could only be achieved, the book claimed, by engaging first in a program of physical consciousness and balance, which in turn would lead to emotional stability and mental clarity. Emphasis was placed on the value of experience, visualization, and humor. Consequently, in the photographs taken of Rambova after the publication of this book, one can find more instances of her smiling than in all the volumes of photographs taken of her previously in Hollywood. *Technique for Living* was followed the next year by another joint effort, *The Road Back,* in which the authors devoted their attention to a program of rehabilitation for returning veterans suffering from physical disabilities, emotional trauma, and mental disorientation.

Since Rambova's exercises concentrated on physical and mental control and were not intended to induce in the practitioner an afterglow of perspiration, there was some misunderstanding as to the worth of these gymnastics. Even some members of her own family, ignorant of the philosophical reasoning behind her drills, parodied Natacha's exercises; they would lie on the floor and extend and contract their index fingers.

Rambova also sought guidance from the stars. Having been introduced to astrology by Evangeline Adams, Iris Vorel, and Leslie Grant, she pursued a study of the zodiac with such enthusiasm that she began to accept appointments from clients eager for her to do a chart and provide counsel. Uneasy with the stigma of superstition attached to astrology, Rambova wrote a number of essays under the title "Astrological Psycho-Chemistry" for *American Astrology* magazine. They appeared monthly, from February 1942 through June 1943. She began her defense of the discipline by claiming that astrology's reputation had benefited from the scientific contributions of Albert Einstein (the theory of relativity), Sir James Jeans and Arthur Eddington (the logical awareness of the cosmic Mind as creative Cause), Robert Millikan (discovery of cosmic rays from outer space), George Crile and George Lakhovsky (the scientific realization of living beings as instruments of reception and transmission of cosmic radiation), among others. These theories had enhanced, she declared, the astrologers' age-old claims that astral bodies have a profound influence on human organisms. She incorporated into her argument a remarkable knowledge of varied fields, including physics, metaphysics, symbology, cosmology, alchemy, mythology, and numerology. After attempting to exonerate astrology, Rambova wrote a detailed analysis of each of the planetary figures for what she called "a zodiacal pattern of creative evolution." As always, the purpose of her writing was to educate and uplift. For the July 1942 issue, she wrote an additional essay titled "America: Her Purpose and Three Great Trials for Liberty—Equality—Unity." Here she plotted the nation's horoscope from an astrological chart calculated upon the place and date of the country's national birth: Philadelphia, July 4, 1776, five P.M. From this she predicted that beginning in the spring of 1945 there would be a new resurgence for equality and unity taking place under the mantle of justice and law. In another essay titled "America's Destiny: The World of our Future," which appeared the following November, Rambova devised a war chart for Washington, D.C., dated December 7, 1941, 12:57 P.M. From this she made predictions on developments that would occur once the war was over. These included the permanent stationing of American military troops around the world, a focus on higher education for mental rather than material gain, an emphasis on parks and sports, a turn in domestic architecture toward more horizontal lines, and a new interest in and appreciation of native American culture and lore.

It is highly unlikely that the last prediction was influenced by the heavenly bodies alone. One of Rambova's closest professional friends was Maud Van Cortlandt Oakes, who regularly attended classes in Rambova's apartment on symbolism, mythology, and comparative religion, came to her for dream analysis, and borrowed books from her "Psychological Research Library."

Like Natacha, Oakes had been born into an affluent family. She had grown up in Washington state, and it was there that her interest in native civilizations began, as she read the legends of the Northwest Indian tribes. Although she circulated in society as a debutante and received an art education in France, her goal in life seemed unclear until, through John Barrett, a family friend, she met Paul and Mary Mellon. They introduced her to the work of Carl Jung, for it was Mary Mellon's intention to publish Jung's work, under the auspices of a foundation she later formed and called "Bollingen," after the castlelike refuge Jung had built for himself on the shores of Lake Zurich. Through the Mellons, Maud also met Olga Froebe-Kapteyn, organizer of the Eranos Conferences at Ascona. It was Olga who challenged Maud to return to her lifelong interest in native culture, and Paul Mellon facilitated this by giving Maud a foundation grant to finance a study of the sand paintings of the Navajo Indians of New Mexico.

The intellectual, artistic, and spiritual quest that motivated people like Maud Oakes, John Barrett, and the Mellons came to be shared by a network of personalities who used the Bollingen Foundation and its publishing arm, the Bollingen Series of Princeton University Press, as a forum and point of intersection. Besides Jung, the Bollingen would promote the diverse endeavors of such personalities as Joseph Campbell, Mircea Eliade, Heinrich Zimmer, André Malraux, Otto Von Simpson, Erich Neumann, Jacques Maritain, Etienne Gilson, Dora and Erwin Panofsky, and Ananda K. Coomaraswamy. It was through Maud Oakes that Natacha Rambova kept abreast of the Bollingen's fascinating projects and came to know many of its key figures.

In the summer of 1945, Rambova traveled to the remote highlands of Guatemala to assist Maud Oakes in her study of the pre-Columbian background of the Indians living there. While the altitude put her health at risk, the adventure of uncovering ancient truths in exotic places satisfied one of Natacha's lifelong dreams. Aaron Sussman, publisher of the work of Alexandra David-Neel, the only European woman to have been honored with the rank of a lama in Tibet, recalled meeting Rambova thirteen years previously when David-Neel's *Magic and Mystery in Tibet* had just been released. Escorted by her chauffeur on an unannounced visit to the publisher's office, Rambova caught Sussman by surprise. He was stunned by her beauty and fascinated by the project she told him she wished to undertake: an anthropological research expedition to study the people of the Pacific islands. Sussman wanted her to sign a contract on the spot, but Rambova, encouraged by his enthusiasm, nevertheless rejected a contractual commitment to the enterprise. Their meeting lasted only thirty minutes, and Sussman never heard from Rambova again, but the encounter left such an impression on him that he recorded the incident in the introduction to a later edition of David-Neel's book. While Rambova's fate took her to an island near Spain rather than the Pacific, her urge to connect with lost or vanishing civilizations endured. It began to find fulfillment when she joined Maud for those few short months in Guatemala, helping her to find symbolic and numerological patterns in the ancient culture of the native people.

Upon her return to New York, and acting on the advice of Mary Mellon, Natacha applied for her own grant to create an archive of comparative universal symbolism. She proposed to collect from museums and private collections sketches and photographs of rare books and manuscripts containing archetypal symbolism. The collection would focus on cosmological symbols depicted in numerical, geometric, and zodiacal form, and animal symbolism. These, she felt, were the hieroglyphic keys to the mysteries and sciences of the ancient temples, from the lost cultures of India to those of the Near East. Knowledge of these symbols was necessary, she argued, if one hoped to understand the nature of religious belief as expressed in the mythology, art, and sacred texts of the ancient world.

A renewable grant of $500 was approved in November 1945, and a month later Natacha was already proposing to Mary Mellon that a book based on the archive be written by Ananda Coomaraswamy, a man she had known and admired since her days with the Roerich Society. It was Natacha's conviction that knowledge of symbols must be made readily available before it could be understood and applied for the benefit of humanity. The symbols "must serve to give people an understanding of themselves, their life and purpose, and . . . provide a key for future students of mythology, ancient art and archaeology. It is useless to have museums if the objects in those museums cannot be made significant so that they play an important part in the life of people."

Natacha told Mary Mellon that the search for root symbolism, which linked her work with Maud's, pointed ultimately to the lost civilization of Atlantis, a culture she believed had disseminated its knowledge to all points of the world before vanishing. The astrological sign of Leo ruled the Atlantean sciences, Natacha declared, and she found it more than coincidental that Jung and Blavatsky were both Leos. Jung's analysis of what he called the collective unconscious pointed to that Atlantean past, she felt, and Blavatsky's *The Secret Doctrine* was, de facto, an encyclopedia of Atlantean religion and symbolism. In a letter to Mary Mellon, Natacha wrote that she also thought it "curious that so many working on this subject . . . have Leo rising—you, your husband, Maud and myself and many others whom I know. . . . Quite possibly old Atlanteans who are here to take their responsibility and opportunity of bringing essential knowledge at this time out of chaos."

Rambova believed that a rediscovery of the past would build a better world for the future, and to this end she began to gather material for a book on "The Myth Pattern of Ancient Symbolism." She wrote Mary Mellon a lengthy letter on the importance of this work:

It is necessary that gradually people be given the realization of a universal pattern of purpose and human growth—which the knowledge of the mysteries of initiation of the Atlantean past, as the source of our symbols of the Unconscious, gives. In this present mess of hatred, greed, and ignorance the only thing we can do individually is to [discover] where and how we can make this deeper knowledge available—to help individuals clear themselves from fear and confusion by giving them an understanding of the great pattern of life to which they belong.

In the same letter, Rambova disclosed to Mary Mellon that, while her interest in legend and mythology began in childhood and continued

Rambova smiles for a passport photo.

in her professional career as a dancer and cinematic designer, she did not begin serious study until December 25, 1925, when she made her "first real contact." This contradicts the rumors, still prevalent in Hollywood, that she and Valentino were seriously involved in Spiritualism prior to that date. "Since then," Natacha continued, "I have known what I wish to do, and all my work and experiences have had the purpose of making this possible."

Because of her work in therapy and counseling, Rambova considered herself an "analytical psychologist," a profession augmented by her astrological endeavors, dream analysis, and her classes in symbolism and myth. In order to pursue her research, however, she would have to suspend these income-producing activities while she devoted her full attention to the development of the archive. "Financially I have a small income, $150 per month, for a sale of stock in payments which will end sometime next year," she wrote Mary Mellon in explaining her need for the grant. "When my income stops I think mother will help me for a time as she is interested that I write—but this I do not know, and do not worry about. I never have to worry about personal expenses," Rambova concluded in her letter, "as I am always taken care of in some way or another. I do want, however, for the work to go on."

From lecturing, Rambova gained much exposure and was frequently offered financial backing for her projects. But she turned these offers down, since the patrons seemed to be insincere. Wealth alone, she believed, should not justify a patron's participation in this spiritual research. Crass materialists, only interested in endowments for the sake of being fashionable, were unwelcome. On this principle she was immovable, carrying her intolerance for what she saw as the duplicitous and greedy to the point of bigotry. "I have seen well meaning students, filled with purpose and enthusiasm, who have accepted the wrong kind of money and have instantly destroyed the very thing they hoped to achieve," she declared. "But things come when the right people come along to do them and the time is ready."

In Natacha's mind, the Mellons were the right people, and the Bollingen Foundation was the right organization through which she could pursue her work. In this alliance she would not be disappointed, for it would enable her to return to Egypt—a land she believed she had already known in a past life.

*I*n October of 1946 Mary Mellon died of heart failure brought on by a serious asthma attack. She was only forty-two. Her husband, Paul, asked John Barrett to help him carry on the Bollingen Foundation. Barrett did so, acting as president and editor of the Bollingen Series. Late in 1946 the foundation awarded Rambova a grant to travel to Egypt to analyze symbolic material gathered from antique scarabs. This, she believed, would forge a link between the belief system of Egypt and that of the ancient American cultures. After sailing nineteen days across the Atlantic and the Mediterranean, Rambova landed in Cairo with nine bags filled with equipment, clothes, medicine, and reference books. She had just celebrated her fiftieth birthday.

"Egypt is one of the most potently beautiful lands of the earth," she wrote "Jack" Barrett in the first of several detailed reports typed during the course of 1947. She found Cairo had changed much since the war and her previous visit in 1936. For one thing, it was now rife with racial intolerance, "much of it created by the thousands of American and British soldiers during the war, with their crude and brutal way of showing their white superiority—awakening resentment, bitterness and hurt where none had existed before." But the countryside and the monuments of Aswan and Luxor impressed her with "the same magic in the air and the same sadness which often comes in lands where the power lies in the memories of the past rather than the life of the present." It

Rambova at home in Egypt

was no wonder to Rambova that Egypt had been chosen "to be the center from which the most sublime of sciences and the purest philosophy spread to all corners of the world." It was to be her quest for the remainder of her life to piece together, through a knowledge of symbols, a greater understanding of the wisdom behind the religion of the Egyptians, the conduit that fed the spirit of successive cultures: "Her temples and her mysteries had been the source from which had come the gods and myths of Greece, the philosophy of Pythagorus, Plato, Apollonius; the new teaching of Brotherhood given by the Galilean; and even in her later days when all was but lost, she could yet speak through Plutarch, Iamblichus and the Neo-Platonists, who were the last interpretors and conveyors of a wisdom now deeply buried and almost forgotten."

Her reports to Barrett were colorful and atmospheric, filled with images of veiled women, turbaned men, and the hubbub of modern shops set against the profound silence of decaying monuments. Driven by her demand for data, she ignored no one. She trafficked with priests, professors, sheiks, collectors, curators, and even forgers. The bogus material, which she quickly learned to identify, had its own significance for her. "So-called fake pieces of ancient art are found to contain much that is of symbolic interest and importance," she told Barrett. Convinced that their manufacture was inspired by a wellspring of symbols based in the unconscious, she declared that, "in an unusual way, they provide another rich source of analytical study."

The persistence of the atavistic cult manifesting itself in modern culture had been demonstrated to Rambova long ago by Howard Carter in an incident that took place as they sailed across the Nile to a restoration site at Luxor. "I remembered Carter years before translating for me words from a chant the workmen were using at the temple of Luxor, as they hauled the heavy stone beams to be put again in place. They were calling on their god A-mon to help them and give them strength," she wrote Barrett. Rambova's previous connection with Carter and W.M.F. Petri proved beneficial on her return trip to Egypt. Dealers were willing to sell her their best objects at little more than cost, and guides were eager to take her to places no foreign woman had ever seen. Two Egyptians in particular, Sayed Mulatam and Mageed Sameda, were enchanted with Rambova, and they provided her with excellent antiques from their shops in Luxor. They also fed her valuable information on archaeological sites and introduced her to many of the ancient religious ceremonies still practiced by the common people.

"Magic is in the very soil of Egypt," Rambova exclaimed as she witnessed case after case of psychic phenomena, from the debilitating effects of the evil eye, to the curative charms of scarabs, and the religious ecstacies experienced by those who danced in dervishes and spoke in tongues. As Rambova understood it, to dance was to invoke the Divine, whether the action is found in ancient or primitive peoples, medieval Mystery Plays, or the folk dances still practiced by men in modern Basque society. "This religious significance of the dance must be kept in mind," she wrote Barrett, "if we are to accurately evaluate and interpret the dancing figures which abound on early dynastic seals—usually dismissed by our archaeologists as trivial or irrelevant."

The dance, the symbol, the ritual, the chant—Rambova examined and compared all these religious manifestations with a respect professional scientists did not give them. Self-taught, Rambova nevertheless approached her thesis with all the diligence of a doctoral candidate, impressing the intellectuals at the Bollingen Foundation with her comparative research. Ignoring warnings of an outbreak of typhoid in the Delta region, Natacha took money her mother gave her and went on a buying spree there, gathering artifacts to support her theories of the unity of ancient religions. She wrote Jack Barrett of her progress:

In tracing the archaic forms and designs backward to their roots and source, I have gone from the scarab, to the earlier button seals, carved rocks and symbols, and to the rich and rewarding field of prehistoric slates and pottery—all verifying the antiquity of the one great pattern of belief which unquestionably united the knowing ones of the ancient world. The same symbols, the same ever-repeating numbers, illustrating the same cosmic conceptions and giving the clues and magical formulas with which to tap the fountainhead of a great lost knowledge, probably derived originally from some Motherland in distant Asia.

While studying in the library of the French Institute of Archaeology in Cairo, Natacha met the director, whose work had impressed her. His name was Alexandre Piankoff, a Russian academician who had left his native country during the 1917 revolution to pursue his Egyptological studies in Germany and France. A gifted linguist with an open mind and broad interests, Piankoff had become a French citizen and a resident of Egypt, where his investigations took him to a variety of locales, from the Coptic monasteries near the Red Sea to the tombs of ancient Egyptian rulers in the Valley of the Kings. Like Rambova, he took an interest in unusual forms of religious expression and felt that the inscriptions found on the walls of the funerary shrines of the pharoahs could not be dismissed as the unimportant fantasies of court magicians and priests. He introduced Rambova to his French translation of the esoteric religious representations referred to as the "Book of Caverns" found in the tomb of Ramesses VI. It so impressed her that she brought her study of scarabs to a halt and eventually returned to New York, urging the Bollingen Foundation to underwrite an expedition to record all the religious inscriptions found throughout Ramesses's tomb and in the vaults of the nine pyramids at Sakkara, dating from the Fifth and Sixth Dynasties. This project, she believed, would be the key to understanding the religious mind of the ancient Egyptian. Maud Oakes, who had joined Natacha at Luxor in November of 1947 for some comparative research, added her voice of support to the project.

The Bollingen Foundation budgeted $50,000 for a projected two-year expedition beginning in October 1949. Piankoff was named director and translator, with Rambova acting as a supervisor and coordinator of the collected material. The Bollingen provided them with photographic equipment and a car, and paid for the added assistance of a photographer, L. Fred Husson, and an artist, Mark Hasselriis. Elizabeth Thomas, an Egyptologist from the Oriental Institute of the University of Chicago, was also attached to the expedition for a short time, to help Piankoff in his translations.

"She was as dignified as a queen when she interviewed me in her apartment in New York," Mark Hasselriis recalled of his 1949 meeting with Rambova. Yet when the expedition was about to be launched that October, Mark saw a less serene side of Natacha. Called to the Mena House Hotel, located near the Pyramids, where the company planned to meet for their final deliberations, Mark heard strange agitated noises coming out of Natacha's room. By their voices, he could tell that Piankoff and Elizabeth Thomas were inside. He knocked on the door repeatedly until Natacha finally answered it, stuck her head out, and hissed, "Keep out!" She had just received the catastrophic news from Elizabeth Thomas that eight of the nine pyramids they planned to record lay buried under drifted sand. This had not been made known to them by the Egyptian Antiquities Service, which presumably expected the American-financed expedition to clear it away. The Pyramid of Unas, dating from the twenty-fourth century B.C., was the only accessible pyramid. Furious that her ambitious plans had to be scaled down to a more modest undertaking, Rambova exhibited a fit of temper that left a lasting impression on the young Hasselriis. Piankoff would refer to these rare outbursts as "her Irish." When she finally calmed down, it was decided that the party should repair to Luxor for the winter months, and investigate fully the inscriptions in the tomb of Ramesses VI.

From October to April, Rambova and Elizabeth Thomas housed themselves in the Luxor Hotel. Piankoff joined them there in February. Mark Hasselriis and Fred Husson were lodged a half mile north at the Oriental Institute. Both young men felt that Rambova intentionally distanced herself from the Institute in order to avoid any possible conflicts of interest with her own mission. She maintained a polite respect for the work of that institution, but felt it suffered from an improper "scientific" orientation, lacking any real appreciation for the spiritual foundation of ancient Egyptian culture.

"Natacha and I would cross the Nile three times a week, from the east to the west banks, that is from ancient Thebes [Luxor] to the Valley of the Kings," recalled Fred Husson. "We did our field work in the mornings before the heat of the day. She would examine the wall paintings, take notes, and do some writing while my native assistants and I photographed the tomb." Fred found that his working relationship with Natacha was always professional. "Natacha was an aristocrat, learned,

The first columned hall of the tomb of Ramesses VI

cosmopolitan and always a lady. The achievements of the ancient Egyptians appeared to be a constant amazement to her, and she was always searching for clues to explain how and why this was so." The photographer, like everyone else in the party, discovered that Rambova was a tough taskmaster. "Natacha demanded the best. She worked hard herself, and she expected no less from others."

During the expedition, Rambova's intellectual preoccupations did not blind her to the sad state of the Egyptian peasantry. Fred Husson recalled that "on many occasions, Natacha would show her empathy toward the plight of the natives. This was demonstrated over and over in the little things she would do to assist them." In a letter to Barrett, Rambova wrote that the peasantry "show strong indications of an inner culture and maturity," while the merchants and upper classes "are very obviously young and crude." Money, she felt, had entrenched the wealthy in materialism, fostering "a deep seated refusal to take obligations seriously or curtail indulgences." The spirituality practiced by the poor, Natacha concluded, was edifying and worth investigating: "Curiously the peasantry of many villages has more inner dignity than most of the privileged class found in the cities. In their dreams likewise they show an inner degree of experience in the purity of the symbolism and the accuracy of their prophetic sense."

Rambova's desire to assist the defenseless extended to animals. When the party concluded their work at Luxor and returned in April to Cairo, Natacha rented an apartment in the suburb of Dokki, just a few hundred yards from the mansion of one of the sisters of King Faruk. As Mark Hasselriis recalled, "some children from the royal household were making a commotion in the street one day as they were playfully torturing dogs and cats. Rambova saw what was happening from her balcony and flew out of the building like Medea. She stopped the cruelty by calling the Royal S.P.C.A. to talk to the people in the neighborhood." Earlier, Rambova had witnessed an Arab beating a donkey unmercifully with a whip. The animal was bearing a heavy load, and its knees began to buckle. "When Rambova saw this," Mark Hasselriis recounted, "she lost her head. She grabbed the whip and beat the man senseless in the street. She was vengeance itself! People gathered around to stop her, and it caused a riot." The artist compared Rambova's love for animals with that of the ancient Egyptians. "Everything in ancient Egypt was steeped with religious significance, and they considered certain animals as theophanies of the divine. Islam wiped away all this, and Rambova considered such torturers as being completely debased." Because of her commanding female presence in the male-dominated society, Rambova came to be addressed by many Egyptians as "Sit Mudir." Roughly translated as "boss lady" or "governess," it replaced Madam as an appellation, used by those who were amazed at the sight of a woman leading an expedition.

While in Cairo, in April 1950, the group was given permission to photograph and study the inscriptions on the four gold-encrusted shrines that had enclosed the sarcophagus of King Tut-Ankh-Amon, part of the much-publicized discovery made by Howard Carter in the winter of 1922–23. The curse that had always been rumored to haunt the tomb's treasures seemed disturbingly real to Mark Hasselriis, as he recalled a peculiar chain of events that took place as soon as the Department of Antiquities allowed them to bring to Natacha's apartment samples of gold gesso from the shrines. They were studying these in order to reproduce them accurately in color plates for a future Bollingen publication. "Natacha's new apartment had just been plastered and it was damp inside because there was no central heating," the artist recalled. "Suddenly her dog Chi-Chi got sick and died of liver trouble. I had liver trouble. Natacha came down with dengue fever. And Piankoff, who came to her apartment to work while she was in the hospital, collapsed on the floor upon his return home." Except for the dog, everyone recovered.

This was not the only time that members of the Bollingen Foundation had encountered something strange in their investigation of tomb inscriptions. After the 1950 Christmas holidays, the group moved south again toward Luxor in order to study the temples of Esna and Edfu. They were joined by Maud Oakes, whom Natacha asked to reenter the tomb of Ramesses VI to check some disputed measurements of the inscriptions they had photographed previously. "As she was doing this," Hasselriis recalled, "she suddenly became aware of a presence behind her. A cold chill ran down her spine. No one was there. She was terrified and started to pray." As the artist later recounted, "Maud was afraid of Egypt, but I loved it." So did Natacha. "She was fearless," her cousin reminisced. "In exploring one of the tombs, she discovered a new channel and slid down it immediately without asking someone else to investigate it first."

"Natacha believed in reincarnation, and thought that she had once been a sybil in Rome—a disastrous one at that," Mark Hasselriis declared. She was also beguiled by Cleopatra, Caesar, and Antony, and bought coins with their images on them. "She asked me one day," Mark continued, "whether I thought she was like Cleopatra. I told her no, I

The great columns in the interior of the Temple of Edfu

thought she was more like Hatshepsut. Rambova didn't believe in the comparison people had been making, since her Hollywood days, between her and Cleopatra, but she found the idea intriguing nonetheless."

The expedition's last important assignment was to record the inscriptions inside the Pyramid of King Unas at Sakkara. The tomb was approximately 4,500 years old and contained the oldest Egyptian texts known. When that project was completed, the group took pride in the fact that they had recorded the religious testimony of three separate periods of Egyptian history. Over the next several years, their data became a series of Bollingen publications known as "Egyptian Religious Texts and Representations," prepared and translated by Dr. Piankoff and edited by Rambova. Before she left Egypt, Natacha had resumed her classes in symbolism and comparative religion, and both Mark Hasselriis and Alexandre Piankoff attended them. While Piankoff had originally harbored doubts about many of Rambova's ideas, he later admitted to Mark that she had convinced him of certain things. "Piankoff wanted a nice codified system with neat labels," Mark reflected, "while Rambova knew that the Egyptian priests took much for granted in their inscriptions, often omitting those predictable labels. She would interpret, showing us how things fit, while Piankoff wanted to be able to read the text literally."

When Rambova returned to New York in 1951, she discovered that the twenty-fifth anniversary of Valentino's death was being commemorated by various branches of the media. She adamantly refused all requests for interviews, and threatened legal action against Columbia Studios if they attempted to portray her in their motion picture biography of the star. *Valentino,* starring Anthony Dexter, a Rudy look-alike, consequently made no mention of the Latin Lover's marriage to Natacha. It proved to be an unsuccessful film, lost in a quagmire of fiction and caricature. Valentino's siblings. Alberto and Maria, did successfully sue for this unauthorized biography. So did Rex Ingram's wife, the actress Alice Terry, for the movie's portrayal of her having had an affair with Rudy both before and after her marriage to her director-husband.

Mark Hasselriis returned to New York at about the same time as Rambova, and for the next fourteen years he continued to do artwork for her, producing skillfully drafted drawings of ancient Egyptian inscrip-

Left to right: an unidentified visiting scholar, Dr. Piankoff, Madame Piankoff, and Natacha Rambova at the entrance to the Temple of Esna

tions and art objects for her archives and publications. He became a master of detail and credited Natacha with having fostered this trait in him. They also had many philosophical discussions, and he remembered how she made a sharp distinction between beauty and glamour:

Natacha was surrounded by glamour early in life and also by beauty. She often spoke of each separately, and never failed to point out that glamour was illusory and a distortion, or false image. She had doubtlessly had her fill of this in the world of movies. She called Hollywood "Piscean," and by implication Neptunian, a watery world of glistening dream images. It not only provided entertainment, but heartache and malice to some of its participants. Beauty, she said, was distinct from glamour, and a reflection of the world's basic essence before it had been misused or distorted.

Rambova believed that the world was witnessing the collapse of the Piscean Age, its spiritual aspirations now clouded by false images. The Aquarian Age was approaching, and it would usher in a period of harmony, peace, and goodwill. "Natacha always considered herself an Aquarian," Mark declared, "yet the glamour aspect seemed to stick to her in the minds of others. Perhaps they were actually in pursuit of Beauty and a kind of perfection, and Natacha somehow represented it."

Rambova never ceased to attract to herself people of high accomplishment and searching minds. When she resumed her classes in symbolism, mythology, and comparative religion in her apartment in New York, a number of celebrated figures became her students. They included the artist and scholar Mai-mai Sze, Academy Award–winning costume designer Irene Sharaff, the painter Buffie Johnson, writer and photographer Dorothy Norman, and Professor Stella Kramrisch, a renowned expert on the art of India. The devotion of Rambova's students and colleagues was made manifest by the various works they dedicated to her. Maud Oakes dedicated to Natacha her study of Mayan ritual, *The Two Crosses of Todos Santos*. Dorothy Norman dedicated to her the catalogue of an exhibition she organized at the Willard Gallery in New York on the symbolic art of the hero. Dr. Piankoff dedicated to Rambova the fourth volume of his series on Egyptian texts and representations, *The Litany of Re*. And Buffie Johnson dedicated to her friend and teacher an impressive volume she published on goddess imagery, called *The Lady of the Beasts*. "There was an abundance of love felt in this intellectual group," Mark Hasselriis recalled, "and we communicated on many levels.

She was my teacher, but she rejected the role of guru and hated anybody sitting at her feet, figuratively or actually."

Part of Rambova's appeal was to be found in the self-assurance with which she pursued her philosophy of life. "She knew precisely where she was going," Mark reflected, "and she conveyed this sense with so natural and disarming a grace that it did not occur to me that it might be otherwise. Each of us has the duty and opportunity, she would say, to put our lives in order, and only by doing so could we possibly realize how we might help others."

Even in middle age Natacha's grace and physical charm did not desert her. "She had the movements of a beautiful, sleek animal," Ann Wollen recounted. "She was graceful and light with an airy laughter that reflected her attitude toward life," Buffie Johnson recalled. "When one came into a room occupied by Natacha," Mark Hasselriis added, "there was an atmosphere of serenity." Stella Kramrisch remembered Rambova as being "utterly enchanting, but she could appear aloof to those she didn't know." That beautiful aloofness caused Dorothy Norman to call Natacha Rambova "an intellectual Garbo." Not surprisingly, Greta Garbo herself expressed a desire to meet Rambova, and she called her *Mata Hari* costar, Ramon Novarro, to make the necessary introduction. The actor asked Natacha to his apartment, but made the mistake of inviting a number of other people, transforming the rendezvous into a reception. When Garbo arrived at Novarro's door and saw the crowd inside, she turned around and fled. Thus the two women never met. But they did have a mutual acquaintance in the screenwriter Mercedes de Acosta.

"I must first say that she is physically very beautiful," Mercedes wrote of Natacha in her autobiography, *Here Lies the Heart,* published in 1960. "Had she wished she could have successfully lived a social or an artistic life, but she chose a more difficult way. She has chosen The Way that all adepts and sincere seekers of Truth must, sooner or later, follow. The Way of anonymity and seclusion." The two women first met briefly when Natacha was dancing with Rudy on the Mineralava Tour. Now, many years later, Mercedes attended Rambova's lectures on religion and art. "Mercedes was rather on the short side," Mark Hasselriis recalled. "She had a pale complexion, jet black hair, and wore a black patch over her one blind eye." A one-time follower of the Indian holy man Bhagavan Ramana Maharshi, de Acosta threw her heart into religious experiences with the same gusto that she pursued celebrities and romance. When her autobiography appeared, it shocked her associates for its allegedly transparent references to her lesbian conquests. Nazimova, Eva le Gallienne, Marlene Dietrich, and Greta Garbo were just a few of the personalities she listed as intimate friends. As one of de Acosta's acquaintances remarked, "She liked collecting beautiful women; Rambova attracted her, but I do not believe there was ever a physical relationship between them —much to Mercedes' regret!" Dorothy Norman recalled how displeased Natacha was to find herself mentioned in Mercedes's book, feeling that she had been cast in an improper light.

Mark Hasselriis never read *Here Lies the Heart*, but he remembered Natacha came to disapprove of Mercedes, refusing to see her when she appeared unannounced at her apartment with a Buddhist monk in saffron robes, expecting to show him Rambova's extensive collection of Tibetan and Nepalese art. Natacha retired to her bedroom as Mark was assigned the task of showing them the pieces. Afterward, as they were leaving, he recalled that "Mercedes gave me a glance with her one eye of sheer naked gratitude; I had apparently helped her to save face."

"I detest lesbians!" Mark remembered Natacha telling him one day. She said the same thing to Dorothy Norman. Both found this odd, since she had a number of lesbian friends. "I don't think she detested lesbians," Mark concluded, "but I think she disapproved of something about them. She felt this male trait in the female was odious and she had a cosmological reason for this that I did not quite understand. It seemed as if she thought that in the male this duality was not unnatural, but in the female it was a travesty. It had something to do with her concept of feminity based on ancient ideas." The artist added that while she could be commanding and critical, "she was not by any means an anima hound. Her femininity never lost its place or its gentle charm, and she never raised her voice."

While Rambova may have harbored a personal disdain for lesbianism, she had to admit that lesbians had influenced her education, career, and beliefs. Elsie de Wolfe, Nazimova, and, if Warren S. Smith's *The London Heretics* is to be believed, Madam Blavatsky were lesbians; all of them helped to develop in Rambova an idealization for the childless, independent, creative, questing woman. The unfounded rumors that her marriage to Valentino had been unconsummated, the control that she exerted over his career, her subsequent divorce from the Latin Lover, who died as an indirect consequence—all these factors helped to forge the false image of her as a male-dominating Amazon. Lesbians were admittedly attracted to her, and there was much curiosity about the

Rambova, in awe of ancient Egyptian ruins, recorded them with her camera during her tour of Egypt.

nature of her relationship with her closest female friends. Maud Oakes was asked outright whether or not she had ever been to bed with Natacha. Her answer was no. Despite all evidence to the contrary, a lesbian mystique clung to Natacha Rambova, much of it fabricated after her death (see Appendix).

By the fall of 1953, it was evident that Rambova had more serious problems than dealing with lesbians. A September letter to Jack Barrett from Wallace Brockway, one of the Bollingen editors with whom Natacha was working, reveals a decline in her health after her return from Egypt: "Natacha needs cheering up. She has been in miserable health, and seemed truly ill when I saw her last. She has a number of ailments (none of them imaginary), and her mood is not infrequently despondant, which is unusual for her. I don't know how one goes about 'cheering up' a nun, but the problem seems—to me—a real one."

The celibate and ascetic Rambova, in her intellectual and spiritual drive to uncover the unifying themes in the religion of the ancients, found herself saddled with a fifty-six-year-old body that was at times not equal to the rigors of the task. In a letter to Stella Kramrisch the following year, she complained of phlebitis and a glandular condition. Shortly afterward, doctors diagnosed scleroderma, a degenerative and incurable disease in which the esophagus and internal organs become fibrous and hard, making swallowing and digestion difficult. Having little faith that the doctors who pronounced her case hopeless could help her, she avoided hospitals and devised her own therapy of mental and physical exercises, substituting herbs for prescription drugs.

All the while, her attention to the Egyptian texts for the Bollingen Series took time from her writing on the mythic patterns behind ancient symbolism. When Jack Barrett pressed her to show her manuscript-in-progress to a Greek classicist for scrutiny, Natacha's patience wore thin. She reminded him that, for the most part of the last five years, her time had been taken up with the typing, editing, and format of the Ramesses and Tut-Ankh-Amon material. "If my own first volume has been written at all," she wrote Barrett, "it is because I work ten or twelve hours a day without vacations. On account of my health I can no longer do this." Sleeping less than four hours every night, she worked tirelessly in her apartment, using a card table as her desk. As her weight declined, her finger tips became raw to the bone with incessant typing. Undaunted, she bought rubber caps, placed them on every finger, and carried on.

In 1954, the Bollingen published the first volume of its series on Egyptian texts and representations. Titled *The Tomb of Ramesses VI,* it was the first complete publication of a royal crypt. The text, accompanied by numerous plates and other illustrations, covered the four sacred books of the New Empire, with a liturgical description of the cycle of birth, life, and death. This was followed the next year by a second volume, *The Shrines of Tut-Ankh-Amon,* also richly illustrated. In 1955, Rambova made her last trips to Egypt via Paris, where she did final research in the Louvre for the third volume of the series, *Mythological Papyri,* published in 1957. For that work, she acted not only as editor, but wrote a chapter on symbolism. The translated texts were from the Twenty-First Dynasty and represented the magic formulations developed by the Egyptian priesthood for use in the afterlife.

Anne McGuire assisted Rambova as copy editor for the third volume, and the two became good friends. Despite her vast accumulation of knowledge, and a facility for languages (French, Italian, Spanish, and some Russian), Rambova was a notoriously bad speller. Anne vetted Natacha's prose, and recalled how the woman paid careful attention to her appearance despite her failing health: "Her hair was impeccable. She would use just a small amount of makeup in a very delicate way. She spent a fortune on just a few clothes—tailored suits and blouses, and adapted to the styles of the day. She was fastidious in dress and cleanliness. She was quite striking for her age." Anne added, "Rambova was immersed in scholarship, but was perhaps too opinionated to be a true scholar. She was somewhat embarrassed by her Hollywood days and her marriage to Valentino, but more open to talking about her life in Spain." Anne thought Rambova had become somewhat bitter about men. She advised the copy editor not to throw away her potential by sacrificing herself to the duties attached to marriage and family. She had given the same advice to Dawn Mundy, who, after Talbot's death in 1940, remarried and raised a family.

While Rambova was burning herself out with work, her mother began to wind down from nothing more than old age. Now in her eighties, Winifred resolved to divest herself of worldly goods in preparation for her death. She moved to the Dorset Hotel at 30 West 54th Street and began to dispose of the art objects, jewelry, and furniture that she had kept in storage. "I spent the first half of my life collecting things," she said, "and the second half was spent giving them away." She gave Foxlair to the Police Athletic League of New York City, to be converted into a recreational center for the poor. (In 1964 the State of New York bought the property with the intention of turning it into a public campsite or forestry school. Due to the lack of funds necessary to restore it, however, the Lands and Forest District ordered the demolition of all the buildings on the estate, allowing the property to return to the wilderness from which it came.) After the war, Mrs. Hudnut gave the Château Juan-les-Pins to General Charles de Gaulle to use as a home for war orphans. But when she later discovered that the French government never used it for that purpose, but merely stripped it of its crystal chandeliers and other built-in finery, she took it back and sold it. The furnishings that she managed to salvage and bring to the United States she donated to the University of Utah, founding in her hometown of Salt Lake City the nucleus of what later became the Utah Museum of Fine Arts, today boasting the finest collection of artifacts in the intermountain region. In April 1951 she made one last visit to the city of her birth and was guest of honor at the gala opening of the Hudnut Gallery, housed on the fourth floor of the Park Building on the university campus. For the next several years she carried on a lively correspondence with the museum director, I. Owen Horsfall, entrusting to his care the continued donation of artifacts she had gathered from Egypt and Spain.

Natacha followed her mother's example. Starting in 1952, she began donating some of her own Egyptian artifacts to the Utah Museum of Fine Arts, writing Horsfall that "as I can, I shall continue to buy small but interesting pieces to add to the collection. Unfortunately I have not the means to do very much, but I have unusual opportunities as most of the best Egyptian dealers are my personal friends." These Utah donations and loans were a meager substitute for the research archive she had hoped to establish. In a letter to Horsfall she wrote: "It has always been one of my fast vanishing dreams to someday start a small museum of religious symbolism—complete with archive, research library, and exhibition room where lectures could be given. In consequence, I keep my fingers on some of the objects which should go there if it ever materializes. You can see from this there is little fear of the loan not being permanent!"

One of the donations her mother made, the Ivanovitch portrait of Natacha descending the château staircase, caused Rambova much consternation when it was reproduced in a Utah newspaper with her name highlighted underneath. She immediately dashed a letter off to Horsfall demanding that he address the matter: "When allowing mother to give my portrait to the museum it was with the understanding that under no condition would my name be used on it. It was to be 'A Portrait of a Lady' or some such usual title—nothing more. Will you please be so kind as to see that this is changed as soon as possible. It could cause a great deal of unpleasantness." Natacha later remarked about the portrait, "I wasn't always a lady, but it's better than having my name on that painting!"

Rambova continued to endow the museum with Egyptian artifacts in additional bequests made in 1954, 1958, 1959, and 1963. In letters to the director she described in detail how the pieces should be exhibited, making stipulations as to the size, color, and lighting of display cases. One day, in 1957, after buying some Egyptian art that had been deaccessioned from New York's Metropolitan Museum of Art, Natacha took a bad fall on the sidewalk. "To add to the joys of life," she wrote Horsfall, "I have a double fracture in my left leg and will be unable to work for a while."

The day she had her cast removed, Natacha was visited by Alvaro de Urzáiz. He had come to the United States to ask her help in getting their marriage annulled. Since divorce was not legal in Spain, only an annullment would enable Alvaro to remarry. After nearly twenty years of separation and no communication, the bad feelings she had harbored against Alvaro evaporated. The work she had been able to accomplish since leaving Spain was, in her estimation, worth more than anything she had ever done before, and their reunion was congenial. Although Muzzie was very ill, seeing the two together again and hearing them laugh lifted her spirits. Natacha agreed to cooperate with Alvaro, and an annullment was eventually granted on the grounds that she had no intention of ever having children.

In truth, Natacha's refusal to bear children did contribute to the failure of her two marriages. "She never felt that she had the right temperament for motherhood," Mark Hasselriis recalled. "The only thing that ever excited her was art." Since the loneliness of her childhood had been alleviated only by beauty and myth, one might suspect that the unhappiness of those formative years dictated her attitude about motherhood. Nevertheless, she did have an interest in the young. In a letter to her cousin, Natacha wrote, "Beauty unfolds many doors to children, and heaven knows they need the stimulation of fairy tales and legends to offset the horrors of the usual fare today with psychologists harping on realism. Let the young have their dreams while they may!" The necessity of educating young people to survive in the hostile atmosphere of a materialist age appealed to Rambova's pedagogical instincts. "Working with young people, I knew how badly they needed help," she once wrote. "We have given them nothing to help them think for themselves and see clearly through knowledge of values."

Rambova's conviction that a woman must choose between her children and a career was born from experience. Her mother became a self-made millionaire in a profession that demanded she consign her daughter to the care of others—or worse, to an institution. This left a scar on their relationship that healed only after a long period. Natacha felt that, sometimes, more than one lifetime was needed to resolve one's problems with another. "I had several lives with mother in Egypt," she wrote her cousin. "That caused our karma together—now at last worked out."

As Muzzie's health quickly deteriorated, Natacha notified Director Horsfall at the museum in Salt Lake City: "Mother is failing as the months go by, but there is nothing to be done. Poor little thing is now bedridden, and I fear will never be up and about again. It is very hard on her as she has always been so active. Her memory is very poor, but as long as she is contented that is all that is important."

Death finally came to Winifred Hudnut on September 1, 1957. She was eighty-six years old. Private funeral services were held in New York, and she was buried in the Hudnut family plot at Woodlawn Cemetery, New York. Natacha sent the remaining antiques and paintings found in her mother's room in the Dorset Hotel to the museum in Salt Lake City. Winifred's obituary in the *Salt Lake Tribune* hailed her for the $300,000 worth of fine art she had donated to the place of her birth.

The inheritance she received from her mother's estate enabled Natacha to exercise a financial independence she had never before experienced. She moved to a more spacious apartment at 24 West 55th Street and bought herself a country home in New Milford, Connecticut. The latter she used as a weekend retreat, decorating it with simple Danish furniture and an assortment of her Asian and Egyptian art objects. "She was very neat, and everything went together in a natural and eclectic way," Mark Hasselriis recalled. "Books abounded, but in suitably sized bookcases. Nothing appeared ill-fitting; it was all thought out carefully. It was the work of a designer, but the total effect was not contrived or stiff."

Rambova's new wealth only made her more generous to others.

"Natacha was not a greedy person," Hasselriis declared. "She might be, in the sense of collecting things, but she was very generous. She would hand people objects of art out of the clear blue sky—beautiful things!" Ann Wollen added, "You wouldn't dare compliment her on any of her art objects for fear she'd have it wrapped for you by the time you reached her door."

Eating had been one of Natacha's favorite recreations. While in New York she would take guests to the Women's Exchange Restaurant on Madison Avenue or eat at Longchamps, where she could park her dogs at a table out on the sidewalk. She loved simple American dishes and employed a cook at her home in Connecticut who was an expert at producing such fare. Later, when scleroderma made it increasingly difficult for her to swallow, let alone eat meat, she would preside at the head of the table to watch others enjoy her country banquets. "Well maybe I can afford to try just one bite," Mark remembered her saying as she surveyed the tasty morsels. As the disease progressed, her diet came to consist mainly of water, rose hips, and crushed caviar. In defiance of all medical predictions that she would be dead by 1960, Rambova continued to be active, and she continued to work on her own manuscript while Dr. Piankoff took over the preparation of the remaining volumes of their Bollingen publications.

She was finally convinced to send a draft of her work on the myth pattern in ancient symbolism to Carl Jung for his appraisal. He was amazed by the ambitious scope of her analysis and the catholic expertise she demonstrated in dealing with related subject matter. Jung handed a portion of the manuscript on number symbolism to one of his pupils for her opinion. The pupil felt that Natacha's hypothesis needed correcting, and advised Rambova to come to Zurich.

Lacking Jung's approval, the Bollingen deferred making a decision on whether to publish her work. "Natacha was devastated by Jung's rejection of her manuscript," Mark Hasselriis recalled. "While she admired him for his appreciation of the spiritual, she felt that there was a strong Freudian influence still at work in him." Rambova wrote to Jack Barrett of her dismay: "Where [Jung's] work on Alchemy is an extremely valuable contribution, the deeper metaphysical meanings of the alchemical transmutation are not touched upon—interpretations which are found in Egyptian doctrine and in Hindu yoga. Dr. Jung's purely scientific interest and focus in these last years to me is regrettable, as much of the deeper side of the work in which at one time he was interested is now apparently being laid aside—for his interest in scientific recognition." Rambova said of her encounter with the venerable Swiss psychologist, "Scratch Jung hard enough, and you'll find Freud."

Although Joseph Campbell believed that Rambova's manuscript merited publication in the Bollingen Series, his support for her work did not spare him similar criticism. In a letter to her cousin, dated October 28, 1963, Rambova delivered an analysis of his classic work: "Yes, I know *The Hero with a Thousand Faces*—the first part is good, but they should have cut all that mess at the end about modern political problems, etc. I know Campbell well, he knows his myth material but knows nothing of the symbolic content or the significance of the myths. He is doing some lectures now on T.V. and what a mess! As he knows nothing of ancient religion or philosophy, he interprets everything from the standpoint of agriculture—the 'scientific' approach of the twenties."

Natacha's critique of Jung, Campbell, and even Piankoff for what she considered their lack of an appreciation for the metaphysical was extended even to celebrated theologians. At a lecture sponsored by Dorothy Norman at her East Hampton home, Paul Tillich was the guest of honor. After his talk, Rambova took a walk in the garden with a group of women that included Hannah, Tillich's wife. One of them was so effusive about the theologian that she turned to Rambova and exclaimed, "Don't you think Paul Tillich is the most spiritual man you've ever met!" With brutal honesty, Natacha replied, "No, my dear, I do not."

"Rambova would have been disinclined to put Tillich on a pedestal," Mark Hasselriis remarked, "because she felt a purely intellectual approach to spiritual matters was simply not adequate." She believed that the intuitive and devotional aspects of a religious life were undervalued in the modern era. She expected anyone labeled "spiritual" should be extraordinary in other ways besides being intellectual. "She probably had nothing against Paul Tillich at all," Mark concluded. "She just didn't feel he was a saint!"

Even as Rambova was quick to criticize, so she was criticized—sometimes by her friends. Asian art expert Dr. Stella Kramrisch, who advised Natacha on her growing interest in Nepali and Lamaistic art, admired the woman's mind, but wanted to give it new direction. She disagreed with Rambova on the subjects of astrology and Atlantis, feeling that there was too much theory and not enough substance to her views. "Natacha never discussed with me the geography or technical achievements of Atlantis," Mark Hasselriis interjected. "But she felt it repre-

Avalokitesvara,
*Natacha's eighteenth-
century Tibetan bronze*

sented a previous stage in the evolution of humanity, a precursor to our present level of consciousness." Dr. Kramrisch knew that Rambova's Atlantean theories were derived from theosophy and Madam Blavatsky, because she spoke of both with lingering respect. She did, however, give a copy of Natacha's manuscript to the famed Egyptologist at the University of Pennsylvania, Professor Rudolf Anthes, and was surprised to hear him say that Rambova's metaphysical interpretations were on the right track.

Rambova was never personally satisfied with her manuscript and was continually rewriting in an effort to perfect it. In a letter to Jack Barrett dated August 25, 1958, she expressed her delight in having the freedom at last to pursue her own work: "For the first time in over a year and a half my work is going well. It is a difficult book on the Religious Origins of the Zodiac, which has to take up all the calendar problems, the religious feasts of the year, plus the animal and body-part symbols of the twelve divisions. It is a work which needs quiet and concentration. For the first time in over fifteen years I have the peace and freedom from worry with which to work." But she ended her letter on an ominous note: "My health is bad and I have not much more time or strength left, and what I have I wish to use to finish at least this work." To ensure her privacy she got herself an unlisted telephone number. "I disconnected my telephone as I had no peace," she wrote Stella Kramrisch. "I shall not be in the book anymore. It rang continuously day and night. The peace and quiet now is heaven!"

As always, she did reserve time to see her closest friends, and even paid for Dawn to fly up from Florida to see her in New York. On one visit in 1964, Dawn brought her daughter Dian, on whom Natacha made a lasting impression: "She was skin and bones, yet very stylish—even pretty. She looked forward to dying in a positive way. She said, 'Maybe this year it will happen and I can go home.' There was no sense that this wasn't a natural completion of things. She had used her body up and was at peace with herself. Her illness didn't seem to distract her from her work. There was no martyr in her."

Dian remembered how Natacha would talk to her mother about Valentino and the reasons for their break-up: "She felt that Valentino allowed himself to be surrounded by Hollywood sycophants who weren't interested in him as a person, only his power and money. She felt he bought into the flattery and false image and did not remain true to himself. She couldn't abide the phoniness any longer, and so she left."

Rambova's cousin, Ann Wollen, remembered being cautioned by older members of the family not to bring up the subject of Valentino in Natacha's presence. But later, in their private conversations, she noticed that Natacha herself would make many references to Rudy, and it was always done in a loving way. "I wish now that I had spent more time talking to Natacha about those Hollywood days, even though she felt the work she was doing later in her life was much more important."

Rambova's work had brought her to a point where corporeal love no longer seemed important to her. She, who had in her lifetime been the object of great physical passion, now wrote to her pupil and disciple Mark Hasselriis of another kind of love: "Yes, I have seen that smile of divinity which warms and breaks your heart as well—it is that smile, my dear, which makes all the thorns of the Way not only bearable but blessed. This sacred glimpse of Love in all its divine purity is that by which we can distinguish between divine and human love. It is the true source of compassion which can wound deeply to awaken, and so bring nearer the day of Unity. When one has contacted this source of Love the human counterpart is poor indeed!"

Eventually Natacha gave up her apartment in the city in order to live full time in her Connecticut country house. While force of will and self-treatment had enabled her to live beyond the expectations of physicians, her wasted body knew that death was stalking it. In September 1965, she returned to New York and booked herself into the Gotham Hotel in order to meet her lawyers and make some adjustments to her will. Codicils were drawn up and signed on September 15. On September 29, hotel personnel responded to a report that a female had gone berserk in one of their elevators. It was Natacha.

She was taken by ambulance to Lenox Hill Hospital, where she was placed under the observation of three psychiatrists, who diagnosed her condition as paranoid psychosis arising from malnutrition. She was emaciated: her weight was listed as sixty-five pounds. Her malnutrition was attributed to an advanced state of scleroderma, which made it impossible for her to swallow. This, in turn, led to delusions in which she refused to eat because she was fearful of being poisoned. The less nutrition she received, the more paranoid she became. The doctors placed her in the neuro-psychiatric ward of the hospital, and a battery of shock treatments was administered.

"I received word from Mrs. Norman that Natacha had collapsed and had been taken to the hospital," Mark Hasselriis declared. "I then phoned one of her students who told me that she had actually been paranoid for several weeks, and had been found screaming at her Connecticut home at night, claiming that she was being attacked by demons from the Netherworld." Dorothy Norman, Mai-mai Sze, and Mark were among her former students who visited Rambova at Lenox Hill. "When I saw her in the hospital she was as thin as a skeleton," Mark recalled. "I remember she had been drinking milk, and she had a little white moustache. She was too weak to even read." When Mark found out that she had been given shock treatment he immediately consulted a lawyer to prevent the hospital from doing it to her again. "I knew from years of conversation that she was morally against shock treatment. Now the very thing she hated and considered so unethical was being done to her." The lawyer informed Mark that since he was not a blood relative, he could do nothing to stop the treatment. Soon, more shock treatment was administered, and Natacha became very subdued.

Finally, news of Rambova's plight reached relatives on the West Coast. Cousins Ann Wollen and her mother, Katherine Peterson, flew out from California to bring Natacha back home with them. "My mother was sick herself at that time and was confined to a wheelchair," Ann recalled. "When we arrived at the hospital, Natacha was surprised to see us. She apologized for causing us any trouble, got up, and made the bed for mother to recline on." She told her cousins that it must have been the effect of two martinis on an empty stomach that caused her to get lost in the hotel and panic. Nevertheless, she was happy to return to California with them and gave Ann a list of things to pick up at her Connecticut home in preparation for their journey west.

On November 23, Rambova was released from the hospital and taken, with her cousins, by ambulance to the airport. "The three of us were quite a sight," Ann recalled. "Mother was in a wheelchair, Natacha was on a stretcher, and I was holding all their bags." When they arrived in Los Angeles, Natacha entered Methodist Hospital in Arcadia, where she remained until her following birthday, January 19, when she moved to a rest home, Las Encinas Hospital, in Pasadena. Having once written Ann that "these damn worn out old carcasses are such a bore; I hope to get rid of mine before too long," Natacha found that the slow process of death was painful. "I'm in purgatory here," she told Ann as her body was hooked up daily, month after month, to feeding tubes.

In May 1966 Maud Oakes drove down from her home in Big Sur to visit her sick friend in Los Angeles. Shortly after, she wrote the Bollingen Foundation to report that Rambova was failing. Natacha no longer took any interest in her appearance or in the outside world, and saw no one but her cousins. Maud reported that while her mental acuity fluctuated, her memory was good. She could remember everything, Maud added, but was suffering from guilt feelings about her past life.

It was ironic that Rambova should have faced death in a town on which she had turned her back in disgust forty years previously. Only a few miles away, the Hollywood studios continued to manufacture their celluloid dreams, and in a crypt not far from Paramount rested the world's Latin Lover, interred with the platinum slave bracelet that symbolized the greatest love he had ever known.

On June 4, Ann Wollen visited Natacha, who was awake, but barely able to speak. Her books and letters by the bedside were no longer of any interest to her. Only an illustrated tile of Anubis, the canine deity to whom a pharaoh's mummy was entrusted, decorated her room. It had been given to her by Mark Hasselriis.

"When you visit me tomorrow," Natacha whispered to Ann, "you'll meet me downstairs." Ann thought the statement was odd, since Natacha's room was on the first floor. Without further reflection, she kissed her cousin good-bye, and drove home.

*I*n an atmosphere of gray light, two dark figures in a narrow barge glide silently through space. In front sits a woman with her face covered by a sheer black veil. Behind her, guiding the craft, stands an unusually tall man in billowy robes. His face is buried under the shadow of an Asian straw hat. As they draw near, their vague forms gain greater definition. The woman seems to raise her hand in recognition. There is no sound other than the cadence of a labored heart beat. Fog and light begin to flood the scene, but not before one startling second when the man beneath the pointed straw hat raises his head to reveal the hollow face of Death.

Intuitively, Ann Wollen understood the meaning of this nightmare, which awakened her the morning of June 5, 1966: Natacha Rambova was dead.

A telephone call from the doctor confirmed it. She had suffered a fatal heart attack. By the time Ann reached the hospital, the staff had taken Natacha's body out of her room and placed it in the basement morgue.

Rambova had left written instructions that no embalming was to take place, and no funeral services were to be held. She was to be simply cremated and her ashes scattered in the woods "to fertilize the earth that I love." In a letter to Katherine Peterson, Natacha gave her reasons for wanting it that way: "What a wonderful thought it is to know that the fire purifies and destroys all the old physical left-overs, and we can start from scratch again, all fresh and new! Cremation is so clean and right—the other way gives me the creeps! But each to his own way of thinking."

These were strange words coming from one who had spent a good portion of her life studying the burial chambers of royal mummies. Yet cremation seemed nothing more to her than common sense. If her spiritual quest was beyond the grasp of the uninitiated, Rambova also had a pragmatic side to her character, turning esoteric theory into a practical way of living. "Her ethics were irreproachable," Mark Hasselriis recounted. "Some have said Natacha was a searcher of truth, and this is true," he added, "but in her search she also came to know certain important aspects of inner spiritual truth. She was not one of those searchers one so often hears about who searches and searches and never seems to find anything in the end except that they must go on searching!"

A perfectionist in her scholarship as she was in her art, Rambova's manuscript on the myth pattern remained unfinished at the time of her death. She left over one thousand pages of text and numerous photographs and illustrations drawn from the resources of her visual archives, which were left to the Brooklyn Museum. Her Egyptian artifacts were given to the Utah Museum of Fine Arts in Salt Lake City, where they are showcased in a gallery called the Natacha Rambova Collection of Egyptian Antiquities. Her Far Eastern collection was donated to the Philadelphia Museum of Art, where the Natacha Rambova Gallery of Nepali and Lamaistic Art is maintained. The remainder of her estate, which was estimated to be worth a relatively modest $368,000, was willed to a number of relatives, friends, and students.

Obituaries placed emphasis on her position as Valentino's wife, with the *New York Times* quoting her as saying that a happy marriage "is the most ideal state of which I can imagine. There is emptiness to all other careers." For a woman of many careers, the question as to whether she ever found true happiness in any one of them is debatable. "I think Natacha's life was basically filled with tragedy," Ann Wollen concluded in speaking of her cousin. Besides losing in love, Rambova met obstacles in every career she pursued. "Aunt Winifred always said that Natacha's talents stretched in too many directions; she strove to be the best in too many fields, and suffered as a consequence." Yet the remarkable mosaic of personalities with whom she came into contact in her professional endeavors was more than most could hope for in one lifetime. Few of

her acquaintances, enemies, or lovers could claim to have had such a full and diverse life.

Elsie de Wolfe continued her career as the arbiter of eighteenth-century decorative taste in Europe and America until her death in 1950. A French newspaper gave her the most appropriate epitaph when it proclaimed that the last queen of Versailles had died.

Theodore Kosloff was finally divorced by his wife, Maria Baldina, in a scandalous proceeding during which she claimed he was entertaining his mistresses in her presence. Despite the divorce, the maestro never carried through his promise to marry Vera Fredova. She and Flower Hujer finally left his employ, and each pursued successful dance careers. Kosloff died of a cerebral hemorrhage in November 1956. He was seventy-five. Up to the day of his death, he taught in his Hollywood dance studio.

Alla Nazimova returned to the Broadway stage after her attempt to bring art to Hollywood films resulted in the loss of her fortune. For financial reasons, she turned her Sunset Boulevard estate into a hotel complex of twenty-five villas her promoters called "The Garden of Allah," reserving an apartment above the garage for her lifetime use. In the 1940s she returned to Hollywood to play bit parts in a number of forgettable films. She died in 1945.

The director Douglas Gerrard, who was nearly killed in a fall while pursuing an intruder one storm-ridden night at Foxlair, died of a skull fracture incurred when he suffered a stroke and fell to the pavement in downtown Los Angeles in 1950.

Nita Naldi's Hollywood career fizzled when silent film vamps went out of style. She left the film industry to marry millionaire J. Searle Barclay, who later died broke. Naldi herself died penniless in 1961. She suffered a fatal heart attack in a Times Square hovel, and her body was discovered two days later.

George Ullman was sued by Valentino's siblings for mismanagement and fraud in his handling of the actor's estate. The court ruled in favor of the family against the executor, forcing him to resign and pay the Guglielmis $187,754 in penalty fees in 1932. Teresa Werner managed to buy back from the estate many of the artifacts that had been Natacha's, and these were passed on to Winifred Hudnut when Mrs. Werner died in the early 1940s.

Another of Rambova's Hollywood nemeses, Joseph Schenck of United Artists, was convicted in 1941 on three counts of tax evasion and one of perjury and sentenced to four months in prison and $432,050 in fines. Nevertheless, he died a very wealthy man.

Luther Mahoney, the Valentinos' faithful confidant, was surprised to read that Natacha Rambova had been living in Pasadena and lamented that he had not been able to see her before she died. Before his own death in 1968, he made a three-hour tape recording of his recollections of Rudy and Natacha, which his daughter, Madeline Mahoney Reid, generously lent me for this book.

Alvaro de Urzáiz remarried. While he remained a shadowy figure after his separation from Natacha, it is known that he eventually wed Esperanza Villagonzalo, the daughter of the marquis of Villagonzalo.

Sources report that he died "like a saint" a few years after Rambova's death. Confined to a sick bed, he ordered that his military uniform be brought to him one morning. He rose, put it on, feebly made his way downstairs to a chapel where he attended Mass, received communion, and dropped dead.

In his memoirs, the artist Erté recalled visiting the island of Mallorca and seeing the villa on the cliffs where Rambova once dwelt as the condesa de Urzáiz. Although they never met, he was an admirer of hers and considered her a "brilliant personality gifted in so many fields." He noted how her legend survived on the island long after she had left it behind.

Dr. Alexandre Piankoff was born the same year as his colleague Natacha Rambova. They also died the same year. He suffered a fatal heart attack in Brussels in July 1966, after having nearly completed *The Pyramid of Unas* and *The Wandering of the Soul*, volumes 5 and 6 in his Bollingen series. Fellow Egyptologist Erik Hornung has stated that the work Piankoff did with Rambova was valuable insofar as it corrected previous misconceptions about ancient Egyptian religious literature, but that it has yet to attain its rightful place in the understanding of religion in that ancient civilization.

Ann Wollen took Natacha's ashes and distributed them in a northern Arizona forest, the state in which Rambova had felt the same cosmic mystery she had experienced in Egypt. When asked what epitaph she might have given Natacha—had Rambova wanted one—her cousin paused thoughtfully and replied: "Natacha was a teacher who opened doors for others when she could. She was a catalyst and a perfectionist. But she made mistakes. She recognized that, and learned from the experience to carry on." The epitaph she would have chosen was a phrase Natacha had used herself to describe the various stages of her life's journey: "I thought it was important at the time."

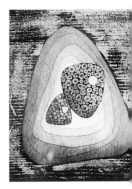

A Jungian portrait of Natacha Rambova, painted in watercolor by her friend Maud Oakes

At 8:30 A.M. on October 31, 1968, a secretary discovered the nude and badly beaten body of actor Ramon Novarro in the bedroom of his Hollywood Hills home. Called to the scene, the police launched a thorough investigation. Two suspects were eventually apprehended and brought to trial. They were brothers: Thomas Scott Ferguson, eighteen years old, and Paul Robert Ferguson, aged twenty-three.

During the trial, the prosecutor introduced an ivory-handled black cane as the instrument used to bludgeon the actor to death. Testimony revealed that the actor had invited the brothers to his home, thinking that they were prostitutes. They were, in fact, thieves, hoping to find a stash of money that the actor reportedly kept. In the early morning hours of Halloween, an argument erupted, the actor was beaten and left to drown in his own blood, and the thieves had gotten no money. On September 17, 1969, a jury found the brothers guilty of first degree murder. They were sent to prison.

What should have remained a homicide statistic or the sad ending of a celebrated actor's life took on new significance in 1975 with the appearance of a book called *Hollywood Babylon,* by Kenneth Anger, an avant-garde filmmaker and a disciple of the English satanist Aleister Crowley. In that tremendously popular, gossip-filled book of Hollywood scandal, Anger alleged that Natacha Rambova was a lesbian and that Rudolph Valentino had presented his friend, Ramon Novarro, with an autographed art deco–style dildo fashioned of black lead. This bizarre sex toy, Anger further alleged, was found at the Novarro murder scene thrust down the actor's throat. Later, in an interview for *Oui* magazine, Anger reiterated his claim and added that, as far as the district attorney was concerned, this was the murder object.

After numerous editions of Anger's work, these allegations have assumed the status of fact, leaving the relationship of Rambova and Valentino (not to mention Novarro) mired in controversy and innuendo.

In writing this biography, I felt it necessary to check the veracity of Anger's story. The coroner's report filed for Novarro revealed no evidence of any object thrust down his throat. Mr. C. Robert Dambacher, the coroner's investigator assigned to the case, has written that no "Art Deco Dildo" was found at the scene of the crime. An interview with the Reverend Edward Samaniego, a Jesuit priest and nephew of the slain actor, revealed that nothing of the sort was ever inventoried in his uncle's estate, and, according to Novarro's relatives, the actor was never even on friendly terms with Rudolph Valentino, since they were in competition for the same roles. Finally, United States District Judge James M. Ideman, who was at the time the deputy district attorney responsible for prosecuting the killers of Ramon Novarro, answered my inquiry on this matter: "With reference to the claim that Mr. Novarro was choked to death by means of an "Art Deco dildo," I can tell you that that did not happen. . . . I certainly never made any statement to the effect that such an instrument was used. I did not even know of its existence."

If this murder weapon is fictitious, then so is the insinuation that Valentino and Novarro were connected to it in "friendship." Likewise, the convenient and related allegation that Natacha Rambova was a lesbian collapses when one scrutinizes the facts.

When Anger's book appeared in America in the 1970s, the gay liberation movement was just getting under way. Coincidently, during that same decade, Robert Florey, who was an intimate friend of Rudy and Natacha, wrote a Canadian biographer of Valentino a letter in which he declared that the stories of Rudy's homosexual liaisons were of recent origin. Nothing of this nature surfaced at the time of Rudy's death.

The same holds true for Rambova. In the numerous interviews I conducted in the United States and Europe, those who had known Natacha Rambova personally presented me with a different picture of the woman than those would-be authorities I questioned who had never met her. This disparity called to mind Voltaire's cynical definition of history as the lie that everyone agrees upon. In the case of Rambova, the media has, for several decades, paraded fabrication as fact. The public has had little chance to know that the truth concerning Madam Valentino was far more compelling than the celebrated fiction.

1917 The Woman God Forgot (costumes)

1920 Why Change Your Wife (costumes worn by Theodore Kosloff)

1920 Something to Think About (costumes worn by Theodore Kosloff)

1920 Billions (costumes and sets)

1921 Forbidden Fruit (costumes and sets, with Mitchell Leisen)

1921 Aphrodite (costumes and sets)

1921 Camille (costumes and sets)

1922 Beyond the Rocks (costumes worn by Rudolph Valentino)

1922 The Young Rajah (costumes and sets)

1923 A Doll's House (costumes and sets)

1923 Salome (costumes and sets)

1924 Monsieur Beaucaire
(art director, sets, costumes, with Georges Barbier)

1924 The Hooded Falcon (supervisor, writer, costumes, with Adrian)

1924 The Sainted Devil (sets, costumes, with Adrian)

1925 Cobra (costumes, with Adrian)

1925 What Price Beauty? (producer, design supervisor)

1926 When Love Grows Cold (actress)

NOTE: Neither *Aphrodite* nor *The Hooded Falcon* was ever fully realized as a film. In both cases production was interrupted and never resumed. *Billions, A Doll's House, Beyond the Rocks, The Sainted Devil,* and *What Price Beauty?* are lost films; only fragments remain of *The Young Rajah* and *When Love Grows Cold.*

Two "Blackmoors," wearing eighteenth-century powdered wigs, peer into an incense pot in Salome.

BOOKS

ALBRECHT, DONALD. *Designing Dreams*. New York: Harper & Row, 1986. APPLIN, ARTHUR. *The Stories of the Russian Ballet*. New York: John Lane, 1911. BEEVOR, ANTONY. *The Spanish Civil War*. London: Orbis, 1982. BENNETT, J. G. *Gurdjieff: A Very Great Enigma*. York Beach, Maine: Samuel Weiser, 1973. BROWNLOW, KEVIN. *The Parade's Gone By*. New York: Knopf, 1968. BROWNLOW. *Hollywood, The Pioneers*. New York: Knopf, 1979. CHAPLIN, CHARLES. *My Autobiography*. New York: Simon & Schuster, 1964. CHIERICHETTI, DAVID. *Hollywood Director: The Career of Mitchell Leisen*. New York: Curtis Books, 1973. COLE, DAVID, ed. *History of Rockland County, New York*. New York: J. B. Beers & Co., 1884. COOPER, GLADYS. *Gladys Cooper*. London: Hutchinson & Co., 1931. CROZIER, BRIAN. *Franco: A Biographical History*. London: Eyre & Spottiswoode, 1967. DAVID-NEEL, ALEXANDRA. *Magic and Mystery in Tibet*. New York: University Books, 1958. DE ACOSTA, MERCEDES. *Here Lies the Heart*. New York: Reynal & Co., 1960. DECTER, JACQUELINE. *Nicholas Roerich: The Life and Art of a Russian Master*. Rochester, Vt.: Park Street Press, 1989. DE MILLE, AGNES. *Dance to the Piper*. Boston: Little, Brown & Co., 1952. [parts reprinted by permission of Harold Ober Associates, Inc.; copyright © 1951, 1952 by Agnes de Mille. Copyright renewed 1979, 1980 by Agnes de Mille]. DEMILLE, CECIL B. *Autobiography*. Englewood Cliffs, N.J.: Prentice Hall, 1959. DE RECQUEVILLE, JEANNE. *Rudolph Valentino*. Montreal: Presses Sélect Ltée., 1979. DEUTELBAUM, MARSHALL, ed. *Image: On the Art and Evolution of the Film*. New York: Dover Publications, 1979. DIAZ DEL CORRAL, LUIS.

Majorca. New York: W. W. Norton & Co., 1963. DOS PASSOS, JOHN. "The Big Money," *U.S.A.* New York: Random House, 1937. EARLEY, MARY DAWN. *Stars of the Twenties, Observed by James Abbe*. New York: Viking, 1975. ERTE. *Things I Remember: An Autobiography*. New York: Quadrangle/New York Times Book Co., 1975. FLOREY, ROBERT. *Filmland*. Paris: Editions de Cinemagazine, 1923. FLOREY. *Hollywood hier et aujourd'hui*. Paris: Editions Prisma, 1948. FLOREY. *La Lanterne magique*. Lausanne: Cinémathèque Suisse, 1966. GODOWSKY, DAGMAR. *First Person Plural: The Lives of Dagmar Godowsky*. New York: Viking, 1958. HORNUNG, ERIK. *The Valley of the Kings*. Translated by David Warburton. New York: Timken Publishers, 1990. KIMBALL, STANLEY B. *Heber C. Kimball: Mormon Patriarch and Pioneer*. Urbana: University of Illinois Press, 1981. LASKY, JESSE L. *I Blow My Own Horn*. New York: Doubleday, 1957. LAVINE, W. ROBERT. *In A Glamorous Fashion*. New York: Scribner, 1980. LOY, MYRNA, WITH JAMES KOTSILIBAS-DAVIS. *Myrna Loy: Being and Becoming*. New York: Alfred A. Knopf, Inc. (copyright © 1987 by James Kotsilibas-Davis and Myrna Loy. Reprinted by permission of Alfred A. Knopf, Inc.) LYNES, RUSSELL. *The Taste Makers*. New York: Harper & Brothers, 1955. MCCONATHY, DALE, WITH DIANA VREELAND. *Hollywood Costume: Glamour, Glitter, Romance*. New York: Abrams, 1976. MCGUIRE, WILLIAM. *Bollingen: An Adventure in Collecting the Past*. Princeton, N.J.: Princeton University Press, 1982. MAEDER, EDWARD, comp. *Hollywood and History: Costume Design in Film*. Los Angeles: Los Angeles County Museum of Art; London: Thames & Hudson, 1987. MANDELBAUM, HOWARD, AND

ERIC MYERS. *Screen Deco*. New York: St. Martin's Press, 1985. MENJOU, ADOLPHE. *It Took Nine Tailors*. New York: McGraw Hill, 1948. MILLER, PATSY RUTH. *My Hollywood: When Both of Us Were Young*. London: O'Raghailligh Ltd., 1988. MOORE, COLLEEN. *Silent Star*. Garden City, N.Y.: Doubleday, 1968. NORMAN, DOROTHY. *Encounters: A Memoir*. New York: Harcourt Brace Jovanovich, 1987. PAUWELS, LOUIS. *Gurdjieff*. New York: Samuel Weiser, 1972. PIANKOFF, ALEXANDRE. *Mythological Papyri*. New York: Pantheon Books, 1957. PRATT, GEORGE C. *Spellbound in Darkness*. Greenwich, Conn.: New York Graphic Society Ltd., 1973. PROVOST, DAWN MUNDY. "Talbot Mundy." In *Talbot Mundy: Messenger of Destiny*, compiled by Donald M. Grant. West Kingston, R.I.: Donald M. Grant, 1983. RAMBOVA, NATACHA. *Rudy: An Intimate Portrait of Rudolph Valentino by His Wife*. London: Hutchinson & Co., 1926. RAMBOVA AND JAMES H. SMITH. *Technique For Living*. New York: Essential Books, 1944. RAMBOVA AND SMITH. *The Road Back: A Program of Rehabilitation*. New York: Creative Age Press, 1945. RHYS, JEAN. "At the Villa d'Or." In *The Left Bank*. London: Jonathan Cape, 1927. ST. JOHNS, ADELA ROGERS. *Love, Laughter and Tears*. Garden City, N.Y.: Doubleday, 1978. SCAGNETTI, JACK. *The Intimate Life of Rudolph Valentino*. New York: Jonathan David, 1975. SHULMAN, IRVING. *Valentino*. New York: Trident Press, 1967. SMITH, JANE S. *Elsie de Wolfe: A Life in the High Style*. New York: Antheneum, 1982. SMITH, WARREN S. *The London Heretics*. New York: Dodd, Mead & Co., 1968. SPEARS, JACK. "Nazimova." In *The Civil War on the Screen and Other Essays*. New York: A. S. Barnes & Co., 1977. STALEY, THOMAS F.

Jean Rhys: A Critical Study. London: Macmillan Press, 1979. ULLMAN, S. GEORGE. *Valentino As I Knew Him*. New York: Macy-Masius, 1926. VALENTINO, RUDOLPH. *Daydreams*. London: Hurst & Blackett, 1923. WEHNER, GEORGE. *A Curious Life*. New York: Horace Liveright, 1929. WELLS, JAMES M. *The Chisolm Massacre*. Washington, D.C.: The Chisolm Monument Assoc., 1878. WESTMORE, FRANK, AND MURIEL DAVIDSON. *The Westmores of Hollywood*. Philadelphia: J. B. Lippincott, 1976. WHITE, PALMER. *Poiret*. New York: Clarkson N. Potter, 1973. WHITNEY, ORSON F. *The Life of Heber C. Kimball, an Apostle*. Salt Lake City: privately printed, 1888. ZUKOR, ADOLPH. *The Public Is Never Wrong*. New York: Putnam's Sons, 1953.

ARTICLES
BELTRAN-MASSES, FEDERICO. *Ciné-Miroir*, June–July 1929. BIERY, R. "Spirit Messages to Natacha Rambova." *Motion Picture Magazine*, January 1929. CARR, HARRY. "Home Life." *Motion Picture Magazine*, November 1925. CHICAGO TRIBUNE. "Pink Powder Puffs." Editorial, July 18, 1926. DEAN, FRANCES SMITH. "Reading Between the Lines in the Valentino–Rambova Separation." *Motion Picture Stories*, December 29, 1925. DORGAN, D. "A Song of Hate." *Photoplay*, July 1922. DRUESNE, MAEVE. "Nazimova: Her Silent Films." *Films in Review*, June–July, August–September 1985. LIFE. "The Great Lover," January 2, 1950. MACGREGOR, HELEN. "A New Portrait of the Well-Known Star." *Shadowland*, August 1923. MENCKEN, H. L. "Valentino." *Baltimore Evening Sun*, August 30, 1926. NEW YORK TIMES. Editorial, August 20, 1926. Copyright © 1926 by the New York Times Company. Reprinted by permission. PHOTOPLAY. "At Home after January First 1923," September 1922. PHOTOPLAY. "Natacha Valentino Inspired Paul Poiret to Create for Her this Exotic Wardrobe," January 1924. PHOTOPLAY. "The Valentinos' Chateau on the Riviera," May 1924. PHOTOPLAY. "Valentino Puts Art Above Good Looks," November 1924. PREDAL, RENE. "Rudolph Valentino." *Anthologie du Cinema*, May 1969. QUIRK, J. R. "Presto Chango Valentino." *Photoplay*, November 1924. RAMBOVA, NATACHA. "Mrs. Valentino on Graft." *Movie Weekly*, July 7, 1923. RAMBOVA. "Astrological Psycho-Chemistry." *American Astrology*, February 1942–

June 1943. RAMBOVA. "Strength . . . Serenity . . . Security." *Harper's Bazaar*, June–July, 1942. RAMBOVA. "America: Her Purpose and Three Great Trials for Liberty—Equality—Unity." *American Astrology*, July 1942. RAMBOVA. "America's Destiny." *American Astrology*, November 1942. REDFIELD, ELIZABETH. "May a Wife Deny Her Husband Children?" *Liberty*, January 1926. SMITH, FREDERICK JAMES. "Does Rudy Speak from the Beyond?" *Photoplay*, February 1927. VALENTINO, RUDOLPH. "Women and Love." *Photoplay*, March 1922. VALENTINO. "An Open Letter from Rudolph Valentino." *Photoplay*, January 1923. VALENTINO. "My Life Story." *Photoplay*, February–April, 1923. VALENTINO. "What Is the Matter with the Movies?" *Movie Weekly*, June 16, 1923. VALENTINO. "Why Marriage Was a Failure in My Case." *New York American*, September 5, 1926. WATERBURY, RUTH. "Wedded and Parted." *Photoplay*, December 1922.

NEWSPAPERS, JOURNALS, CATALOGS, PUBLIC RECORDS
The author wishes to acknowledge those publications that provided dates, reviews, and general information on the personalities discussed in this book: *The Bioscope, Bollingen Foundation Report: 1945–1965, Boston Evening Transcript, Catalogue of the Estate of Rudolph Valentino, Chicago Tribune, Deseret Evening News, The Dramatic Mirror and Theatre World, The Ledger* [Newark, New Jersey], *Los Angeles Times, Motion Picture Magazine, Movie Weekly, The Moving Picture World, The New Republic, New York Times, Photoplay, Portland Express, Rockland County Journal, Salt Lake Herald, San Francisco Bulletin, San Francisco Chronicle, Screenland, Seattle Post-Intelligencer, Seattle Times, United States Census Record* [for Salt Lake City: 1860, 1880, 1890], *Variety*.

NON-PRINT MATERIALS
THE SHEIK. Screenplay by Monte M. Katterjohn. Based on the novel by E. M. Hull. Copyright © 1921 Famous Players–Lasky Corporation. Renewed 1948 Paramount Pictures, Inc. All Rights Reserved. MAHONEY, LUTHER. "Taped Recollections of Rudolph Valentino and Natacha Rambova" [1968]. Collection of Madeline Mahoney Reid.

UNPUBLISHED MATERIAL
ABBE, JAMES. "Memoirs." Copyright ©

Kathryn Abbe. BROWN, VERNAL A. "The United States Marshals in Utah Territory to 1896." Masters Thesis, Utah State University, 1970. CLARKSON, ELIZABETH HUDNUT. "One Family's Adirondack Story." Copyright © Elizabeth Hudnut Clarkson. HUDNUT, MRS. WINIFRED. Letters to I. Owen Horsfall. University of Utah, Collection of the Utah Museum of Fine Arts. OAKES, MAUD. Bollingen Correspondence. Bollingen Foundation Papers in the Manuscript Division, Library of Congress. RAMBOVA, NATACHA. "Up Spain." Collection of Ann Wollen. RAMBOVA. "The Myth Pattern in Ancient Symbolism." Collection of Ann Wollen. RAMBOVA. Letters from Egypt to Jack Barrett [1947]. Collection of Ann Wollen. RAMBOVA. Bollingen Correspondence, 1945–1967. Bollingen Foundation Papers in the Manuscript Division, Library of Congress. RAMBOVA. Letters to Mark Hasselriis. Collection of Mark Hasselriis. RAMBOVA. Letters to I. Owen Horsfall. University of Utah, Collection of the Utah Museum of Fine Arts. RAMBOVA. Letters to Stella Kramrisch. Collection of the Philadelphia Museum of Art. RAMBOVA. Letter to Mary Mellon. Collection of Ann Wollen. RAMBOVA. Letters to Relatives: Winifred Hudnut, Katherine Peterson, Teresa Werner, Ann Wollen. Collection of Ann Wollen.

INTERVIEWS
Kathryn Abbe, Antonio Altamirano, Dewitt Bodeen, Kevin Brownlow, Susan Dinwoodey Burton, David Chierichetti, Elizabeth Hudnut Clarkson, Samson De-Brier, Agnes de Mille, C. Robert Dumbacher, Winifred Edwards (Vera Fredova), Daniel Entin, Erté, William K. Everson, Leslie Flint, Harold Grieve, Jane Hampton, Mark Hasselriis, Flower Hujer, L. Fred Husson, the Hon. James Ideman, Paul Ivano, Buffie Johnson, Charles Kidd, John Kobal, Stella Kramrisch, Craig H. Long, Anne McGuire, William McGuire, Patsy Ruth Miller, Alden Nash, Joaquin Nin-Culmell, Dorothy Norman, Katherine Peterson, Dian Provo, Mark Provost, Madeline Mahoney Reid, Raymond Rohauer, the Countess of Romanones, Rev. Edward Samaniego, S. J., E. F. Sanguinetti, Jack Scagnetti, Joseph Simms, Anthony Slide, Jack Spears, Gordon Stone, Brian Taves, Alexander Walker, John Wayne, Lois Wilson, Ann Wollen, Loretta Young.

The photographers and sources of photographic material other than those indicated in the captions are as follows: copyright © Kathryn Abbe, courtesy of the Washburn Gallery: jacket front, pp. 2, 122, 139; Courtesy of the Academy of Motion Picture Arts and Sciences: pp. 10, 51, 58 (top), 59, 67 (left), 70, 71 (top), 73, 75, 78, 81 (top and center), 88 (bottom), 97, 103, 109, 117, 128 (left), 149, 165–66, 266; Author's collection: pp. 40, 43 (right), 48, 57, 71 (bottom), 84, 86 (top right and bottom right), 92, 128 (right), 137 (right), 146, 148 (right), 158, 169, 173, 177, 179, 182, 189; Courtesy of Paul and Patricia Chamberlain: p. 86 (top left and bottom left); Courtesy of David Chierichetti: p. 58 (bottom); Courtesy of Elizabeth Hudnut Clarkson: p. 120; David Cole's *History of Rockland County, New York*: pp. 24–25; Courtesy of the Robert Florey Collection: p. 113; Courtesy of Vera Fredova (Winifred Edwards): pp. 37, 44, 54; Courtesy of Jane Hanson: p. 154; copyright © Fred Husson, courtesy of Lancaster Ultra-Graphics, Inc.: pp. 239, 242–43; Courtesy of The Library of Congress: p. 130; Courtesy of The Museum of Modern Art Film Still Archive: p. 148 (left); Courtesy of the National Film Archives and Stills Library of the British Film Institute, London: endpapers, pp. 67 (right), 83, 85, 88 (top), 107, 111, 137 (left), 140–41, 142 (bottom), 143, 150, 160, 178; Courtesy of the Philadelphia Museum of Art: pp. 253, 261; *Photoplay* magazine: p. 133; Courtesy of Madeline Mahoney Reid: pp. 4, 77, 94, 100 (right), 156; Courtesy of the Nicholas Roerich Museum: jacket back; Courtesy of the Billy Rose Theatre Collection, New York Public Library at Lincoln Center, Astor, Lenox, and Tilden Foundations: pp. 43 (left), 64, 192; Courtesy of Jack Scagnetti: pp. 14, 17, 81 (bottom), 112; Courtesy of the Department of Special Collections, University of Southern California Libraries: p. 195; Courtesy of the University of Utah, Utah Museum of Fine Arts: pp. 184, 260; Courtesy of the Utah State Historical Society: p. 23; Courtesy of Ann Wollen: pp. 1, 6, 18, 26–36, 38, 46, 53, 61–62, 68, 100 (left), 126, 131, 142 (top), 170, 186, 200–34, 262.